Bonded in Christ's Love

other books from the authors
published by Paulist Press

DENISE LARDNER CARMODY
What Are They Saying About Non-Christian Faith?
Caring for Marriage

JOHN TULLY CARMODY
Ecology and Religion
Holistic Spirituality

Bonded in Christ's Love

An Introduction to Ecclesiology

Denise Lardner Carmody
and
John Tully Carmody

PAULIST PRESS
New York ◆ Mahwah

Library of Congress Cataloging-in-Publication Data

Carmody, Denise Lardner, 1935–
    Bonded in Christ's love.

    Includes bibliographies and index.
    1. Church.   2. Catholic Church—Doctrines.
I. Carmody, John, 1939–   .   II. Title.
BX1746.C277   1986   262   86-5016
ISBN 0-8091-2791-1 (pbk.)

Published by Paulist Press
997 Macarthur Boulevard
Mahwah, New Jersey 07430

Printed and bound in the
United States of America

Contents

Page

Preface 1

Chapter

1. Introduction: Contemporary Questions.................... 3

2. Scriptural Sources 32

3. Church History.. 68

4. Theological Models..................................... 105

5. Worship 128

6. Mission 151

7. Governance 173

8. Conclusion: Contemporary Answers 196

Index 225

For Joan and Warren Armstrong

Preface

On several occasions we have presented courses or lectures dealing with the Christian church. When the opportunity to fashion a book from these materials arose, we decided to stress contemporary questions and answers, since these had proved the items of most interest to our students. This book therefore begins with a survey of the questions facing the Christian church. To set these questions in perspective, it then devotes two rather full chapters to historical background: the scriptural sources on which the Christian church depends and the nineteen hundred years or so of experience that the church has generated since its scriptural beginnings.

Chapters four through seven probe topics that today's systematic theologians usually spotlight in their ecclesiological reflections: models of the church, community worship, the church's mission, and Christian governance. We then conclude by returning to the focus of our beginning and trying to use the historical and systematic materials we have surveyed to answer the key questions of current ecclesiology. We hope that this rather comprehensive coverage, along with the minimal assumptions that we make about readers' theological background, will make the book suitable for introductory college courses and church study groups.

On the whole, we have written from a Roman Catholic perspective and with principally Roman Catholic audiences in mind. Still, we have tried to indicate the nuances that Protestant and Eastern Orthodox traditions would suggest, and to make most of our exposition relevant to any churches open to ecumenical sharing. For further study we recommend the bibliography of Avery Dulles, S.J. and Patrick Granfield, O.S.B., THE CHURCH: A BIBLIOGRAPHY (Wilmington, Del.: Michael Glazier, 1985).

1

Our thanks to the several audiences before whom we worked out our positions, especially to the members of the class we taught at Boston College in the summer of 1984, and to Larry Boadt, C.S.P., who sponsored the project at Paulist Press.

Chapter 1

Introduction:
Contemporary Questions

**Faith and Liberation ◆ Christian Sinfulness ◆ Post-Christianity? ◆
Community ◆ Summary, Study Questions, Notes**

Faith and Liberation

Anyone beginning a work on the Christian church today is only prudent to wet a finger and raise it to the wind. As the American Catholic bishops make plain in their pastoral letter "The Challenge of Peace," effective church teaching demands a keen sense of the signs of the times. In our view probably the dominant sign of the times is the groans of billions for liberation. The pastoral letter addresses liberation from the bondage of war and nuclear threat. Church teaching and work as a whole must address the manifold liberation from sin that the billions who are starving, or politically oppressed, or economically deprived, or racially abused, or sexually harassed, or spiritually bereft are begging. It is a tall order, requiring nothing less than the mediation of the Creator's recreative love. Still, this has always been the main task and central gift of Christ's people. From the beginning, the faith of the community called into being by Jesus has intended nothing less than the Pauline "new creation": an order in which the love-life of God might oust human destructiveness and communicate a foretaste of heaven, a down-payment on the time when God will wipe every tear from our eyes.

There is nothing contrived, therefore, in coupling faith and liberation. Whatever new accents "liberation" may carry at the end of the twentieth century, it translates human needs and hopes as old as

3

lapsarian Adam. Nor has "faith" greatly altered. Despite all the changes in worldview that separate us from Jesus, the authors of the synoptic gospels, John, Paul, and the rest, faith remains the attitude stipulated by the divine mystery, the primordial fact that we human beings never understand the most basic features of our situation. We don't know where we came from. We don't know where we are going. We don't understand why our time between origin and term is such a confusing mixture of joy and sadness, fulfillment and frustration. As a result, we are all forced to accept ignorance as the bedrock of the human condition. In every life, ancient or modern, God has been present as the fullness far too great for us to comprehend, or the void so threatening that we flee in distraction.

Under close examination, therefore, most lives exhibit an obvious theology. Regardless of what the people involved may say about their motivations and resources, their actual living depends on assumptions and hopes that pass far beyond empirical proof. Thus the brazen atheist comes to use Lenin or Bertrand Russell to prop up an intellectual position that is by no means certain. The agnostic in effect chooses not to choose between the mystery of why there should be so much evil and the mystery of why there should be so much good. The believer of Eastern religious allegiance takes the teaching of the Buddha or devotion to Krishna as a path through the wilderness of doubts. The Jew clings to Torah, despite all the horrors of the holocaust, while the Muslim depends on the Qur'an. Virtually nowhere do Christians find people whose essential spiritual build differs dramatically from their own. In almost all lives there are positive data, calling for a hopeful interpretation of life's ultimate mysteriousness, and there are negative data, making hope and commitment difficult.

We think it important to stay close to such nearly universal human experience of a puzzling, challenging, seldom certain ultimate mystery, because if the church is to carry the significance it should it must make itself meaningful in quite basic terms. If it requires people to accept a strange jargon, or participate in separatist rites, it cannot accomplish the outreach to the ends of the earth, to the center of the heart, that Jesus' first followers intended for it. In the wake of the Master's own approach to people, the differences between Cardinals and hoboes are dramatically thin. Jesus was mainly interested in calling people to the justice and joy of the Reign of God. If a scarlet robe would help people respond generously to his call, Jesus would be the first to order up a dazzling dozen. If tattered rags, even a tattered spirit, would bring the demand for a change of mind, a conversion of heart, home with effective force, Jesus would be the last to bar the door against hoboes.

One gets a fair sense of this rather democratic setting of the ecclesiastic task and question in the fine volumes of interviews produced by the child psychiatrist Robert Coles. Perhaps especially in the two books of interviews with women that Coles has recently done with his wife, one sees the pervasive impact of religion, even of church life, in the struggles and dreams the interviewees reveal.[1] Whether they are people from the underside of history, whom we would locate among the have-nots, or people from the fortunate half that has done quite well, the women show themselves acutely aware of the connections between what they have been brought up to believe, have hope in and love, and where they have stood on the socio-economic ladder. With virtually no explicit tutoring from Karl Marx or the other analysts who have made this sort of linkage the first strand in a full interpretation of history, the women struggle after the attitudes, the commitments and beliefs, that will make it possible for them to call their lives good. Again and again, what they find making it possible for them to sacrifice for their children, hold their marriages together, and finally bless the earthly time they have been given is an acceptance of trials they cannot understand and the friendship or support of fellow-sufferers.

For example, a woman who eventually becomes a successful executive is most helped on her way by an intern who helps her through her teen-age sister's death. The intern is the only woman in her class of medical students, and her wry comments on male-female relations in medicine plant seeds that the executive-to-be later develops into an articulate feminism. Because the intern effectively treats the young girl's grief, the further dimension of what sort of career might suit the girl and help her contribute to lessening other people's grief easily can surface. Eventually it turns out that the girl judges herself unsuitable for medicine, but the bond they have first struck in the context of pain keeps the two women close enough to discuss other, later sufferings, including the painful marital situations both find themselves in.

Another example is a woman from a terribly poor family who is ridiculed at home for aspiring to become a nurse. Her family is basically kind, and certainly hard put-upon by the Depression, but in their inability to understand her desires to find a profession they deal with her quite cruelly. So the kindly attentions of a young doctor (again) prove immensely influential in the girl's finding the confidence to strike out after her dream. For a while the doctor is her boyfriend, but the differences between his Jewish faith and her Catholic faith finally prove too great. Nonetheless, the closeness they have shared, and above all his understanding of her desire to do something helpful with her life, something of which she can be proud, give her the key to a self-respect that never leaves her. In later life, when she goes back to nursing part-time to help support her bustling family, she finds herself amazed at the path she has trod, the strength she and other members of her family and social class have been able to muster.

This second woman has a quite traditional and reflective religious faith. The first woman, who becomes a successful executive, would not describe herself as religious. Yet the two women would have little difficulty communicating across their differences because both have consciously struggled to find convictions strong enough to carry them through disappointments with men, painful encounters with crude business systems, hard decisions about child-rearing, and much more. In the Coles' skillful presentation, all the women in the two volumes are soul-sisters, because all have grown wise through painful trial and error. Regardless of their degree of explicit allegiance to or protest against the Christian church, all exhibit a posture in the world that can only be called faith.

The brother and sister who dominate the moving film "El Norte," which depicts the struggle of Guatemalan campesinos to flee their tyrannized land and find riches in the United States, may stand for the myriad other human beings whose posture in the world is set by systemic injustices. They lose their father and mother because these elders have opposed the oligarchy that controls the politics and the military. They struggle to make their way north through Mexico and finally can celebrate their arrival in the promised land, where they practically expect to find the streets paved with gold. But of course their status as "illegals" in a Southern California all too eager to exploit such cheap labor writes them but a third chapter of suffering. Slowly they start to contemplate the grim possibility that no place truly wants them. The girl dies of illness brought on by rat bites. The last scene of the film has the boy selling the brute labor of his strong arms, exactly as his peasant father was forced to do. The father lost his life for revolting against those who wanted to reduce him to the status of a beast of burden. The son's range of cho' s hardly seems much wider.

Who will liberate the people of Central America, South America, and even North America from the systematic abuses that make so many of their lives sub-human? Who will give the world a more excellent way? One would like to be able to point to the nations historically considered Christian, but the lamentable fact is that very often politicians, military leaders, corporation officials, and even ordinary citizens of those countries have to be counted among the oppressors. The will to liberate the world from poverty and fear is not the first motive that flashes forth from any of the Northern nations' foreign policies. The conversions necessary to move the historically Christian nations onto the side of the angels are far too radical to permit any serious observer easy optimism. And this is the green wood, less liable to the flames of murder and brutality than the totalitarianisms. When one gazes unflinchingly at the current five billion of us human beings, Augustine's "damned mass" comes to mind. Unless a column, a file of holy subversives musters and sets out on a thorough-going guerilla campaign, the inertia that Robert Heilbroner wrote into a dolorous scenario for the human prospect[2] will roll us all toward oblivion.

The Christian church ought to think of itself as such a subversive group. Not in military or political terms, of course. In terms of basic values, ultimate commitments. The roots of the bondage that liberation theology sets out to overthrow are the sins that keep people from cooperating. The church is by definition counter-cultural whenever its primary values of faith, hope, and love contradict the operative values of a given culture. Any time, for instance, that financial profit is the dominant goal, the church has to start to clear its throat to demur. That m~ans that a majority of the time Christians ought to be coughing in the boardroom. As the first draft of the American Catholic bishops' pastoral letter on the American economy made plain, there are many conflicts between capitalistic views, as recently they have dominated the American economic system, and traditional Christian values. In this judgment the bishops were but echoing verdicts at least strongly implicit in Pope John Paul II's encyclical on labor. The Christian instinct that work-relations ought to aim at a fair connection between labor and management, a teamwork in which laborers are by no means the subordinate or disadvantaged (let alone the abused) party, means that again and again today's Christian economists or labor theoreticians find their positions counter-cultural. Let the goods of the earth be seen to exist for all the earth's people, and one cannot do business as though the have-nots were of no account. Let the needs of the poor take priority over the wants or superfluities of the well-to-do, and you have a revolutionary impulse.

The church today is compelled by both love of God and love of neighbor to endure this marginalized, counter-cultural situation. As is becoming clearer to American church leaders, speaking the bare truth about Christian moral instincts means taking on many of the high and mighty, and perhaps even a majority of the electorate. So, for example, the bishops' very hedged approval of nuclear arms as a temporary means of deterrence on the way to negotiations that would reduce, and ideally one day eliminate, all armaments, gives them only a short pause to draw breath. After coming to this difficult, challenging position they then have to cast an unblinking eye on what the nuclear nations actually do by way of movement toward arms reductions. The bishops, like any who read the Scriptures, know all too well that love is shown by deeds. It is not those who say "Lord, Lord" who enter the Kingdom but those who do the Father's will. So too in the judgment of the nations' real will to peace. It is not those who say that more arms will stabilize the situation and bring the adversary to the bargaining table that make the real case. It is those actually moving toward peace, actually proposing the practical steps and making the imaginative or generous overtures.

In the economic order the situation is quite analogous. It is not those who claim that the capitalistic system (let alone the Marxist system) is the best means to raise the standard of living of the whole world that make the case for Christian support. It is those who turn initiative, stimulus, ambition, free enterprise and the rest to making a new order in which the graphs of the economic indicators will dramatically change, the shares of the poor will go on the rise and the shares of the rich will decline. Most of the critics of the bishops' economic pastoral, like most of the critics of other egalitarian visions, profit too much from the current system to allow our taking their protests without considerable skepticism. You can't be chauffeured to work in a re-built Cadillac, jet here and yacht there to hobnob with the mighty and down the best caviar, and be taken seriously as an expositor of an economy or a lifestyle compatible with the New Testament. You've got palpably to intend the flourishing of all God's people, the needs of the many in preference to the wants of the few. You've got to know from the bottom of your soul that any respectable, acceptable God groans with all people who are in bondage, is always on the side of the Hebrews against the oppressive Pharaoh.

Liberation therefore is ingredient in what it means for Christians to be the church. They are "called forth" (the root image of *ekklesia*) to serve God and help usher in God's reign. In the present context, they (we) are called forth to keep alive a justice, mutual regard, love, forgiveness, commitment to recreative new beginnings, and the like that the darkness of warfare and starvation, political oppression and economic manipulation, constantly threatens to overwhelm. The amazing resilience of people like the women interviewed by the Coles, the little brother and sister featured in "El Norte," shows that God is doing God's part. Hope continues to flicker whenever it gets a chance. The part of the people supposed to be knowledgeable about God's "program" for human prosperity, the ways God would have the race relate, is to put forth the ideas and practices that adumbrate a world fit to live in.

So ecclesial faith, as we shall be pondering it here, from the outset takes aim at human liberation. Simply by being faithful to their tasks of preaching God's word and celebrating God's love, the people called forth by Jesus become opponents of all those who would justify oppression and suffering.

Christian Sinfulness

If the theme of faith and liberation stands high on today's ecclesiological agenda, so does the theme of Christian sinfulness. Gone are the days, if ever they legitimately existed, when a triumphalist tone can prevail. The victory that the church preaches is the victory of Christ. Christ's followers participate in that victory, to be sure, but seldom through great merits of their own. Today this quite traditional theological teaching takes sharp form when one considers the roles Christians are playing in warfare and economic injustices, as we have already indicated. Not to put too fine a point on it: Elie Wiesel's rather gentle, sad observation that the victims of the Nazi holocaust are a problem for Jews, but the perpetrators of the holocaust are a problem

for Christians, illumines a massive Christian participation in evil-
doing.

Much of this participation, we may hope, has been inadvertent
or only half-knowing. God alone can mete out the degree of responsibility for the holocaust that the ordinary German citizen, the pope,
the leaders of the free nations, and others deserve. But the fact is that
Nazism developed on soil long considered Christian. One would think
that a vigorous Christian faith would have been able more effectively
to denounce so unChristian a phenomenon. Indeed, one would think
that live Christian faith anywhere would almost surely innoculate
people against the perversions of racism, sexism, pornography, and
the rest, to say nothing of genocide. The conclusion that much modern Christianity has had little lively faith seems unavoidable, and with
it comes the need for all the churches thoroughly to rethink their situations. Have we not seriously underestimated the degree to which
our faith has become merely cultural, a bland form of civil religion?
Have we not grossly ignored the incompatibility between professing
Christian faith and doing business as though Christ had never appeared? If the church is to be alive, Christ must reign as our central
treasure. All too often this is not the case. All too often, we list Christ
alongside our other assets—career going well, kids turning handsome,
sex life quite satisfying—to round out a nice portfolio. The middle-
class prosperity on which American Christianity has thriven in outward terms shows signs of being an inward desert. The mercy of God,
of course, is that the Spirit of God can turn the desert fertile. If we
but confess our sinfulness we may recapture God's power and wisdom.
Nonetheless, we must soberly face the fact that it will not happen automatically. Automatically, things will continue along the same very
questionable track.

Sinfulness, in this perspective, is Godlessness. Without a central
allegiance to the divine mystery, a love that flames forth to offer whole
mind, heart, soul, and strength, we quickly become idolaters. It takes
considerable grace, of course, to discern what is idolatry and what sacramentality. Where one critic finds a capitulation to the world, another may find a winsome appreciation of the goodness of creation. But
over the long haul the patterns are sure to come clear. If a culture
systematically marginalizes large portions of its population, that culture's claim to being Christian or devoted to God is seriously dubious.
If an economy is driven by profit, rather than by service of all the peo-

ple's most basic and important needs, that economy is godless and sinful. Too often we diddle with the external signs of sin, worry over snide remarks or lusty glances. We should take first things first. The gross sins of our time are the stupidities and injustices that wrench the entire international community out of joint. The non-Christian nations have a full share of responsibility for the disjointed state of our world, and there is no good reason why theologians should be shy about documenting their whys and wherefores. On the other hand, it is always an instinct of health to let judgment begin with the household of God. Christian theologians are also not doing their job when they fail to turn the spotlight on their own nations and churches.

Fortunately, we have been blessed with many prophetic theologians whose love of the church is beyond question. Karl Rahner, among Roman Catholics, stands out for his willingness to probe the deep reforms that his tradition needs, and also for his support of his student J. B. Metz, whose socio-political critique has gone even deeper. Among Protestant theologians Robert McAfee Brown has been almost a case study in increasing involvement with liberational and prophetic themes, and were we more familiar with Orthodox theologians we no doubt could summon obvious examples from that tradition. Many of the churches themselves have struggled to redefine their positions on pressing matters of nuclear armaments, social justice, racism, sexism, economic imbalances, ecology, and the like. So certainly the household of God is alert to its present need to submit itself to the judgment of God. We merely would like to make this submission simpler, deeper, and more central to ecclesiology than often it tends to be.

Among many television preachers and right-wing fundamentalists, for example, a sense of election still prevails. Logically enough, this tends to go hand in hand with a moralistic concentration on the supposed sins or faithlessness of the devil-ridden, but on the whole the atmosphere of the airwaves is remorselessly upbeat. In fact, it is remorselessly simple-minded, to the point where one soon suspects that smiling and thinking positively have become a shield against repenting and thinking deeply. No doubt, to be fair, one can find many good deeds done and many prayers sincerely cast upon the waters. In its linkage of Americanism and Christianity, however, the religious right reveals the horrifying possibility that election and rebirth have become warrants for quite gross pride and destructiveness.

So, for example, one finds defenses of profit-making and preparations for nuclear warfare that seem straight out of a manual of Satanic smokescreens. Years ago C. S. Lewis wrote THE SCREWTAPE LETTERS as a warning about the wiles of the enemy in the arena of spirituality. Today one gets a sense of déjà vu, but the stakes are considerably larger, and the topsy-turvyness considerably more serious. Thus we find preachers trying to justify what they call the free enterprise system (in effect the selective defense of certain corporations by the government) by appeals to the book of Proverbs. We find the evils of Soviet or Southeast Asian Communism used to justify American support for Latin American butchers. Our President, who has been willing to let himself be considered reborn, calls the Nicaraguan Contras the "moral equivalent of our Founding Fathers," ignoring such documented atrocities as the following: "Item: Doroteo Tinoco Valdivia, testifying about a large Contra attack in April, 1984, on his farming cooperative, near Yali, Jinotega: 'They had already destroyed all that was the cooperative: a coffee-drying machine, the two dormitories for the coffee cutters, the electricity generators, seven cows, the plant, the food warehouse. There was one boy about fifteen years old, who was retarded and suffered from epilepsy. We had left him in the bomb shelter. When we returned . . . we saw . . . that they had cut his throat, then they cut open his stomach and left his intestines hanging out on the ground like a string.' "[3] The account from which this is taken lists four other items, several if anything worse, and describes all five as simply samples from a pool of over one hundred forty affadavits. To the Christian reader probably the most perverse account is the last, where a female Indian doctor, one of several victims of an extended raping, describes the rapists as chanting "Christ yesterday, Christ today, Christ tomorrow" while they degraded the women.[4]

What is one to say when such perversion gets the implicit approval of the leader of a nation that likes to think itself Christian? The deeper observation, perhaps, is that the rapists were quite correct: They were abusing the contemporary body of Christ.

The simpler observation is the dilemma so frequently set us by the news: Are we dealing with simple fools, who don't realize the idiocy of their judgments, or are we dealing with truly wicked knaves, who know very well their every twisting of the truth? Either way, the throat gags to modify any tolerance of such evil, let alone any sanction or support, with the adjective "Christian." For any part of Christ's body to condone the rape of Christ's body is the worst sort of self-hatred or self-abuse. It is so far-fetched, in fact, that one quickly concludes that it is impossible. No living member of Christ's body could bless the rape, castration, murder, degradation, or other violation of other members. In no meaningful way are people who pass out such blessings Christians. The kindest thing one can say about them is that they haven't the slightest notion of what the Christian church actually is.

What the Christian church actually is is more than sinfulness, of course, and we shall spend most of this book accenting the church's positive graces. We will not get to the level of the people who are most provocatively choosing their church allegiance, however, unless we are willing to sound the depths of putative Christians' complicities in today's disorders. The people most provocatively choosing their church allegiance, to our mind, are the victims of oppression who find Christ their great reason for saying "nonetheless." Many of the Nicaraguans abused by the Contras, and by the Contras' kinsmen who served the dictator Somoza, mourn their dead and try to heal their slashes while saying, "Nonetheless, God will provide." Many of the black Christians who suffered decades of racist abuse said their prayers similarly. For every victim of abuse who curses God probably there are at least two who follow Christ in saying God's will be done. At the deepest level of the spirit, where the mystery of evil brings into focus the mystery of the whole, God has many who are not so much defenders as accepters. One doesn't have to trot out exercises in theodicy, supposed defenses of God, to hand oneself over to the divine darkness. The rabbis in the camps who put God on trial came to a verdict of "Guilty"—and then they turned to God in prayer. Wiesel has said that were he to write a character who would try to defend God's ways in dealing with the victims of the camps, that character would turn out to be Satan. We never do God justice by watering down the wrongness of any great evil. On the other hand, we never do either God or ourselves justice by assuming that any great evil proves the non-existence or uselessness of God, any more than we do either God or ourselves justice by assuming that a great good proves the existence or helpfulness of God. God is always beyond our justification or condemnation. We are always in the position of Job, unable to reckon the proportions of the one who gave the earth its foundations and set the seas their boundaries.

Yet the testimony of many victims of evil-doers is that in the no-man's land to which their experiences took them their hearts or souls dealt with absolutes that their minds were unable to handle. This suggests something important for any significant ecclesiology. What the church finally brings before us, in both its sinfulness and its sanctity, is the true God, the mystery nothing created can either fathom or control. If there is scandalous infidelity among the members of Christ's community, torpor or outright evil so massive as to take our breath away, the final upshot is the divine darkness. Crazily enough, God has somewhat entrusted the fortunes of salvation to the weak flesh of human beings. No matter how lovely the Spirit's firings and glazes, the vessels of election remain quite humble clay. So the sinfulness of the church beckons us toward a deeper faith, as does the church's sanctity. If Stalin could leave the seminary and become one of history's worst butchers, Mother Teresa could go deeper into her religious vocation and find herself called to minister to the most wretched of the earth. Either way, we have before us a sign of the mysteriousness of God's having been willing to take our flesh.

Ecclesiology therefore doesn't do its business apart from the greater Christian tracts on God, Christology, and Redemption. Most of what the gathered people signify depends on the revelation granted in Jesus Christ. To be sure, the church in turn reads us further lessons in such greater theological tracts. For the topic at hand, the sinfulness of the church certainly adds nuance to the more general issues of sin and conversion. At the least, the sinfulness of the church forces us to go below such extrinsic denominations as "Christian" and "Non-Christian," as we might enter them on a census form. Belonging to the social entity of the church certainly is part of ordinary Christian existence, but simply being on the membership rolls or showing up for a Sunday worship service hardly gets to the heart of the Christian matter.

The heart of the Christian matter, in our view, is living the divine life. The divine life, come through the grace of Christ, is the love of Father-Son-Spirit. As Eastern Christian theology especially has made clear, Christian faith immerses us in a process of divinization. If we believe to the extent of truly opening our hearts, the Spirit that we receive is a Spirit that makes us adopted children of God. When this Spirit groans in our depths, with sighs too deep for words, God prays to God. When this Spirit waters what is arid, washes what is dirtied, God serves us as the prime agent of our sanctification. Becoming human, in this perspective, is becoming more and more lost in God. The worldly self that we lose by taking Christ seriously is but the pale shadow of what we can hope to become when the divine mystery really takes us over. On the model of Christ, the divine mystery will become parental, an inmost intimate whom we wouldn't think to doubt. As Christ defined himself by his relationship with his Father, so might any of the baptized, or even any of the simply generously human, were they to see clearly their utter dependence on their Creator.

There are simpler words for these thoughts, of course, and the church should be able to translate its message into them. Our suggestions would include saying that profound faith inculcates the sense that nothing need be lost, no defeat is ultimate, the power that made the world and keeps it going can knit any happening, however apparently destructive or sordid, into the tapestry of the human spirit's victories. Before you call this wishful thinking or merely pious patter, consider the occurrences that are almost routine on any cancer ward, the victories that even the insane, the retarded, the imprisoned, or the brutalized victims of war have won in every generation. Christ on the Cross is for the believer the ultimate index of human sinfulness, and what does Christ on the Cross finally say? "Fear not."

God has overcome the world of evil, torpor, hatred, stupidity, and abuse. God knows all of our losses, all of our church's failures, down to the smallest spot and wrinkle. Yet God still makes the sun to rise, the rain to fall, on just and unjust alike. We do well to strive for a similar tolerance. Between agreeing to evil and constantly focusing on evil lies a central point of balance. The sinfulness of Christians may bulk larger today, when so much evil is structural and shaped by the Northern nations, than it did in past centuries, but the church has never been free of sin. The perennial truth in the Protestant Reformers' slogan, "the church is always to be reformed," shines from every chapter of ecclesiastical history. Peculiar to our day, however, are the threats of nuclear war, and an increased appreciation of how much human misery could be relieved, were our technology to target the world's most pressing problems, our economies to serve the needs of the many rather than the militaristic or luxurious wants of the few.

We know that proper care of the land, proper control of human population, and a fair distribution of wealth and goods could give virtually all the earth's people a shining future. We know that the resources wasted on preparations for war are a major church failure. Thus we know much of the agenda of any liberationist ecclesiology. It must call believers away from their connivance in the modern world's dehumanizing rush after riches and power. It must present the community of Christ as a people with a much more fulfilling way to live.

Post-Christianity?

To describe the ecclesiological agenda in this way is directly to raise the issue of post-Christianity. Have we passed out of the time when Christian values do, could, or should dominate the cultures of the Western nations? Has the great impulse that flowed out of Jerusalem and Rome turned in to the retirement home to nod its way to oblivion? Or do the crises of modern culture but reclarify the need for a conversion to religious values, among which the Christian ideals of love and self-sacrifice can very well hold their own? Is the church, in this latter case, once again a missionary group with an exceedingly relevant message?

No doubt analysts sharply divide in their answers to many of these questions. On the simple matter of demographics, however, it would be premature indeed to sound any death knell. The figures given in the 1984 Yearbook of the Encyclopedia Britannica list well over one billion people as Christians, and probably the figures are conservative. In North America about 25 out of every 39 people are Christians. In South America about 10 out of every 13. Europe shows the ravages that modernity has made in traditional Christian allegiance, for there the figures are below 50%: about 17 out of every 38. In Asia Christians now number about 5 out of every 14 people, while in Africa, where both the Protestant and the Catholic churches have been growing rapidly, the tally is now about 15 out of every 52. In Oceania, finally, the estimate is that 19 out of every 24 people now are Christians. Worldwide, the figures are about 53 out of every 236, or about 23%. Since less than 60% of the world population assigns itself to a religious tradition, Christians are an even more impressive fraction of the world's explicit religious believers: about 40%.

To be sure, there are all sorts of questions that would arise if one tried to run these figures to ground. How they were compiled, and what in fact a self-naming as "Christian" tends to be worth, are only two issues that could spark great debate. But the gross features of the world population surely force us to pause before we accept any facile relegation of Christianity to the past. It is a quite present phenomenon, and of course wherever Christians live, move, and have their being the church of Christ is in play.

What is clear in the figures but perhaps still bears underscoring is that Christianity both remains a significant force in the traditionally Christian portions of the world and now has a vigorous presence in portions traditionally foreign to it. If there are in Africa and Asia together just about a quarter of a billion Christians, the African and Asian churches are hardly insignificant. And while it is true that a Europe less than fifty percent Christian is rather shocking to contemplate, it remains provocative that about 11 out of every 12 Europeans who consider themselves religious have a Christian allegiance. In North America the proportion is even higher: 25 out of every 26 people who claim a religious allegiance name one of the Christian churches.

As our reflections on Christian sinfulness perhaps implied, no eccesiological analyses of present demographics or cultural trends would be wise to base itself on statistics. Many of the people pushing the policies that appear to bring the world great portions of its grief show up in Christian pews on Sunday mornings. The indices that a wise ecclesiology will pay more heed are the indices that Jesus himself would study: the fruits the people produce. Such criteria cut both ways, however, by no means augmenting the case for post-Christianity. For example, surely an analysis of the European majority who profess no religion would find many people of spiritual depth and ethical integrity. Equally surely, it would not be hard to read the "humanism" of such people as owing a great deal to both Jesus and the Christian tradition. Just as many commentators have shown the similarities between the humanism of Karl Marx and the programs of the biblical prophets,[5] so other commentators have argued that modern science is inexplicable without assumptions or confidences (in the intelligibility of creation) that ultimately depend on the biblical depiction of creation.[6] Wherever Shakespeare is played, the audience is exposed to character developments deeply indebted to Christian psychology. Where Mozart is played, people hear a music never very dis-

tant from the cathedral. One can over-gild this sort of cultural
Christianity, of course, but equally one can too lightly dismiss it. The
simple fact is that wherever a humanistic depth or heroism surfaces,
but especially in the nations historically Christian, some Christian influence or analogue is discernible.

As a case study, let us consider the writings of Lewis Thomas,
the Chancellor of Memorial Sloan-Kettering Cancer Center in New
York. His most recent work, THE YOUNGEST SCIENCE,[7] is sufficiently
autobiographical in its early chapters to show a significant Protestant
church upbringing. The rest of the book, like Thomas' other collec-
tions of essays, only nods now and then toward religion, but the language is so knowing and well-wrought that the Bible frequently
hovers, while the humanism, reverence for the mysteries of nature,
and career of social service all easily can be fitted to an at least loosely
Christian mold. Thomas is a man of learning and dedication who
could only have come to think the thoughts he thinks and do the work
he does in a culture beholden to Christian influences. This is no de-
meaning of other, non-Christian cultures. It does not imply that one
could not find even more admirable writers or public servants in other
cultural areas. It is simply a cultural fact. The man thinks his so discerning thoughts, has lived his so public-spirited life, in an ecology
certainly derived from and perhaps even formed by Christian attitudes. If he would list himself among the Christians of North America, he would only be confirming this judgment. But if he would not,
as many of his fellow physicians and scientists probably would not, it
would hardly tell against the vitality of the Christian message, or
hardly tell for the dominance of post-Christianity.

Many of Thomas' virtues and values, of course, grow in other
scientists from Jewish roots. For the simple sort of analysis we have
been making thus far, the distinction between Jewish and Christian
forms of biblical outlook is certainly not very sharp. Moreover, we
shall feel little need to trace down in great detail the differences between the collectivity of religious Jews and the churchly life of Christians. Apart from the obvious fact that they differ in their final
evaluation of Jesus, they share much more than they hold separately.
No, the "other" with whom the church must deal when the question
is post-Christianity is the humanist who has repudiated intellectual
and emotional allegiance to the gospel and the Christ, at least on the
conscious or deliberate level. Thomas shows himself a possibility for

such a description in that little in his writings confesses dependence on Christ or looks to Christ for its ideals. A sort of Deism wafts through his pages, most strongly when he is speaking of the mysteries of nature, all we don't know about the incredibly vast and complex universe. The mood is post-Christian in the at least attenuated sense of not feeling it necessary or fitting to pivot from this appreciation of nature's mysteries to a praise of the Creator. Similarly, when Thomas is referring to the victims of cancer, or other suffering people to whom his long career in medicine has introduced him, no overt connection to the suffering Christ appears. His brooding reflections on the possibility of nuclear holocaust deal more with the music of Mahler than with the themes of divine providence. The move to theology proper is not considered, or is rejected as bad form, in such a way as to put well the church's present apologetic problems.

The church's present apologetic problems differ from group to group, but a central, recurring theme is so many people's refusal to take the basic person of Christ or demands of Christian faith fully seriously. In middle America such a charge may seem hard to sustain, so forcefully do pictures of Jesus and references to the Bible present themselves. Yet again and again one finds the basic person of Jesus wrenched from the community focus that Jesus himself assumed and perverted into a justification for an unbiblical individualism. Or one finds the demand for conversion that the New Testament makes chapter after chapter shunted from the realms of business and politics. People assume that they know what Christian faith means and requires, but their assumption both dilutes the gospel and confuses it with a rather bland form of American patriotism. The middle American culture is post-Christian in its rush after money, its worship of entrepreneurship, and above all its ignorance of the contemplative life necessary to make the Spirit our wellspring.

Among the intelligentsia this bastardization of Christianity merely helps make the case that Christianity is passé. The more honest post-Christian intellectuals rely little on such arguments, however, since they know that one cannot fairly judge a position or way of life by its superficial adherents. The church's apologetic task among the intelligentsia therefore frequently allies it with them in criticism of the emotionalism or ignorance of the culture at large. Christians have the responsibility to make such criticism kindly and without arrogance, of course, but we also have the obligation to make it very clearly. The militarism and injustice of current Western culture are too closely allied with superficial religion and phoney patriotism for the churches not to have a strong responsibility to take to themselves all the valid reasons why people of good mind and heart find so much that goes on in the churches repulsive.

Thus it will be an effective apologetic for those who never would consider taking the church or Christianity seriously to find committed believers by their side at the sorts of events that express a lively, critical spirit. Be such events demonstrations against preparations for war, demonstrations on behalf of people being treated unjustly, practical expressions of help for the poor, or programs (educational, musical, artistic, scientific) of higher culture, a strong Christian presence will be the best argument that the church really does know the proportions of the human struggle, really can be a mother and teacher of what gives light and life.

Beyond this, the apologetic we favor is asking people disaffected from Christianity to put forward their alternatives. Too often the critics of the church are allowed to snipe and pull down without having to carry the burden of proposing a more excellent way. The problem of evil, suffering, death, injustice—what do *you* make of it? Christianity can point to Christ crucified as a powerful "answer" from God. What can you bring forth from your repertoire? Or the mystery of goodness, creation, love, forgiveness, sacrifice—how do you propose to deal with it? Christianity speaks of a good, creative God and a gracious power of redemption. What in your set of symbols, or fund of experience, or programs for political renovation makes more sense of the surplus, gratuitous side?

Most often the supposedly post-Christian respondent has little to match the riches of the Christian tradition. In terms of an articulate worldview, a beautiful sacramental system, and a long list of benefactions on behalf of human beings, Christianity is a most formidable challenger. Even when the opponent legitimately enough can point to the many abuses of human beings that lie on Christianity's head, the many inhibitions and malformations, the alternative still has to be produced, and the alternatives usually suggested either are suspiciously close to positive Christian ideals or have no historical record obviously better than the Christian.

This is the case, for example, with post-Christians of Marxist persuasion. We shall agree, with many of the liberationist ecclesiologists, that Marxist insights into the construction of ideology, class conflicts, the ties between economics and power, and the like offer all social analysts powerful tools that they ignore at the peril of being superficial. But nothing in classical or updated Marxist theory that we have seen comes near to matching the cross and resurrection of Christ in symbolic or experiential power. Similarly, no one from the lists of Marxist heroes, least of all Lenin, is comparable to Jesus for depth, sanctity, or compassionate love. The history of Marxist-Leninism, despite its relative brevity, makes the evils of Christianity seem like kindergarten. The interdict placed on further questions by Marx himself leads Eric Voegelin (no simple-minded proponent of the Christian church) to brand him intellectually dishonest.[8]

Where we travel, along the university circuit, post-Christianity shows in the relative unhappiness and impotence of the professorial class. There are exceptions, of course, and we gladly acknowledge them. But on the whole those in the state universities supposedly learned in the humanities, even in religious studies, present Christianity only a rather pathetic challenge. They tend to talk much and say little. They are as distracted and dominated by worldly tinsel—money, status, gossip, ambition—as any group of callow youths one would send to a monastery for seasoning. So they backbite, philander, and often laze their way through thirty unproductive years, all the while dismissing Christianity, with its riches of asceticism and accomplishment, as having nothing to offer "people come of age." It is bizarre, a most illuminating species of pathology. Because they don't know the depths of their selves, have not mastered the Socratic abcs of self-knowledge, let alone the permutations wrought by Christ's cleansing Spirit, they are T.S. Eliot's "hollow men" (and women), finally more to be compassionated than despised. This would be easier to do, were they less overbearing and condescending, but after a while one sees that pride and pretense also frequently are just masks. Wherever the church has intelligent, healthy people living lives of deep prayer and good, socially significant work, it has a full apologetic to answer the derisions of most of its academic critics.

Thus, to our mind, the issue is not so much post-Christianity as "post-modernity." The spiritual malaise and political impasses of the present age are such that only the foolish now take the program of modernists seriously. Their rationalism, irreligion, and set of liberalist dogmas based on mechanistic science is the program really passé.

It has virtually nothing to say to those wanting a profound cosmology, a profound political science, an educational theory equal to the hunger of our best minds, or a personal way of life properly mystical. No, modernity as epitomized in the Enlightenment enthusiasm for human autonomy, in Laplace's rejection of God as an unneeded hypothesis, had its death knell sounded in the twentieth century's world wars. We are moving away at lightning speed from the eighteenth and nineteenth century problems that absorbed the cultured despisers of the Christian church. The challenge to the church, however, is not to read the disarray of the post-Christians as a vindication of its own conservative or fundamentalist instincts. Only by being more critical than the best moderns, critical to the point of seeing in full clarity how the mind finally is fulfilled by a mystery that criticizes it, can Christians develop the programs needed in the twenty-first century. Only by taking the best of Marxist and other socialist idealism and producing from Christian love of neighbor, Christian realization of the unity of all human beings, economic and political programs both more effective and more generous, can the church be the wave of the future. We have miles to go before we can sleep confident that we are making present in the world the humanizing riches and power of our Christ. If "Christianity" be defined as the medieval synthesis of church and state, or the current American amalgamation of religion and patriotism, we have the almost amusing task of making ourselves the strongest post-Christians.

Community

We have considered the pressing contemporary questions of liberation, sinfulness, and post-Christianity. If the church of Christ is to publish glad tidings at the end of the twentieth century, it must offer persuasive answers to these questions. Moreover, the answers must be more than intellectual or academic. The consoling fact is that when the church really lives as the community of Christ, the branches expressing the life of the vine, it itself *is* the basic answer that honest post-modern people are seeking.

For the most pressing problems of post-modernity boil down to our loss of ultimate meaning, and so our loss of the basis for a profound

common life. No doubt the pluralism of contemporary American life
has its advantages, especially in the realm of personal freedoms. Focusing the spotlight on community therefore is no call for the church
to return to the authoritarianism or monolithic ideals that too often
dominated past ecclesiology. Rather we have in mind an essentialist
concentration on Christ that would make Christian community the
fruit of deep prayer and radical social service.

The unity of the Christian church comes from the common life
that faith, baptism, and the rest both inculcate and express. Far more
important to any significant ecclesiology than statistics on church allegiance, on demographic or ethnic patterns, is the coincidence of allegiance to Christ and a fulfilling humanism. When people share a
radical appreciation of Christ's beauty, a genuine conviction that he
has the words of eternal life, they are bonded at the deepest level. No
matter how much they may have to discuss, even debate, the theological, political, liturgical, and other forms that best express their common conviction, they are members of one body. Compared to what
they hold in common by making Jesus Christ their path through the
wilderness, the pioneer of the faith they hope will make their lives full
successes, what they hold separately as Protestants, Catholics, and
Orthodox, or as Irish, Italians, Polish, and Scots, is relatively insignificant.

This implies quite a definite position in the debates over Christian ecumenism, and elsewhere we have spelled out such a position in
some detail.[9] It also requires a Christian allegiance that is more mystical than sociological—that takes its form more from prayer than from
the patterns of the neighborhood. The patterns of the neighborhood
have their beauty, and certainly their significance, of course, even in
a culture where mobility makes the very notion of "neighborhood"
problematic. But we have left the time when the church can indulge
the partialism, and the anti-ecumenism, that neighborhood parochi-
alism tends to foster. The churches have been seriously derelict in
preferring their separate identities to the welfare of the whole Christian body. To be sure, from the beginning local churches have had
strong rights, and the diversity of ecclesiastical styles just within the
New Testament era is impressive. But nowadays the world has become smaller, through contemporary means of travel and communication. So nowadays the separateness of the Christian churches, and

even more their divisiveness, is a more egregious disobedience of the Johannine Christ's farewell command that his followers be one (John 17) than it has been in the past.

To be blunt about it, the Christian church will be no persuasive herald of liberation from oppression, no bride fit for Christ, no obviously superior alternative to the rag-tag community of agnostic post-Christians, so long as its own house is in manifest disarray. The major Christian bodies—the Roman Catholic church, the World Council of Churches, and the pan-Orthodox assembly—have to become ruthlessly serious about ecumenical unity, which to date they have not been. To date they have all been serving their own preservation, if not their own advantage, more than the cause of Christian unity. They have made very significant progress in doctrinal matters, and they have learned to cooperate in social services. But politically they remain sinfully self-centered. Thus their witness to a world desperately in need of alternatives to the pattern of self-seeking nation-states is to say the least muted.

The history of the church, we must admit, shows few eras when the various church groups in fact lived differently than they do today. Achieving a fine balance between local autonomy and pan-Christian unanimity has long been a grievous problem. Further, we must also admit that the human cultures as a whole regularly have found this balance hard to achieve. In the smallest of groups, such as the family and the cadre of fellow laborers, the tension between individualism and collectivism has been constant.

It is all the more instructive, therefore, that the best solutions to this central problem, the best indicators of where genuine community lies, seem regularly to stem from the moments when the people involved can go below their workaday personas and share their problems and ideals from the heart. In a word, the best indicators of the solution to the problem of community are the contemplative and practical times when people interact with an explicit reference to and reliance upon the Spirit of God.

Apart from reference to the Spirit of God and reliance upon the Spirit's support, all people tend to focus on what they hold separately, rather than on what they hold in common. The danger of individualism, in our experience, is best overcome by forcing or helping people to see that in fundamentals they very much share the same human condition. We all are mortal. We all hunger for love and meaning.

None of us knows the Beginning or the Beyond. These may seem quite abstract or profound issues, but in fact they are both utterly concrete and utterly elementary. It is only the distraction and trivialization dominating so many cultures that makes them seem extraordinary. In themselves they are the most glaring features, the most dominant "controls," in any life or community.

Thus, in any life or community profound connection to other human beings is as close as descent to the center of one's own spiritual life. Any discussion, prayer, or work that takes us to this center, or that waves out from this center, builds up our sense of community. All of us are simply people, and our lives are all short. None of us has ever seen God. In any of our lives there is the memory, if not the present reality, of sore disappointment. In all of our lives fear, self-doubt, and anxiety about the future have had a toehold. Equally (one may hope), in all of our lives there have been Spring flowers, crisp Fall days, sunny children, and good friends who have given the world a bright glow. We need only tell our stories of good times and bad, and let such stories take us to the central silence, the mystery, that all of us must hope and pray is good, to be brothers and sisters, fellow-pilgrims, far below the level of superficial rhetoric.

The danger at the other extreme, that we might become lobotomized into lockstep, people taken out of themselves by the animal contagion one senses in the films of the Nazi rallies or the riots of huge masses of soccer fans, certainly demands attention, but it is not our usual foe. Moreover, the antidote to this contagion again is our becoming deeper, more mature and conversant with the central mystery. The people who lose themselves in mob-psychology are shells of real human beings, masks and outer forms that house no solid individual selves. They are in flight from the silent mystery of God, the radical darkness of the human Beginning and Beyond. Their ec-stasis is an effort to drop the burdens of serious existence, just as the distractions of the average fractious, uncooperative person are an effort to avoid the basic levels where human beings are more like than distinguished or separate.

The community that human beings seek therefore is part and parcel of their aspirations after the reign of God, the state of affairs where the divine Spirit makes life what we sense, in our best hours, it ought to be. Consequently, the vital church life that would answer the major questions of our time amounts to showing the world the togetherness that both human destructiveness and human creativity, in their quite different ways, postulate as necessary for our survival and flourishing. In the church the Spirit ought to be able to make plain, utterly concrete, the alternatives God offers to war and violence, loneliness and separation. When the Spirit finds people sufficiently open to accomplish that, one cannot doubt that the branches mainly have been made to abide in the vine and express the best wine God has.

Anyone who doubts that "community" can serve as such a central symbol of the answers that contemporary humanity is seeking ought to reflect on the major results of contemporary humanity's worst failings, its worldwide recourse to violence and its inability to achieve socioeconomic justice. The nations' rush toward war, their immense outlays for military arms, and their internal violence in so many geographic areas (from Latin America to India, from Africa to Southeast Asia) have as perhaps their worst consequence a despair over the possibility of world peace. Without strong counter-examples of cooperation and community—dramatic happenings much better than what the United Nations has been able to offer—humankind at large has no rational basis for thinking that large-scale peace is possible. Similarly, the gross imbalances in the nations' standards of living mock the notion that all people are created equal, endowed by their Maker with inalienable rights to life, liberty, the pursuit of happiness, and the rest. What person of the slightest critical capacity could link the economic ways of the United States, let alone of the worldwide economic community, with such a profession of faith? When some people starve while other people waste all sorts of resources, the equality that any deep view of human nature comes upon seems derided and degraded. One is forced either to reject "deep views" or idealisms, calling them utterly unrealistic, or to condemn the large fractions of the world population who won't honor such idealisms as stupid, inhuman, or sinful. Either way, the dreams that lead to the Kingdom of God, the bone-deep desires for justice and sharing, come under cruel assault. Either way, the very idea of a "church" or "people of God" can seem chimerical.

All the more powerful, then, are the times and places where the church or the people of God actually occurs. The medieval scholastic philosophers had the dictum, "from being to possibility is a valid illation." If something exists, actually occurs, there is no denying that it can exist, really could occur. So, whenever people make a family,

the worst implications of a cynical Freudianism, in which we spend
our lives trying to undo the maiming inflicted by our parents, stand
countermanded. A single instance in which children grow up whole,
happy, enjoying good relations with their parents, proves that a successful family is possible. The same with teams at work, grass roots
liturgical communities, towns and cities and nations. If even a single
instance of shining success makes the charts, the charts have to provide for the real possibility of human community.

This is not to say, of course, that a single instance is enough to
make prudent people expect successful family life, teamwork, liturgical communities, towns-cities-nations. If the statistics show only a
10% incidence of signal "success," the prudent person will have sober
expectations. Yet on the deeper level of hope and possibility, which is
by no means the same as the level of pragmatism and minimalist prudence, even a single instance saves the day and God's interests. For
what we need if we are to keep going, not give up, is merely possibility:
a chance that our efforts are not wasted. Moreover, as long as we have
a few instances of success to which we can point—for example, a few
saints, who show that full humanity can happen—God's justice is am-
ply protected. God would be unjust, we instinctively think, to give us
hopes, ambitions, aspirations, that *never* are fulfilled. But God would
not be unjust to give us a freedom that, by our own fault, often fails
to come to fruition. God would not be unjust, for example, to make a
world of sufficient natural bounty that, were human beings to use it
wisely and justly, very few people would starve—even though, since
human beings actually use creation unwisely and unjustly, very many
people do starve.

To bring this sort of reflection to bear on the central problem of
community, and wind up our introductory considerations, we can focus on Christ on the cross. Is God unjust to have created a world in
which human beings might have accepted a message and person who
could lead them to God's reign but in fact did not? Or does the success
Christ did have, the acceptance of the Kingdom Christ did witness,
"vindicate" God as wise beyond human calculus? Certainly the Christian instincts, and indeed the Christian dogmas, force us to the second
option. The ways of God with the world are best discerned through
what happened to Jesus of Nazareth. Some people accepted him and
his message. Many other people did not. In some instances he was
successful. In many other instances he was not. His summary failure

was his hanging from the cross, condemned as a criminal. His summary success—not to be separated from his summary failure—was his being raised by the Father to heavenly life. The pattern is very comprehensive and very mysterious. Just about all varieties of "success" and "failure" can be fitted in. Yet, overall, the Christian proclamation is the glad tidings that where sin abounded grace has abounded the more. Overall, Easter Sunday outshines Good Friday.

If the life of Christ is the inmost pulse of the church, this same pattern will hold for the common life of Christians. The church will, both through its overall history and in any given era, display ambiguous data, reasons to call it both a failure and a success. It will succeed in its main task of uniting people to Christ and so to God's communitarian life, but it will also fail. The theologian, working somewhat from the top down, will predict that the church always will succeed enough to keep alive human hopes for community, salvation, a good God who loves humankind. The empirically minded observer, trying to sift out the elements of the church's performance in any given era, will have to struggle to get quite conflicting data and opinions in focus. Indeed, the observer or analyst will have, quite frequently, to test his or her own prejudices or presuppositions. For example, how significant ought one to consider papal prestige, or the influence of the World Council of Churches? Is the higher esteem in which most Westerners hold Jesus than the church to count for failure or success?

Ultimately, of course, these judgments pass into the mystery of divine providence, so the analyst comes to question their profitableness. What the discerning analyst never will question, however, is the value of the times when the church manifestly is the community of Christ, manifestly does show the world a strange human group of which it must be said (with considerable awe): See how they love one another. People who love one another are united, bonded, allied. They show the many other people who do not love one another an alternative. And since the many other people who do not love one another are those most likely to end up going to war or finding themselves less violently (but perhaps no less bitterly) divided, the alternative proves extremely significant, perhaps even a life or death matter. Indeed, in view of the potential in our nuclear weapons, it seems likely that we either will develop this alternative, show the world more striking instances of love and community, or find ourselves shrinking before a Creator furious at our self-destruction.

Summary

Our chapter has been concerned with contemporary questions that set the stage for today's investigations of the Christian church. The first question we considered was the relation between faith and liberation. The basic relation is that faith either responds to the massive, if not indeed universal, cry for liberation from suffering (above all the suffering of meaninglessness) or it (quite rightly) is dismissed as irrelevant. The church, as a community of faith in Jesus Christ, therefore is bound to be concerned with liberation. We used some of the women in Robert and Jane Hallowell Coles' WOMEN OF CRISIS to illustrate the omnipresence of the struggle for liberation. We referred, as well, to the brother and sister of the film "El Norte." The love of Christ would seem to make one the enemy of the values and systems responsible for such suffering. The recent pastoral letters of the American Catholic bishops on peace and economics gingerly agree.

One cannot take this tack, however, and not face up to Christians' complicity in the structures that make so many people groan for liberation. From early on, therefore, any honest ecclesiology has to contend with Christian sinfulness. Such sinfulness, most frequently, is the actual godlessness or faithlessness of people who pretend to Christian allegiance but support ungodly policies or persecutors. Fortunately, the main churches have all been blessed with prophetic theologians who have made it plain that the service of mammon—money, pleasure, worldly power—is idolatry. Fortunately, also, any serious study of the church's sinfulness leads one to the more significant reality of the church's holiness through Christ's Spirit.

Our third contemporary question was whether it is even legitimate to look to the church as a significant cultural factor, granted the claims that history has become post-Christian. In dealing with this question we first turned to some demographics, which showed that Christians continue to be a significant fraction of the world's population, and an even more significant fraction of the people in the world who consider themselves religious. Second, we started to go below such figures, into the difficult matter of what tells for and against "post-Christianity." Lewis Thomas served us as a concrete example of the problems in this matter. Third, we considered some of the apologetic tasks that the apparent demise of Christian influence sets the church, stressing the need to criticize superficial Christian allegiance, and also the need to force those who would dismiss Christianity to come up with positive alternatives. Our conclusion was that "post-modernity" may be more significant than "post-Christianity."

To bring our brief survey of contemporary questions to a summarizing conclusion, we dealt with the issue of community, sensing that when the church palpably is the community bonded in Christ's love it serves the world most of the answers the world nearly desperately seeks. This led us to some depressing considerations of Christian disunity, and to some sober recollections of church history, but also to some lines for hope. The nations' warmaking and injustice does its worst damage by destroying our belief that peace and justice can occur. Consequently, whenever instances of genuine human community do occur, as in the church's presentation of groups of people who really do love one another, the positive effects are incalculably helpful.

STUDY QUESTIONS

1. How valid is the claim that "faith" and "liberation" are virtually universal issues?
2. Of what oppressive values must the church be subversive?
3. What do you find the most glaring examples of contemporary Christians' sinfulness?
4. What does the mysteriousness of God imply for our judgments of evil and goodness?
5. What are the implications of the fact that non-Christian Europeans now outnumber Christian?
6. How valid is the claim that deriders of Christianity have the obligation to propose (better) alternative responses to the mysteries of both evil and goodness?
7. What place ought ecumenical unity to have on the church's agenda?
8. Why is world-wide injustice so devastating to human hope?

NOTES

1. Robert Coles and Jane Hallowell Coles, WOMEN OF CRISIS and WOMEN OF CRISIS II. New York: Delta, 1979, 1980.

2. Robert Heilbroner, AN INQUIRY INTO THE HUMAN PROSPECT. New York: W.W. Norton, 1980.

3. See "Notes and Comment," THE NEW YORKER, March 25, 1985, pp. 34–35.

4. Ibid., p. 35.

5. See, for example, José Miranda, MARX AND THE BIBLE. Maryknoll, NY: Orbis, 1974.

6. See, for example, Stanley Jaki, THE ROAD OF SCIENCE AND THE WAYS TO GOD. Chicago: University of Chicago Press, 1978.

7. Lewis Thomas, THE YOUNGEST SCIENCE. New York: Viking, 1983.

8. See Eric Voegelin, SCIENCE, POLITICS & GNOSTICISM. Chicago: Regnery, 1968, p. 28.

9. See John Carmody, THE HEART OF THE CHRISTIAN MATTER. Nashville: Abingdon, 1983.

Chapter 2

Scriptural Sources

The Old Testament Background ♦ The Pauline Churches ♦ The Synoptic Churches ♦ The Johannine Churches ♦ Conclusion: The Biblical Christian Community ♦ Summary, Study Questions, Notes

The Old Testament Background

Jesus was a Jew, completely immersed in the religious heritage of his people. The first Christians were mainly Jews, formed through and through by the many centuries through which their people had lived covenanted to the God whom Jesus called "Abba": "Father." The self-conception of the Christian people that we find in the New Testament therefore makes little sense without the Jewish background that we can glean from the Old Testament. Christ's followers first considered themselves a portion of Israel, God's elected people, and then the heir of Israel's privileges. Either way, to understand the Christian community one must understand something of "Israel."

As was true of virtually all traditional (pre-modern) peoples, biblical Jews made no significant distinction between their religion and their overall culture. Their God was Lord of their whole lives. And, by comparison with the peoples who were their neighbors, the Israelites were distinctive for having a non-mythological God who was utterly sovereign and free of the world: "The basic idea of Israelite religion is that God is supreme over all. There is no realm above or beside him to limit his absolute sovereignty. He is utterly distant from, and other than, the world; he is subject to no laws, no compulsions, or powers that transcend him. He is, in short, non-mythological. This

32

is the essence of Israelite religion, and that which sets it apart from all forms of paganism."[1]

The practice of this conviction was expressed in or shaped by the law that Israel accepted under Moses. The people considered themselves to have been freed from slavery in Egypt by their singular God. On Mount Sinai, they believed, God had established a special bond with them—what they called a "covenant"—and the Teaching or Law (Torah) that guided their life was meant to express, protect, and forward this bond. At the core of Israelite religion and life, in fact, was the distinctive belief that the whole people (traditionally pictured as gathered at Sinai) had received God's revelation of the responsibilities that the covenantal bond imposed: "The new Sinaitic covenant superimposes upon the ancient individual obligation a new, national one. Morality ceases being a private matter. Because the covenant was accepted en masse, by all, all become responsible for its observance. When the Israelites stood together and heard the command 'I am YHWH your God,' a new moral subject was created: the community of persons that know YHWH."[2]

The Old Testament uses a variety of words to describe or indicate this community. The word *am,* for example, points to the group insofar as it is bound together by such ties as blood, common speech, traditional mores, and a shared history. For the early period of Israelite history, when life was clannish and nomadic, *am* suggests tribal relationships. So, for instance, Genesis 25:8 describes Abraham's death as his being gathered to his (clan) people: "Abraham breathed his last and died in a good old age, an old man and full of years, and was gathered to his people." Later *am* can suggest whatever body of people or population is at hand, as in the prophet Elisha's usage in 2 Kings 4:41: "He said, 'Then bring meal.' And he threw it into the pot, and said, 'Pour it out for the men [*am*], that they may eat.' " To render *am,* the Greek (Septuagint) translation of the Hebrew Bible normally uses *laos.*

The second leading word for the Old Testament collectivity is "Israel" itself. This name goes back to Jacob, whom the people considered a common ancestor. In Genesis 32:28 Jacob's name is changed to Israel, after his wrestling with the angel: "Then he said, 'Your name shall no more be called Jacob, but Israel, for you have striven with God and with men, and have prevailed.' " The etymology of this

word is uncertain, but the usual scholarly conjecture is something like
"he who strives with God."

Of "Israel" Josef Scharbert has written: "As far as is known from
the Old Testament the name stood from the outset for something conceived to be sacred. Those who bore it comprised all the tribes together
assembled round the ark of the covenant and united in the worship of
Yahweh, that is, the people of God whom Yahweh had chosen."[3]
When the kingdom split in two, the northern portion became known
as Israel and the southern as Judah, but "Israel" still had the connotation of the whole, all the twelve tribes. After the exile to Babylon,
both Jews returned to Palestine and Jews living dispersed outside Palestine used the word to signify their identity as a religious and ethnic
community.

A third important word was *qahal,* the root sense of which was a
crowd or an assembly. The occasion for the assembly could be mus-
tering for war or gathering to take decisions affecting the collectivity,
but the more usual reason was common worship. The Septuagint almost always translates *qahal* as *ekklesia.* The New Testament then
takes *ekklesia* to designate the Christian people, and the usual English
translation of *ekklesia* is "church."

Through these various designations of the Jewish collectivity, the
Bible expresses the conviction that individuals only gain access to God
and salvation by belonging to the people that God has chosen. This
people have an organic unity, based on ties of blood, outlook, desires,
social standards, and the like. Certainly their most central bond, however, is their confession and worship of their God Yahweh. Yahweh
has chosen them (not vice versa). They walk in the line of the patriarchs with whom God communicated, and the Torah that they observe
outlines their covenant with God. As mediators between themselves
and God they have first of all Moses, through whom the covenant and
its law were delivered. They also have outstanding priests, prophets,
and kings (the ideal of whom was David). These individuals function
less for themselves than for the whole people. In both its origins and
its development, the covenant is a collective, social affair.

Even within the Old Testament, however, the covenant became
a rather complicated or rich concept. It had a legal side, in that both
the people and Yahweh were pictured as pledged to certain obligations. Yet it was far from being a deal struck by two equals. On the
whole Israel inclined to picture the covenant as the mercy of God, a

great gift: "Yahweh was a *personal* God who demanded personal loyalty. The sides were by no means equal. Israel recognized that the covenant was a gift from God and an honor for them and not the other way around. God freely chose to bind himself to this people, but not blindly no matter what they did in return. As the centuries went on [many biblical authors] expressed the conviction that Israel's continual sin and rebellion would bring divine punishment that would lead to the end of the covenant blessings. Violations of the solemn agreement would bring consequences against God's people just as fidelity would bring divine favor. Both were aspects of the one covenant."[4]

Within the framework of reward and punishment, the inmost pulse of Israel's religious life was a conviction that its God was gracious, more inclined to do good and forgive than to count sins and rush to judgment. One of the loveliest expressions of this central conviction occurs in Exodus 34:6–7. Moses has gone up Mount Sinai. God descends to Moses in a cloud and describes himself as follows: "The Lord, the Lord, a God merciful and gracious, slow to anger, and abounding in steadfast love and faithfulness, keeping steadfast love for thousands, forgiving iniquity and transgression and sin. . . ." Despite the fact that verse seven goes on to promise God's remembrance of sin, the deepest intuition or hope is of God's mercy and love.

From this sense of God's special love, Israel developed a sense of election. This is clear in several of the prophets. Amos 3:2, for example, suggests both special privileges and special obligations: "You only have I known of all the families of the earth; therefore I will punish you for all your iniquities." The price of Israel's warm and close relation with God was the requirement that the people keep the Torah of the covenant. Since the ethical demands of the Torah were considerably more stringent than what most other people asked of themselves, the Israelites came to think of themselves as set apart. Samuel Sandmel has summarized much of the upshot as follows: "The concept of Israel as God's chosen, elected for obligation, but first in divine concern and affection, became a cornerstone of Israelite thought. In the variety of abundant passages reflecting the concept (e.g., in Psalms), one voice might stress God's universalism, virtually ignoring the particular people, while another voice might stress the particular people, virtually ignoring the heritage of universalism."[5]

Second Isaiah is a milestone in the development of the notion that Israel is God's elect servant, chosen by God for God's own purposes.

The question of whether Gentiles (non-Jews) could join Israel was answered differently at different times. Thus Zechariah 8:20–23, Isaiah 2:2–3, and Micah 4:1–2 allow for proselytes, while Ezra 4:3 and Nehemiah 13:23–30 suggest an Israel closed to outsiders. On the other hand, again, both the book of Ruth and the book of Jonah have a universal outlook, seeing God as having a salvific care for the Gentiles. It seems safe to say, therefore, that Israel had a variety of thoughts about the degree of its specialness. Throughout, however, it praised God for electing it to the covenant relationship, while never doubting that (the one) God also controlled the fate of the Gentiles.

The holiness that Israel came to demand of itself, or to be convinced that God demanded of it, was both ethical and cultic. One sees this especially in the book of Leviticus. Leviticus 1, for instance, speaks of the different kinds of sacrifices one was to make to the Lord. Leviticus 19 links holiness, reverence for parents, keeping the sabbath, and avoiding idols: "And the Lord said to Moses, 'Say to all the congregation of the people of Israel, You shall be holy; for I the Lord your God am holy. Every one of you shall revere his mother and his father, and you shall keep my sabbaths: I am the Lord your God. Do not turn to idols or make for yourselves molten gods: I am the Lord your God.' " This refrain, "I am the Lord your God," suggests the central reasoning of the "holiness code" (Leviticus 17—26) that summarizes much of the moral law demanded of the covenant people. To be bonded to Yahweh, Israel has to be holy like Yahweh. It would not do to bring an unclean spirit before the immaculate deity. The power of God coincided with God's holiness, so uncleanness or sin was risking a destructive backlash from God.

The carry-over into social relations is also significant. The people are to be holy not only in their cultic relations with God but also in their neighborly transactions. Thus Leviticus 19:17–18 lays it down as a commandment of God: "You shall not hate your brother in your heart, but you shall reason with your neighbor, lest you bear sin because of him. You shall not take vengeance or bear any grudge against the sons of your own people, but you shall love your neighbor as yourself: I am the Lord."

In his illuminating study of the popular religion of ancient Israel, Moshe Greenberg focuses on the spontaneous prayers of common people, showing how they are structured on the model of personal communications between two human beings. Every Israelite had the right to deal with God directly and personally. The priesthood and official cult was never meant to supply for less formal and more personal prayer. This was part and parcel of an egalitarian tendency that Greenberg finds at the roots of Israel's self-conception. Allied to the call for holiness was the notion that all the people, not just the ritual priests, would have familiar interactions with God: "Constant familiar intercourse with God, unmediated by priest or other ritual expert, could only have strengthened the egalitarian tendency (a tendency verging on anarchy) that was rooted in Israel's self-conception. The express purpose of God in offering to make Israel his covenanted people is to convert them into his 'kingdom of priests, a holy nation' (Exod. 19:6)—that is, a holy commonwealth in which all members enjoy priestlike intimacy with God."[6]

Although the covenant made with God through Moses on Mount Sinai was the central determinant of Israel's self-conception, two other covenants had significant influence. Abraham, the father of the people, receives a pledge that the land of Canaan will belong to his descendants forever, while David, the founder of the kingdom, receives an analogous pledge that his dynasty will go on endlessly. Moshe Weinfeld has contrasted these two covenants with the Mosaic covenant as follows: "The covenant with David constitutes a pledge given by God to establish David's dynasty forever and is typologically similar to the covenant with Abraham, which is an oath by God to give his children the land of Canaan forever. Both covenants are diametrically opposed to the Mosaic covenant, in which the people pledge loyalty to God. The Abrahamic and Davidic covenants are then a promissory type, while the Mosaic covenant is an obligatory type."[7] For our purposes, both the Abrahamic and the Davidic covenants increase Israel's sense of being chosen by God for special intimacy and special functions in God's historical plans.

The social solidarity of Israel in its covenant relations with God remains in force even when one comes across apparently individualistic passages such as Jeremiah 31:29–35 and Ezekiel 18 or 33:1–20. John L. McKenzie has explained this very well: "No relation of the individual to the deity was known except the relation of membership in a cult group identified with the social group. The collapse of the Israelite political society in the time of Jeremiah and Ezekiel left no relationship of the individual Israelite with Yahweh. In the ancient world a god without a people simply vanished. Jeremiah and Ezekiel were not exactly the creators of personal religion, as many scholars have called them, although one cannot deny that they made statements about personal responsibility that have no parallel in earlier OT literature. Rather, the emphasis of their statements is an assurance that Yahweh has not ceased to exist and that Israel is still his people."[8]

What, then, are we to conclude about the overall Old Testament background to the New Testament understanding of the community God had fashioned in Christ? First, that the Jews of Jesus' day, for all the changes that more than three centuries under Greek and Roman rule had wrought in their self-conception, still had deep in their heritage the notion that they were bonded to God as a special people. Second, that the Mosaic covenant, with its ethical and cultic requirements, was the form in which much of their response to God was worked out. The "Law" that plays so prominent a role in Jesus' teaching and the theology of Paul shows that the Judaism of their day took the Mosaic covenant very seriously. Third, that the vocabulary available to Jesus' followers, when they sought to express their sense of being a group formed by God's new actions in their day, inevitably ran to words that carried overtones of election and covenant. If they decided to conceive of themselves in the lineage of Israel, they were bound to struggle with the newness of their election, covenant, assembly for worship, or social relationships. Above all, they were bound to compare the love they held responsible for their creation with the love that had created Israel. Just as texts such as Isaiah 54:10, Jeremiah 31:3, and Micah 7:20 entrusted Israel to God's covenantal *hesed* (steadfast love), so Christians would entrust their community to the love of Christ.

The Pauline Churches

In fact, the Christians who entrusted themselves to the love of Christ constituted a variety of communities. The impression one receives from the earliest Christian literature is that the local church was more significant than the church universal. It took some time for the church universal to develop structures that would connect all the Christian believers. No doubt a sense that all followers of Jesus shared a great deal and were significantly bonded together existed from the beginning. But what strikes the impartial observer about the first Christian generations is the diversity of the different communities' theologies and political styles. We see this even within "schools" such as that formed by several generations of Christians whose basic outlook was formed by the apostle Paul. As the years raised new problems, and missionary activities took Paul's followers to new cultural areas, Pauline ecclesiology changed considerably.

We may consider these changes as constituting three phases. First, there is the sense of the Christian community that we find in the letters that almost certainly came from Paul's own hand. Second, there is the ecclesiology of Colossians and Ephesians, which probably did not come from Paul's own hand but from a second generation of the apostle's followers. Third, there is the ecclesiology of the Pastoral letters, which likely are later still and represent a period of consolidation, when the church's leaders felt the need to stress orthodoxy and discipline.

In 1 Thessalonians, which is probably the earliest of Paul's own writings (indeed, probably the earliest writing in the entire New Testament), we find the word *ekklesia* used in two senses. 1:1 speaks of "the church of the Thessalonians in God the Father and the Lord Jesus Christ," while 2:14 describes the Thessalonians as having become "imitators of the churches of God in Christ Jesus which are in Judea." Recalling that *ekklesia* was the regular Septuagint translation of the Hebrew *qahal* or "assembly," we get the sense that Paul thinks of the "church" as the local assembly of Christian believers. The second instance cited above (2:14) further suggests that initially this designation of Christ's followers was used in Judea, the area of Jerusalem. If so, it would be applied to the Thessalonians by way of extension, saying in effect that the sort of gatherings of Christians that were established in Judea in the first decade or so after Jesus' death were now in place as far away as Thessalonia.

Finally, we note that the Thessalonian church has for Paul a sort of theologico-spatial "location." It exists "in" God the Father and the Lord Jesus Christ, or it is like the churches of God in Judea that exist "in" Christ Jesus. This is metaphorical speech, no doubt, but already it suggests that the Christian assembly takes its orientation from God and Christ so essentially that its placement in the world, its siting in reality, is within the spiritual being of God. For Paul the churches therefore certainly are not in the first instance organizations just like other social bodies. They take their identity from something other-worldly.

In the "great letters" that Paul is thought to have written to such communities as the Corinthian, Galatian, Philippian, and Roman Christians, the local church remains to the fore. Thus Galatians 1:22 has Paul describing a prior stage of his Christian career with the words, "and I still was not known by sight to the churches of Christ in Judea." 1 Corinthians 11:16 seems to retain a primary reference of "churches" to the early communities of Judea, but implicitly to extend it to the Corinthians. Paul is trying to win the Corinthians over to his point of view in the somewhat confusing matter of whether women ought to pray with their heads uncovered. He buttresses his opinion by saying, "If anyone is disposed to be contentious, we recognize no other practice [than covered heads], nor do the churches of God." The sense would be, then, that the Corinthians are a church (or a group of churches) like the assemblies of Judea and should fit themselves to the customs of their venerable predecessors. Implied, however, would be a linkage or even an equality between Corinth and Judea: a sameness of custom would argue for a sameness of identity or being, maybe even for a sameness of status. Other citations in the Corinthian correspondence (1 Cor 1:2, 6:4, 10:32, 12:28, 14:5,12; 2 Cor 1:1, 8:11) support the sense that Paul is broadening the notion of *ekklesia,* so that it covers not just the local Christian assembly but the commonality or bonding of the local churches in a federation or body that unites them all. Romans, the greatest of Paul's letters, somewhat surprisingly says little about the church, except in chapter 16 (which may well be an add-on), where the usage refers to the local assembly.

The disciples of Paul who wrote Colossians and Ephesians extended his thought so as to make "the church" a more universal entity. Colossians, in fact, makes the Christian assembly Christ's "body." So, for example, the famous hymn of Colossians 1:15–20 speaks of the Son of the (divine) Father as not only the image of the invisible God and first-born of all creation but also "the head of the body, the church." (1:18) Colossians 1:21–22 may also have the church in mind when it says to the Colossians of Christ the Son: "And you, who once were estranged and hostile in mind, doing evil deeds, he has now reconciled in his body of flesh by his death, in order to present you holy and blameless and irreproachable before him." The body being discussed here certainly is the body of Jesus that hung on the cross, but reconciliation also has taken place in the Christian assembly, since it is there that Christians have found peace with God and one another. 3:15 in fact links the peace that comes with Christian faith to the one body of Christ's followers: "And let the peace of Christ rule in your hearts, to which indeed you were called in the one body." A generation or so after the ministry of Paul, therefore, his followers were conceiving of the Christian collectivity as a unified body. No doubt a major stimulus to this conception was Paul's own use of this metaphor in 1 Corinthians 12:12–13: "For just as the body is one and has many members, and all the members of the body, though many, are one body, so it is with Christ. For by one Spirit we were all baptized into one body—Jews or Greeks, slaves or free—and all were made to drink of one Spirit."

It is Ephesians, however, that most fully develops the image of the church as the body of Christ. For example, 1:22–23 has the Father giving Christ full dominion: "He has put all things under his feet and has made him the head over all things for the church, which is his body, the fullness of him who fills all in all." This use of *ekklesia* is quite an advance over the common-sensical use with which Paul began, which seems to have had in mind only the local assembly. Indeed, the church now becomes the fullness of Christ, who as a spiritual power already fills all in all. The church therefore is expanding its connotation in the direction of the vast outreach of the eternal Word of God or resurrected Christ.

Ephesians 3:9–10 indicates how the church functions in the mysterious divine plan of revelation and salvation. "Paul" speaks of his grace to preach to the Gentiles and make all people see "what is the plan of the mystery hidden for ages in God who created all things, that through the church the manifold wisdom of God might now be made known to the principalities and powers in the heavenly places." Clearly, the author has put in the mouth of the apostle a sense of the church as a heavenly reality, a basic component in the structure of God's whole plan, which embraces both time and eternity, both earth and heaven. 4:15–16 is explicit that Christ is the head of the ecclesial body and the source of its growth, while Ephesians 5:22–30 develops the famous simile according to which Christ stands to the church as a husband to his wife: "Wives, be subject to your husbands, as to the Lord. For the husband is the head of the wife as Christ is the head of

the church, his body, and is himself its Savior. As the church is subject to Christ, so let wives also be subject in everything to their husbands. Husbands, love your wives, as Christ loved the church and
gave himself up for her, that he might sanctify her, having cleansed
her by the washing of water with the word, that he might present the
church to himself in splendor, without spot or wrinkle or any such
thing, that she might be holy and without blemish. Even so husbands
should love their wives as their own bodies. He who loves his wife
loves himself. For no man ever hates his own flesh, but nourishes and
cherishes it, as Christ does the church, because we are members of
his body."

In another context we might point out the problems that this parallel between the headship of Christ and the headship of the husband
in a marriage has created for women. Here, however, our principal
concern is to underscore the intimacy between Christ and the church
that the author sees. The mystery of human union, in fact, is deep-
ened by the union between Christ and the church. The identity of
Christians with their Lord is that of a common life, an organic oneness
and compenetration.

Before moving to the behavior that Ephesians, and then the Pastoral Epistles, stipulate for church members, we should pause to consolidate the central theological strands of the Pauline ecclesiology,
because they have been immensely influential in Christian history. In
the contemplative rumination of the Pauline communities, the *ekklesia* of God or Christ moved from a primarily local to a universal or even
cosmic significance. At first the assembly in mind was the Christians
of a given locale: Thessalonia or Corinth. Indeed, "church" on this
level might be the very small group that would gather regularly at one
or more of the members' houses. Wayne Meeks has studied the Pauline letters from a sociological perspective and eked out several stimulating hypotheses about the wealth, ethnic background, social
status, and the like of the Pauline Christians.[9] At the local level, they
no doubt appeared to outsiders as merely members of another one of
the many clubs or religio-social organizations that dotted the urban life
of the Hellenistic world. But through the Pauline literature we can
see a deepening of Christians' internal sense of what their assembly
meant. At an intermediate stage, the many local churches reached toward one another to make an ecumenical network—an international
assembly that could stretch as wide as the inhabited world. Insofar as

they shared a similar faith, their brotherhood and sisterhood passed beyond local boundaries.

By the time of Ephesians, however, even this ecumenical outreach has passed from the center of attention. Without denying the local or ecumenical dimensions, the author of Ephesians is absorbed with the place of the church in the divine plan of salvation. The later usage that we find, for example, in the encyclical of Pope Pius XII on the church, derives from this theology of Ephesians. For Pius XII the church is the "Mystical Body" of Christ, and we have seen the texts that support this view. The later church also thought of itself as the bride of Christ, another motif from Ephesians. Clearly the farthest reaches of the Pauline ecclesiology could encourage a grandiose, even a triumphalistic self-conception. The author of Ephesians has his head in the clouds, because the final significance of the Christian assembly is the union with Christ, the fullness of Christ, that the angels and principalities witness.

Both Colossians and Ephesians (which borrows considerably from Colossians) have ethical instructions for the Christian community that are borrowed from the family mores of the Hellenistic world. Scholars sometimes refer to these instructions as *haustafeln*: household codes (see Colossians 2 and Ephesians 4). The basis for the purity of behavior asked in such codes is the life in Christ that church members should be living. Apparently the authors of these letters felt that this life was threatened by false teachings that were circulating, some of which carried the danger of moral laxity. This fear has become a substantial factor in the composition of the Pastoral epistles, the primary tone of which is cautionary and conservative. Allied with this tone is the prominence of the leader of the local church, and a clearer sense of church governance or structure than what we find in the earlier Pauline literature. (Like Colossians and Ephesians, the Pastoral letters probably come from disciples of Paul rather than from Paul himself.)

In dealing with the death of the first generation of church leaders such as Paul, the local churches had to fashion a means both to ensure fidelity to the traditions they had received and to adapt those traditions to new circumstances. The Pastorals stress fidelity to the traditions, while other parts of the New Testament (for example, the Johannine literature, with its spotlighting of the Spirit), stress the means of adaptation.

The figure highlighted in the Pastorals is the elder or bishop, who becomes the main defender and interpreter of tradition. Raymond E. Brown has summarized the background to the rise of this figure to prominence as follows: "Although the word *presbyteros* (comparative of *presbys*, 'old,' meaning 'elder' in Greek) refers to age, the custom of seeking advice from the senior men of a community meant that the 'elder' or 'presbyter' came to designate a functionary chosen ideally for wisdom, often elder in age but not necessarily so. Jewish synagogues had groups of elders or presbyters who set synagogue policy. Christian presbyters, however, had a pastoral supervising role that went beyond the Jewish counterparts; and so we find them designated by a second title, *episkopos*, 'overseer, supervisor, bishop.' The oft-made claim that the *presbyteros* is a role borrowed from Judaism while the *episkopos* is a role borrowed from Gentile (pagan) secular and religious adminis-tration is oversimplified and ignores the evidence of the Dead Sea Scrolls. In the century and a half before Christianity the Essenes de-scribed in the Scrolls had, besides presbyters, functionaries called 'ov-erseers' with teaching, admonitory, and administrative roles almost identical to those of the bishops of the Pastorals."[10]

The presbyter-bishop who dominates the churches of the Pas-torals has two main duties. First, he (apparently only men are eligible) is the official teacher in the community. So "Paul" tells Timothy: "Command and teach these things. Let no one despise your youth, but set the believers an example in speech and conduct, in love, in faith, in purity. Till I come, attend to the public reading of Scripture, to preaching, to teaching. Do not neglect the gift you have, which was given you by prophetic utterance when the council of elders laid their hands upon you. Practice these duties, devote yourself to them, so that all may see your progress. Take heed to yourself and to your teaching; hold to that, for by so doing you will save both yourself and your hear-ers." (1 Tim 3:11–16) The implication is that Timothy was commis-sioned for this task of leadership and teaching and so can be confident he has God's help and approbation in it.

Second, the presbyter-bishop is to serve the household of God like a reliable and prudent father, administering its goods honorably and setting it a fine moral example. 1 Tim 3:1–7 lists some of the virtues that a church leader must have, and the basic line of reasoning is that he should have been proved successful in managing his own household of wife and children. The good character that the head of the local church ought to display aims at impressing his Christian subjects, yes, but also the outside society. By the time of the Pastorals the church has become a somewhat settled institution that has to reckon with the surrounding Gentile society. Many of the somewhat bourgeois virtues that the Pastorals extoll probably derive from this sensitivity to the opinion of outsiders. If the church can present the world a membership, and even more importantly a leadership, of admirable character, it will be likely to receive little harassment and maybe even will elicit outsiders' respect. The church has come to grips with the delay of Christ's return.

The Synoptic Churches

Among Mark, Matthew, and Luke-Acts, it is the latter body of writing and ecclesiastical tradition that bears closest connection to the Pauline. For while the author of Luke-Acts is not especially Pauline in his theology, the mission of Paul to the Gentiles obviously has greatly shaped his sense of the good news. The second half of Acts clearly enough is dominated by Paul, and throughout Acts uses the word *ekklesia* for local churches, as we saw was the dominant use in writings by Paul himself. To be sure, Acts shows none of the mysticism of the church so important to the Pauline theology of Colossians and Ephesians. But in his emphasis on the role of the Holy Spirit in the spread of the church (through the missionary impulse that Paul most dramatically exemplified), the author gives the network of Christian communities both a central place in the divine economy of salvation and a powerful source of interiority.

The divine economy of salvation that structures Lucan theology often has been likened to a triptych. The first panel is the history of Israel, the people of God with whom the history of salvation began. The second panel is the life of Christ, who for Luke brought the promises of Israel to fulfillment. And the third panel is the time of the church, which under the Spirit is extending salvation to the Gentile world. The church therefore "inherits" the mantle of Israel, as the people of God, and also some of the functions of Christ. Christ is present to the church, alive within the church, but the Spirit is at least equally prominent in the inspiration of church life. Thus one of the early designations for the Christian community is "the way" (of

Christ, under the Spirit). In other places Luke refers to members of the Christian assembly as "disciples" or "brethren." Both terms suggest the fellowship (*koinonia*) that faith in Jesus produced.

A final Lucan contribution to the New Testament's sense of Jesus' community shines through in the place he, along with the other Synoptics, accords to "the twelve." As Joseph Fitzmyer has summarized it: "Luke too is aware of a group in the early church called 'the twelve.' Like the other Synoptic evangelists he traces the origin of this group to the ministry of Jesus himself (Luke 6:13; cf. Mark 3:14; Matt 10:1–5). That there is much to be said for this origin can be seen in the way the early church remembered with horror that Jesus was betrayed by Judas, who was 'one of the twelve' (Mark 14:10, 43; echoed by Luke 22:3, 47; Matt 26:14; cf. John 6:71). Luke follows Mark in making further use of them in his Gospel (see 8:1; 9:1, 12 [their mission]; 18:31; 22:3, 47; cf. 24:9, 33 [the Eleven, minus Judas]. That they serve as an important link between Jesus and the early church is seen in the beginning of Acts, where the initial nucleus of disciples feels that it is necessary to reconstitute the Twelve and Matthias is chosen by lot to be with 'the Eleven' in the place vacated by Judas' death (1:26). Luke sought to explain this necessity by the relation of the new community to be fashioned on Pentecost to that of Israel (represented by its twelve tribes)."[11] Later in Acts, however, when James, another of the twelve, is put to death, no one is appointed to take his place. Whatever the actual historical occurrence, it seems clear that Luke's theology did not feel the need to keep the twelve prominent in the regular reconstitution of church authority.

Mark, whom the majority of New Testament scholars consider the earliest of the evangelists, has little treatment of the church as such. Rather Mark's interest is presenting the drama of Jesus' life in such a way that Jesus' followers will hang on until Jesus' return. Thus Mark stresses the demands of Christian discipleship, mainly by keeping before his readers what sort of a Messiah Jesus was. No doubt the sharpest example of this Marcan stress occurs in 8:31–38: "And he [Jesus] began to teach them that the Son of Man must suffer many things, and be rejected by the elders, and be killed, and after three days rise again. And he said this plainly. And Peter took him, and began to rebuke him. But turning and seeing his disciples, he rebuked Peter, and said, 'Get behind me, Satan! For you are not on the side of God, but of men.' And he called to him the multitude with his disciples, and said to them, 'If any man would come after me, let him deny himself and take up his cross and follow me. For whoever would save his life will lose it; and whoever loses his life for my sake and the gospel's will save it. For what does it profit a man, to gain the whole world and forfeit his life? For what can a man give in return for his life? For whoever is ashamed of me and of my words in this adulterous and sinful generation, of him will the Son of Man also be ashamed. . . .' "

For Mark's community, the suffering and death of Christ have become the key to Christian life. If Jesus experienced so sorry a fate, the dedicated follower can hardly expect to have it easy. Mark clearly displays a skeptical, even a negative view of the time after Jesus' death, probably meaning to castigate both believers and outsiders. Indeed, such prominent students of Mark as Norman Perrin and Dennis Duling liken the author's purpose to that of John of Patmos, the author of Revelation.[12] Mark thinks that Jesus will soon return, to consummate history and bring the drama of salvation to its denouement. The first act in Mark's drama was the preaching and being "delivered up" of John the Baptist. The second act was the preaching and being "delivered up" of Jesus. The third act has begun with the preaching of the church, and it is hurrying toward the climax of the church's being "delivered up" when Christ returns on the clouds. Mark's depiction of Jesus' preaching and ministry is geared to supporting the church in this critical time: "Mark takes the bold and imaginative step of telling the story of the ministry of Jesus so that the concerns of the risen Jesus for his church in the present come to the fore. For him the ministry of Jesus in the past in Galilee and Judea, the ministry of Jesus in the present in the churches for which Mark writes, and the ministry of Jesus that will begin in the future with his parousia [return] in 'Galilee,' are all the same ministry and can be treated together in a narrative in which past, present, and future flow together into the one apocalyptic [revelatory of the end of history] time."[13]

Of all the synoptic writers, however, it is Matthew who is most concerned with the Christian community. Indeed, his concern for the needs of the church is probably the reason why Matthew became the "first gospel," placed at the very beginning of the New Testament canon. To be sure, Matthew derives much of his material from Mark, and he shares with Luke a second source usually called "Q." However, in his use of all his sources Matthew regularly adapts the traditions about Jesus to serve his own purposes, high among which

ranks the need to sketch out a balanced yet demanding view of life in
Jesus' community.

For Matthew, Jesus' community has intimate ties with Israel.
Matthew presents Jesus as dealing almost exclusively with Jews
throughout his ministry, and for Matthew Jesus fulfills the Torah
(rather than, as for Paul, superseding the Torah). Many students of
Matthew describe him as a Jewish Christian, who probably came to
faith in Jesus after training as a Jewish scribe. If so, Matthew 13:52
has an autobiographical ring and reveals a lot about Matthew's goals
in writing: "And he [Jesus] said to them, 'Therefore every scribe who
has been trained for the kingdom of heaven is like a householder who
brings out of his treasure what is new and what is old.' " The old is
the riches of Torah, guidance for God's people. The new is the riches
of Jesus, who brings Torah forward to a greater perfection.

The Matthean church therefore will be structured by a both/and-
ness, and in this it will follow its master. On the one hand, Jesus assures his followers (5:17) that he has not come to abolish the Law and
the Prophets but to fulfill them. On the other hand, Jesus does not
hesitate to legislate anew, with amazing authority. In the Sermon on
the Mount (5–7), for example, Jesus lays out the new, visionary way
of conceiving human relations that the Reign of God has made possible. The refrain, "You have heard that it was said to the men of old
. . . But I say to you" makes it plain that what Jesus derives from the
Reign of God is quite innovative, if not indeed revolutionary.

Still, Matthew's sympathies seem to be with those who would
keep ties with Torah and the Jewish community. In other words, he
does not think that law in itself contradicts the freedom of Christ's
kingdom. No doubt this balanced attitude reflects the situation and
make-up of the church for which Matthew was composed. John Meier
has argued that Antioch is the likeliest locale for this church, and he
has described the background of the gospel as follows: "Matthew's gospel must be seen as a theological and pastoral response to a crisis of
self-identity and function in the Antiochene church, a crisis that was
social and structural as well as theological in nature. A Christian community formerly under strict Jewish Christian control had suffered a
traumatic break with some of the most vital religious symbols and institutional structures of Judaism: the Temple, the holy city Jerusalem,
and the local synagogue. Concomitant with this loss had been the loss
of the revered mother church in Jerusalem, which had provided close

ties with the Jewish past and Christian origins. Liberals and moderates had likewise lost their heroes, Paul and Peter. These major changes, all occurring in a relatively short time-span, created a crisis of identity: what is the church and how does it define itself over against both Jews and pagans."[14] The traumatic event to which Meier refers was the Roman destruction of Jerusalem in 70 C.E. (era common to both Christians and Jews). To the Romans there was little difference between Jews and Christians, and Jewish Christians, deeply attached to Jerusalem and the Temple, could well have been devastated by the tragic destructions.

For the Matthean church the transition from the relative security of a past closely tied to Jewish traditions (whatever the growing strain between Christians and Jews due to their different evaluations of Jesus), to a time when Gentiles constituted more of the church and leaders of the synagogue were becoming hostile to Christians, involved a considerable crisis over authority. Chapter 7, for example, warns against false prophets who don't conform to Jesus' will. Chapter 24 fears an increase of immorality (lawlessness) and a time when Christian love will grow cold. Matthew's response is an attempt to preserve the moral intensity that Jewish dedication to Torah fostered but to take it up into a new synthesis suggested by Christ and the kingdom of God.

Along with this nuanced view of the Law, Matthew develops a correlative view of salvation history. Like that of Luke it has three phases: the time of Old Testament prophecy, the time when the earthly Jesus fulfilled this prophecy, and the present time of the church when salvation is being extended universally. Unless we appreciate the subtlety of Matthew's scheme, we will not be able to understand how he can have Jesus both prohibiting a mission to the Gentiles (10:5–6, 15:24) and commanding a universal mission (28:16–20). The risen Jesus who commands the universal mission has inaugurated a new phase in the history of salvation. Like Paul, Matthew sees the death and resurrection of Christ as an apocalyptic pivot: the revelation and actual beginning of the last phase of history.

In Meier's interpretation, the materials in Matthew that have Jesus approving the teaching of the scribes and Pharisees (for example, 23:2–3) bear more on Jesus' acceptance of the somewhat limited conditions under which his own mission was to transpire than on the later situation of the church. 16:12, with its warning about the doctrine of

the Pharisees and Sadducees, is more indicative of Matthew's position
for the life of the church in his own day. For what happened to Jesus
amounted to a judgment on Israel. Because his own people did not
accept him, the kingdom passed to the Gentiles (see 8:11–12). This
point of view must have seemed buttressed by the entry of many Gentiles into the church and the rising hostility of the leaders of the Jewish synagogues. Indeed, Matthew adds to the materials that he takes
from Mark concerning the parable of the evil tenants of the vineyard
the bitter lines: "Therefore I tell you, the kingdom of God will be
taken away from you and given to a nation producing the fruits of it."
Similarly, in Matthew's account of Jesus' passion all the Jewish people
cry out, "His blood be on us and on our children." (27:25) This is no
justification, of course, for the history of Christian anti-semitism. It
does indicate, however, the strong negative strain in Matthew's interpretation of the church's Jewish heritage.

Characteristically, Matthew is at pains to improve Jesus' image,
giving him more dignity and power than he has in Mark. As well, Matthew is at pains to link this improvement with the status of the
church. So Jesus is more the sovereign teacher and less the suffering
prophet, while the church inherits Jesus' teaching authority. Matthew's reworking of Mark's story of the healing of the paralytic, for
example, underscores that this authoritative power has passed "to
men," implying that the church has inherited it (see 9:8). Chapter 16
has the famous verses that consolidate Christ's grant of authority to
the church—verses that Roman Catholicism long has used to justify
its sense of the papacy (as the continuance of the Petrine ministry):
"And I tell you, you are Peter, and on this rock I will build my church,
and the powers of death shall not prevail against it. I will give you the
keys of the kingdom of heaven, and whatever you bind on earth shall
be bound in heaven, and whatever you loose on earth shall be loosed
in heaven." (16:18–19) Matthew places after this the verses of Mark
about Peter's misunderstanding the need for Jesus to suffer and about
the need for disciples to take up their crosses. He is well aware, in
other words, that the authority of the church cannot be separated
from the sacrificial character of its Master. But he does want to present the Christian community as the place where the power that broke
forth in Jesus continues in the world. Insofar as this point of view
frequently has been congenial to church leaders, Matthew has been
much employed.

From the three instances where Matthew uses the word *ekklesia* to designate the Christian community, Meier argues that for Matthew the assembly of those who have received a Christian calling definitely has a visible structure and authoritative officials. It is a society or an institution, not just an accidental grouping of disciples whose ties are wholly spiritual. This does not mean that Matthew favors a clericalism, as we might call it, in which the officials of the church outweigh the membership at large. The critique of this sort of attitude among the Pharisees (chapter 23) makes it plain that Christian authority is to be quite the opposite of self-promotion.

Chapter 18, which many commentators treat as a sermon on church order, strikes this tone from the outset. Jesus' disciples ask who is the greatest in the kingdom of heaven, and Jesus answers, "Whoever humbles himself like this child, he is the greatest in the kingdom of heaven." (18:4) The rest of the chapter deals with the attitudes that members of the Christian community should foster.

They should, for example, take care lest they not scandalize vulnerable members. They should be concerned for the one sheep who has wandered away, even though ninety-nine are safe. In disputes they must blend firmness with gentleness, always being willing to offer forgiveness ("seventy times seven"). The conclusion of the chapter, with its harsh punishment of the wicked servant who, though he himself had been forgiven a great debt, would not forgive the tiny debt of a fellow-servant, suggests Matthew's bottom line. All members of the church have been offered the unfathomable mercy and largess of God. For any member to treat another harshly or unforgivingly is an outrage. As Raymond Brown has well drawn the contemporary implications: "The number of people who have turned away from the church because they have found it too forgiving is infinitesimal; the number who have turned away because they found it unforgiving is legion."[15]

The Johannine Churches

If Matthew is the best evangelical treatment of ecclesiology, because of its balanced concern for the both/and-ness of church life— both law and liberty, both structure and forgiveness—the Johannine writings are the most radical. Because of their insistence on the di-

vinity of Jesus and the powerful presence of Jesus' Spirit, the Gospel
of John and the Johannine epistles lay more stress on Christian freedom and egalitarianism than either the synoptics or the Pauline writings. On the other hand, the strife among the Johannine Christians
(the followers of "The Beloved Disciple") gives the lie to the claim that
love or the inspiration of the Spirit alone can produce an adequate ecclesiology. By the time that the Johannine Christians limped into full
communion with the "great church" that included the synoptic and
Pauline groups, they had learned all too painfully about the need for
clear lines of authority, church structure, and the interpretation of
Christian tradition.

The Gospel of John, which probably preceded the Epistles by
about a decade, emphasizes the relation of the individual Christian to
Jesus. It does not deny that all individual Christians are related, or
that Jesus gathered a community of followers, but its main interest is
the bond of the individual believer to the Word made flesh. The background here is the Johannine "high Christology," which is more em-
phatic than the other New Testament writings that, as the divine
Word, Jesus existed with God (the Father) before creation (see John
1:1–3, 8:58, 17:5). The many "I am" sayings in the Gospel of John ("I
am the bread of life," "I am the good shepherd," "I am the light of the
world"), culminating in the claim of the Johannine Jesus to have existed before Abraham (8:58), are most intelligibly read as an echo of
God's self-naming in Exodus 3:14. The author believes that Jesus and
the Father are one, so that whoever sees Jesus sees the Father (10:30,
14:9). No wonder, then, that the gist of Johannine ecclesiology is the
union of the branches with the vine (15:1–8).

From this instinct for the organic life that believers share with
Jesus, the author of John achieves a depth that only the Pauline theologians can match. The Johannine theology goes to the foundations
of what Jesus has brought about, reaching the bottom line of divinization. The life that faith in Christ brings is the very life of God. As
such, it not only rescues the believer from sin, it takes him or her up
into the deathless light of the Father. Compared to this foundational
gift, the other charisms that believers may receive are quite secondary.
Relatedly, the place they have in the federation of Jesus' followers is
secondary. By faith, baptism, and feeding on the body and blood of
Christ (the main ways that believers receive divine life and nourish
it), the lowest member of the community (sociologically) is very much

the equal of the highest. In the gift of the Spirit to be the advocate of the followers whom he must leave behind, Jesus has shown all of his disciples where they ought to focus their attention.

Indeed, the main ecclesiological model that one derives from the Johannine literature is of an egalitarian band of disciples. So, for example, the leading figure of this community is not a prominent member of the original twelve, not the famous apostle Paul, but the unnamed "disciple whom Jesus loved" (13:23, 19:26, 20:2). To be a Christian on the model of this hero was to regard Jesus as one's teacher, master, and friend. The bond in all of these relationships was love. Indeed, the Johannine writings are famous for the emphasis they place on love. Some commentators point out that the Johannine love is limited to God and fellow Christians, making a sharp distinction between the realm of divine light and the realm of darkness (the world ultimately ruled by Satan) that cuts outsiders off. Other commentators find a sectarian background in the Johannine community itself: the writings show a special concern with Samaritans, and a special hostility toward "the Jews" (probably adherents of synagogues in Judea), that suggest the rather bitter division of a Jewish Christianity with many Samaritan converts from the Jewish orthodoxy that prevailed in Jerusalem and Judea. Despite these qualifications in the Johannine interpretation of divine life as love, the theology that looks back to the beloved disciple has been a constant stimulus to the church to make its center a warm, holy love that credibly would reflect the transforming presence of Jesus, the Father, and the Spirit.

The Gospel of John contrasts the beloved disciple with Peter in such a way as to relativize the authority of Peter. For the other early churches, both Pauline (see 1 Cor 15:5) and synoptic (see Luke 24:34), Peter was the paramount disciple and apostle because he had been the first among the twelve to see the risen Jesus. The Gospel of John spices its accounts of Jesus' appearances after the resurrection with indications that the beloved disciple was more attuned than Peter to the resurrected Lord. Thus 20:8 implies that when the two looked into the empty tomb it was the beloved disciple who believed in the resurrection, while 21:7 has the beloved disciple explaining to Peter that the mysterious stranger who has directed them to a marvelous catch of fish is the Lord. Later in chapter 21 John recalls Peter's threefold denial of Jesus, through a threefold charge to feed Jesus' sheep, and when Peter asks about the future of the beloved disciple he is in effect told to mind his own business. The obvious conclusion is that the Johannine communities felt themselves possessed of a formative figure and a tradition very much the equal of the Petrine tradition or any other. The further obvious conclusion is that in the first generations after the death of Jesus and the inner circle of disciples Christian communities were, at the least, quite independent. At the most they were jealous of their own traditions and interpretations of faith, to the point of going out of their way to assert them over-against the ways of other Christian communities.

Moreover, the egalitarianism that the Johannine groups derived from the beloved disciple and their high Christology led them to an appreciation of women that other parts of the early church definitely lacked. Chapters 4, 9, and 11, for instance, show that women (the Samaritan woman, Martha, and Mary) were more than the equal of men in their openness to Jesus. The confession of Jesus' messiahship that Matthew accords to Peter (Matt 16:16–17) John accords to Martha (11:27). The honor of announcing the resurrection to the disciples falls to Mary Magdalene, one of the faithful women who had stood by the cross (20:1–18, 19:25). Compared to the Pauline tradition preserved in 1 Tim 2:12 and 2 Tim 3:1–9, which saw women as gullible and to be silenced, the Johannine tradition was blessedly free of patriarchal biases.

In the decade or so that followed the writing of (the first versions of) the Gospel of John, the followers of the beloved disciple apparently fell into bitter strife. Some wanted to push the divinity of Jesus to the limit, so much so that their more conservative opponents thought the humanity of Jesus was being denied. As well, the radicals were exacerbating the split between the followers of Jesus and traditional Jews, since the claims for Jesus' divinity were anathema to Jewish monotheistic instincts. Raymond Brown has sketched a rather complicated hypothesis about the evolution of the Johannine community, and his sense is that the majority finally went in the direction of Docetism, the (later) heresy that denied the true humanity of Christ, and Gnosticism (the heresy that claimed special enlightenments and often considered a strict moral code unnecessary). The two sides (to simplify; there may well have been many intermediate positions) both claimed to be interpreting the materials we now find in the Gospel of John. Both claimed, therefore, to be speaking for the traditions of the beloved disciple. The Epistles of John probably represent the more conservative groups (later judged the better representatives of "orthodoxy"), for their stress on Jesus' having come in the flesh, on the importance of Jesus' historical death for the work of salvation, on the need for an upright moral code and practical love of others, and the like seem directed against an overly-radical interpretation of Jesus' divinity. As well, their attacks on other Christians (presumably other Johannine Christians) as anti-Christs and children of Satan bespeaks the intensity of the threat the author felt. The first Epistle (for example, 2:27) still assumes that the Spirit given to believers is the main authority of church life and ought to suffice to enable believers to distinguish truth from falsity. But one can see how easily opponents could claim to be equally anointed, and consequently how inevitable the question of an institutionalized authority became.

Indeed, Raymond Brown thinks it inevitable that the Johannine Christians represented by the Epistles would themselves have reflected upon the more institutional answers that other New Testament churches had developed for the problem of community division: "Inevitably, as the author's adherents faced such a bleak prospect [of becoming the minority party in the Johannine circle], they would have had to reflect upon other Christian churches that were more successfully surviving divisive movements because they had developed an authoritative church structure and official teachers to correct error— the churches that would become the Great Church. Could the Johannine churches accept a similar structural development in order to survive, or was it indigestibly alien to their theological tradition, which emphasized the Paraclete as teacher and the believers as equal disciples (or branches of the vine)?"[16]

3 John 9–10 may be reflecting this question when the author complains about one Diotrephes "who likes to put himself first." John 21, despite its tendency to humble the figure of Peter, does in Jesus' threefold command to Peter to feed his flock stress the pastoral office of Peter (and perhaps other church leaders). In other words, John 21 may represent a nearly final phase of the written Johannine tradition where the followers of the beloved disciple have made an accommodation with other traditions, such as the Petrine, that had developed authoritative pastors.

When the church catholic took the Johannine writings into the New Testament canon, however, it added not so much an agreement to the legitimacy of official teachers and overseers as a strong vote for a high Christology and the centrality of the Spirit in Christian life. The other portions of the New Testament more than adequately provided for church governance. What the Johannine writings contributed was a sacramental sense of Jesus' flesh (as the revelation of the divine Word) considerably stronger than either the synoptic or Pauline senses. This Johannine christology, in fact, dominated the great christological councils of Nicaea and Chalcedon, where the divinity of the Logos received very formal definition. Ultimately the Spirit, too, was formally declared equal to the Father in divinity. The passages in the second half of the Gospel of John where the disciples are instructed to abide in Jesus, are promised the indwelling of the Spirit, and are assured of the coming of Jesus and the Father to make their home in them (15:4; 14:17, 23) combine into a powerful argument that the center of Christian life (certainly individual Christian life, and by implication communal Christian life as well) is the trinitarian Godhead. No other portion of the New Testament so forcefully spotlights the trinity. Without the "farewell speeches" of the Johannine Jesus (14–17), in fact, all three of the Christian doctrines that Karl Rahner has called cardinal—trinity, grace, and incarnation—would be much the poorer. With these speeches, it is virtually impossible for the church to dominate the Christian worldview, at least as more reflective theologians would propose such a worldview.

For the Pauline communities, the church took its deepest location from the plan of God that had been hidden for long ages. As we saw with Ephesians, the centrality that Christ had as the Logos and first-born from the dead could be focused on his headship of the ecclesiological body. The Johannine theologians in principle might have thought through a plan of universal salvation that grew from the figure of the vine and the branches, but in fact they did not. They had relatively little concern for either outsiders or the church as an organized, prominent, historical entity. Moreover, had they turned their minds to ecclesiology conceived as a meditative speculation (had they, that is, dealt with the theme of the church the way they dealt with the themes of christology, trinitarian theology, and grace), every likelihood seems to be that they would have developed the distinctive Johannine theory of "signs" that is so prominent in the first half of the Gospel into a more sacramental view of the church than what we find in either Pauline or synoptic theology.

We shall see more of this sacramental view of the church when we come to the models that recent ecclesiology has developed. Here, staying closer to the actual Johannine texts, we probably should emphasize the indications that baptism and the eucharist were conceived as the major formal ways in which Christians would come into divine life and nourish it.

The discourse in chapter 6, on the bread of life, makes plain the author's conviction that feeding sacramentally on Christ is essential to growing in divine life: " 'Truly, truly, I [Jesus] say to you, unless you eat the flesh of the Son of man and drink his blood, you have no life in you; he who eats my flesh and drinks my blood has eternal life, and I will raise him up at the last day. For my flesh is food indeed, and my blood is drink indeed. He who eats my flesh and drinks my blood abides in me, and I in him' " (6:53–56). Thus, if asked how to let or make Christ (and the Father and the Spirit) abide in Christians, the Johannine theologians might well have answered: "By regular reception of or participation in the eucharist." It seems obvious enough, from the author's consistent use of metaphor, irony, and other conscious literary devices, that the eucharistic elements of bread and wine are (real) signs of Jesus' nourishing presence. The dominant theme is divine life, so the flesh and blood are taken in to develop divine life. Any sense of cannibalism depends on a literalism, or an ignorance of the entire Johannine sacramentality, that makes hash of the gospel's literary character.

One senses that the Johannine author already had met such a pernicious literalism, for frequently his use of irony plays off of the flatfootedness of Jesus' interlocutors. In an example that bears directly on baptism, Jesus and the Samaritan woman at the well go round an almost amusingly ironic dance: "Jesus answered her, 'If you knew the gift of God, and who it is that is saying to you, "Give me a drink," you would have asked him, and he would have given you living water.' The woman said to him, 'Sir, you have nothing to draw with, and the well is deep; where do you get that living water? Are you greater than our father Jacob, who gave us the well, and drank from it himself, and his sons, and his cattle?' Jesus said to her, 'Everyone who drinks of this water will thirst again, but whoever drinks of the water that I shall give him will never thirst; the water that I shall give him will become in him a spring of water welling up to eternal life.' The woman said to him, 'Sir, give me this water, that I may not thirst, nor come here to draw.' " (4:10–15)

The water clearly enough is the water of baptism, which for Johannine theology leads into eternal life and slakes the soul's deepest thirst. The Johannine church therefore might be conceived of as the place or group or gathering that structures itself by baptism and the eucharist, as primary modalities of abiding in the divine life. The symbolism is too rich or manysided to be captured so simply, but the centrality of divine life is certain. The Johannine church existed to nourish divine life.

Conclusion: The Biblical Christian Community

We have considered the Pauline, synoptic, and Johannine ecclesiologies. It remains to indicate three other strands of reflection on the church that one can find in the New Testament, and then to generalize about the ecclesiological orientations Christians have received from the Bible.

The references to the Christian community that one finds in 1 Peter bear some affinities to Pauline thought. Many scholars think that this writing originated from a disciple of Peter in Rome around 90 C.E. It reflects a community with strongly Jewish origins, and of the Pauline writings it is closest to Romans (no doubt because it was contemplating the same community). The Jewish origins come through in 1 Peter's use of such Old Testament motifs as the exodus, the wandering in the desert, and the promised land. As God's people the Israelites experienced these motifs, so the Gentiles who have joined God's people can expect to experience their equivalents. The author knows well the Old Testament interest in fashioning for God through the Torah a holy people, and 2:9 brings this tradition to bear on the identity of the Christian community: "But you are a chosen race, a royal priesthood, a holy nation, God's own people, that you may declare the wonderful deeds of him who called you out of darkness into his marvelous light." Thus, 1 Peter is a strong warrant for the conception of the church as "the people of God" (with the attendant strength of symbolizing well how believers belong to God and the attendant weakness of exclusivity).

The Epistle to the Hebrews, which focuses sharply on the high priesthood of Christ, adds a liturgical motif somewhat understated in the rest of the New Testament (apart from Revelation). Jesus stands above the "house of God" that Christians compose. Edward Schille-beeckx, who seems unusually appreciative of Hebrews, makes the correlations as follows: "As minister of the whole of the tent of the covenant, the holy of holies and the holy place, Christ is also the chief minister in the church's liturgy on earth, the heavenly forecourt. The church's liturgy is a participation in the heavenly liturgy of Jesus the Christ or high priest, who sits in prayer in the midst of his heavenly hosts (9.24–28; 12.23). The church is that part of humanity which is already reconciled and redeemed, still a kind of heavenly limbo, but already 'taken up' into the dwelling places of the angels and saints (12.22f.)."[17]

In the typological thought of Hebrews, heaven and earth stand to one another as primal reality and lesser reflection. The church is the earthly anteroom to the heavenly holy of holies. Through the church one gains access to the mysteries, worship, and reality of the holy God. The author stresses not the union of believers in Christ (there is no discussion of Christ's "body"), but the community of God that Christ serves as mediator. As Moses mediated between God and the Old Testament people, so Christ mediates between God and the people of this new dispensation. Jesus stands above the house of God's people, and those who hold fast, believing in his mediatorship, become partners of him, the high priest.

Revelation regards the Christian faithful from two points of view. First, as the letters to the various churches (chapters 2 and 3) show, there is a great appreciation of the local church, which must struggle against the threats to faith peculiar to its given area. Second, there is the confederation of these local churches, who are all addressed by the same Risen Lord, and whom the later chapters of Revelation, where the accent is on the heavenly dimension of the church's struggles, tend to collectivize. The great beast (presumably the Roman Empire) that afflicts Christ's followers is opposed by the Christ the champion (Word of God and Lamb). The woman whom the dragon wants to devour (chapter twelve) seems to be the church cast in the lineaments of Mary, the mother of Jesus.

The several passages that depict the heavenly liturgy either focus on the redemptive work for which the Lamb and God ought to be praised or present heavenly fulfillment as constant service and praise before the splendid throne of God. Thus 6:9–10 describes the song of the four living creatures and twenty-four elders before the Lamb as follows: " 'Worthy art thou to take the scroll and to open its seals, for thou wast slain and by thy blood did ransom men for God from every tribe and tongue and people and nation, and has made them a kingdom and priests to our God, and they shall reign on earth.' " The 144,000 of the elect seem clearly to be a mystical multiple of the twelve tribes of Israel: the new confederacy of God's people. Revelation conceives of Christ's rule as being effected through the sending of his people or church into the world, but where other New Testament authors might stress the church's preaching of the gospel, Revelation stresses the church's resistance to the wicked worldly powers. Thus the sufferings and struggles of Christians become the locus of salvation-history. The power of God shows through when God's people oppose the sinful, rapacious regimes of the secular powers.

Revelation recently has been subjected to interesting sociological analyses, the general upshot of which tends to be that the communities it represents were experiencing great dissonance from their pagan surroundings.[18] This may not have been to the point of bloody persecution, but it brought the challenge to rethink just what "redemption" or the successful work of Christ was supposed to mean. Where was the deliverance, even the this-worldly prosperity, that "good news" seemed to import? How could God delay in transferring his people from the position of underlings to the position of victors? Through its quite creative adaptation of the rich symbolism of the Old Testament, Revelation gave the New Testament perhaps its most forceful contrast of faith and worldliness, and perhaps as well its boldest assurances of final victory.

Thus 21:1–4 has long rung out as a great pledge of final victory: "Then I saw a new heaven and a new earth; for the first heaven and the first earth had passed away, and the sea was no more. And I saw the holy city, the new Jerusalem, coming down out of heaven from God, prepared as a bride adorned for her husband; and I heard a loud voice from the throne saying, 'Behold, the dwelling of God is with men. He will dwell with them, and they shall be his people, and God himself will be with them; he will wipe away every tear from their eyes, and death shall be no more, neither shall there be mourning nor crying nor pain any more, for the former things have passed away.' "

Insofar as the church thought of itself as the new Jerusalem, the bride of God, and God's people, it followed in the trail of these symbols from Revelation. And that trail, of course, had collateral paths to a nature or creation that, as a whole, would be renovated by God's consummation of salvation. It also had conceptual paths to other people. A generous reading of passages such as this could stress the generic dimension of "men," making God's dwelling wherever human beings opened themselves to the divine mystery. Finally, the utopian goal of overcoming death and suffering entered into the overall Christian conception of "heaven," so that salvation became the complete redoing of the creaturely condition. Through what Christ had worked, what Christ manifested as the first fruits, the great enemies of the creaturely condition would receive their final defeat.

Thus from Revelation one could think of the church as the place where one might anticipate a glorious liberation from present injustices and pains. The liturgy of the church could be a prefiguring of the constant praise of God that would be the main business of heaven. Since the God of Revelation is both holy and powerful, the people of God ought to be holy and powerful in their faith. In the perspective of the new Jerusalem, the transformed conception of the holy city of God, martyrdom and suffering could become bearable, if never what ought to be. So the vision of John of Patmos gave the church a heavenly relocation. Accepting his symbols, Christians could locate themselves among the 144,000.

If we try to conclude from the foregoing description of the ecclesiological outlooks of the different schools and books of the New Testament, with their Old Testament background, we find that most of the patterns or emphases prominent in later history are present. The community itself is the body of Christ, or the people of God, or the branches of Christ the vine. It is holy, royal, priestly, and espoused to Christ. By the gift of the Spirit, and through its union with Christ, it is filled with divine life. Sacraments such as baptism and the eucharist exercise or channel this life. The divine Word, as inherited from Israel through the Hebrew Bible or preached in the Christian assembly, mediates the community's understanding of its experiences. It has a mission to the rest of the world, and the good reception many Gentiles give this mission is a strong sign that God guides its outreach.

The church has a constitutive connection to Israel, the first people covenanted to God, whose ongoing significance is not clear. On the one hand, the general thrust of the New Testament makes Christ the fulfillment of Israelite prophecy and makes the church the recipient of Israel's privileges. On the other hand, Israel continues to fulfill

the Torah that God required, and whether that Torah should continue in the church is much debated. Matthew is a good representative of the balanced view that eventually came to predominate. To the
triadic historical schema of Matthew and Luke, Hebrews and Revelation add a heavenly dimension rich with liturgical overtones. The
church continues to be in the world, but its heavenly archetype is the
community that even now hymns the victory of the Lamb.

Concerning the authority that should direct the church, we have
seen several styles. The Pastorals spotlight the presbyter-bishop, the
synoptics recall the role of the twelve, the letters of Paul show the
power of the individual church-founder, and the Johannine writings
lay most emphasis on the Spirit that all believers enjoy. For Howard
Clark Kee, several traditions in the New Testament emphasize the
charismatic aspects of the authority that both Jesus and Paul exercised. Thus Mark stresses Jesus' powers against the forces of evil,
while in 1 Corinthians Paul derives his authority from his personal
encounter with the Risen Lord (1 Cor 9:1, 15:8). In contrast to this
charismatic power that is obviously present in an individual's divine
gifts, the New Testament also deals with a delegated power. So Luke
10:16 and Matthew 16:16–18 portray Jesus delegating to his followers
or Peter the authority he himself has been wielding. The beloved disciple who stands at the font of the Johannine tradition has, like Peter
and Paul, received the authority to interpret the gospel of Jesus and
hand it on.

Thus 1 John 1:1–5 places the author's writing in a rather solemn
or authoritative context: "That which was from the beginning, which
we have heard, which we have seen with our eyes, which we have
looked upon and touched with our hands, concerning the word of
life—the life was made manifest, and we saw it, and testify to it, and
proclaim to you the eternal life which was with the Father and was
made manifest to us—that which we have seen and heard we proclaim
also to you, so that you may have fellowship with us; and our fellowship is with the Father and with his Son Jesus Christ. And we are
writing this that our joy may be complete. This is the message we have
heard from him and proclaim to you, that God is light and in him is
no darkness at all." The authoritative tone of the message cannot be
separated from the tradition or witness that the author is representing. As well, it cannot be separated from the fellowship that its proclamation is to create.

Summarizing his sketch of New Testament authority, Kee writes: "Here, then, are the two different functional models of authority in the New Testament: (1) as decision-making, defining rules, specifying authentic and inauthentic perceptions of tradition, designating worthy persons for other authority roles within the structure; (2) as spiritual insight, discerning hidden depths of meaning within the tradition, sensitive to symbolic values, prizing most highly affectionate relationships. Clearly, Peter came to represent the first model, while John embodies the second."[19]

With its rich self-conception as variously connected to God, and its rather complicated sense of its authoritative powers, the Biblical Christian community faced the world as the privileged locus of salvation. When we boil down the implications of the various references to the church, both the explicit and the glancing, that is what finally emerges. God has changed history, accomplished the essence of salvation, offered divine life, and the rest in and through Jesus of Nazareth, the Christ and resurrected Lord. The Christian community is the primary place, in its own mind, where God's history-changing power, accomplishment of salvation, and offer of divine life continue to be present. Alternatively, the Christian community is the primary place where Jesus and the Spirit and the Father, who unify, direct, and create these realities or powers, continue to be present.

The New Testament authors are somewhat fuzzy about what happens outside the Christian community. Both Jews and non-Christian Gentiles figure in God's plans, but precisely how, or with what consequences for the church's self-conception, is far from clear. The New Testament writings do not so much deny that God continues to operate in Israel or the pagan world as to pay such operation little attention because their concern is riveted to what preoccupies their own communities. This is understandable, given the psychological nearness of Jesus. The early churches had been formed by a generation of disciples who either had themselves known Jesus or were the pupils of eyewitnesses.

As well, many of the churches for whom the New Testament authors wrote still expected Jesus to return to complete salvation. Only toward the end of the first century did the Christian body as a whole come to grips with the delay of the parousia and, consequently, with the demands of an ongoing relation to civil society. The Pastoral letters show one line of response to this situation, while the Johannine writings show another. For the Pastorals the solution lay in establishing authoritative teachers who could control the church's relations with the world (and the church's internal developments as well). For the Johannine writings the essence of salvation came when the Word took flesh, and the Spirit that Jesus gave his disciples is the key to the church's vitality. If the faith displayed in the Pastorals seems diluted or bourgeois to the point of making one long for a shift of focus to the Spirit, the disarray of the Johannine communities makes one acknowledge the wisdom of establishing authoritative teaching and administrative organs.

The biblical Christian community ultimately is defined by Christ. Its reason-to-be is the teaching, life, and hope that Jesus personified. As Jesus assumed the traditions of Israel, so did the biblical Christian community. As Jesus tried to work changes on those traditions, in the light of his sense of the dawning Reign of God and gift of the Spirit, so did the biblical Christian community. Where the parallel breaks down, however, is in the dependence of the biblical Christian community upon Jesus. Jesus depended upon God, his Abba, to whom he directed his hearers' attention. The early Christians knew that they completely derived from Jesus, so they made him the prism or mediator or incarnation of the God whom he had preached. To their mind, Jesus was the Word of this God made flesh. To the mind of the Jews with whom they disputed, that could not be. The Gentiles whom the early church received found Jesus the fulfillment of their longing for salvation and wisdom. Although his cross was to many a sign of the folly of his life, to others it represented a wisdom beyond human judging. To the Jews who rejected Jesus and his community, the Torah said that salvation could not come as Christians claimed. To the Jews who accepted Jesus, his death and resurrection were not a stumbling block but a new chapter in the career of covenantal love. So the biblical Christian community was from the beginning focused on the love of God shown in Christ Jesus.

Summary

We have considered the Old Testament background to the Christian notion of the church, the eccesiological orientations of the main schools within the New Testament, and have then drawn some conclusions about the biblical Christian community.

The Old Testament background focuses on Israel's sense of itself as God's people. The covenant welded the people to God, and the covenant relationship was what made Israel distinctive. Although Israel understood its election or chosenness differently at different times, it never doubted that God's covenanted love was the greatest marvel in its history. As well, God's *hesed* was the best reason for Israel to strive to be holy (through keeping the Torah) and so like its God.

The Pauline ecclesiology was first dominated by the local Christian assembly, which drew on the Hebrew notion of the *qahal Yahweh*. Paul's great letters expand the sense of "church" to at least a network of local communities, while in the deutero-Pauline ecclesiology of Colossians and Ephesians the church swells to become Christ's body and the locus of salvation. The Pastoral epistles, representing a stage of consolidation, stress the role of the presbyter-bishop in safeguarding traditional doctrine and assuring good order.

The synoptic theologies obviously vary significantly, but Luke-Acts is close to Paul himself in stressing the local Christian assembly. For Luke the church dominates the last panel in the triptych of salvation-history, the Spirit is active to guide the church, and "the twelve" stand for the proto-church that Jesus himself gathered. Mark is more apocalyptic, pointing his readers to the return of Jesus and asking them to stay faithful to their suffering Master. The ecclesiology of Matthew is the most sophisticated and detailed, making it the "first" gospel. Matthew struggles for a balanced view of Torah, not wanting a jot to pass yet seeing Jesus as a new Moses with a new teaching authority. This gospel reflects the tensions of an early community trying to accommodate both Jews and Gentiles, as well as the hostility that had arisen between Christians and Jews after the destruction of the Temple in 70 C.E. Matthew has Jesus pass authority over to the church, yet he insists that the proper pastoral stance of the church is to stress mercy and reconciliation.

The Johannine churches stress the individual's union with Jesus as branches to vine. The center of the Johannine community is the divine life that Jesus brought and the Spirit now defends. The sacramentality of these writings helped to sponsor a rich liturgical life, but the aversion from formal authority and organization led to bitter struggles and finally schism. Thus the Johannine love is an ambiguous legacy, always calling the church to live out the divine life but seldom showing how to adjudicate spiritual disputes.

The biblical Christian community, as these four strands plus such other sources as Hebrews, 1 Peter, and Revelation describe it, is complex and richly endowed. A wealth of figures suggest the union between God and the followers of Jesus: body, people, house, vine, and more. The center of the community is Jesus himself: the memory of him, experience of his presence, power of his Spirit, enjoyment of his divine life of love, and commission to spread his word. Thus acceptance of Christ became the crux of real entry into the Christian community, while doubts about Christ or rejection made one an outsider.

STUDY QUESTIONS

1. Explain the description of Israel as "the community of persons that know YHWH."
2. What is so wonderful about God's *hesed* or covenanted love?
3. What are the advantages of the focus on the local community that one finds in the early letters of Paul and Acts?
4. Explain the marital symbolism of Ephesians 5.
5. How does Matthew depict Jesus' grant of authority to his disciples?
6. Summarize the main themes of Matthew's treatment of church order in chapter 18.
7. What is the significance of John's making the beloved disciple a figure in many ways superior to Peter?
8. What is the ecclesiological significance of the Johannine concern for close, abiding relations with Father, Son, and Spirit?
9. Explain the liturgical accents of Hebrews and Revelation.
10. How validly may one summarize the biblical view of the church as "a community of disciples of the Lord"?

NOTES

1. Yehezkel Kaufmann, THE RELIGION OF ISRAEL. New York: Schocken, 1972, p. 60.

2. Ibid., p. 234.

3. Josef Scharbert, "People of God," ENCYCLOPEDIA OF BIBLICAL THEOLOGY, ed. J. B. Bauer. New York: Crossroad, 1981, pp. 652–653.

4. Lawrence Boadt, READING THE OLD TESTAMENT. New York: Paulist, 1984, pp. 175–176.

5. Samuel Sandmel, "Israel, Conceptions of," THE INTERPRETER'S DICTIONARY OF THE BIBLE, SUPPLEMENTARY VOLUME. Nashville: Abingdon, 1976, p. 462.

6. Moshe Greenberg, BIBLICAL PROSE PRAYER. Berkeley: University of California Press, 1983, p. 52.

7. Mose Weinfeld, "Covenant, Davidic," INTERPRETER'S DICTIONARY OF THE BIBLE, SUPPLEMENTARY VOLUME, p. 189.

8. John L. McKenzie, "Aspects of Old Testament Thought," THE JEROME BIBLICAL COMMENTARY, Vol. II, ed. R. Brown, J. Fitzmyer, R. Murphy. Englewood Cliffs, NJ: Prentice-Hall, 1968, p. 749.

9. See Wayne Meeks, THE FIRST URBAN CHRISTIANS. New Haven: Yale University Press, 1983.

10. Raymond E. Brown, THE CHURCHES THE APOSTLES LEFT BEHIND. New York: Paulist, 1984, pp. 32–33.

11. Joseph A. Fitzmyer, THE GOSPEL ACCORDING TO LUKE (I–IX). Garden City, NY: Doubleday, 1981, p. 253.

12. Norman Perrin and Dennis C. Duling, THE NEW TESTAMENT: AN INTRODUCTION, Second Edition. New York: Harcourt Brace Jovanovich, 1982, p. 255.

13. Ibid., pp. 255–256.

14. John P. Meier and Raymond E. Brown, ANTIOCH AND ROME. New York: Paulist, 1983, pp. 57–58.

15. Raymond E. Brown, THE CHURCHES THE APOSTLES LEFT BEHIND, p. 145.

16. Raymond E. Brown, THE EPISTLES OF JOHN. Garden City, NY: Doubleday, 1982, pp. 106–107.

17. Edward Schillebeeckx, CHRIST. New York: Seabury, 1980, p. 276.

18. See Adela Yarbro Collins, CRISIS AND CATHARSIS. Philadelphia: Westminster, 1984.

19. Howard Clark Kee, UNDERSTANDING THE NEW TESTAMENT, Fourth Edition. Englewood Cliffs, NJ: Prentice-Hall, 1983, p. 398.

Chapter 3

Church History

The Patristic Era ♦ The Middle Ages ♦ Eastern Christianity ♦ The Reformation ♦ Modernity ♦ Summary, Study Questions, Notes

The Patristic Era

The first centuries of the Christian church are dominated by leaders on the model of the presbyter-bishop of the Pastoral epistles. It is their sense of the church's nature and mission that guides its evolution from a small band of disciples to the leading religious institution of the Roman Empire. By the end of the New Testament era the church had passed from being a Jewish synagogue to being a community filled with Hellenistic Gentiles. The conviction that the church was a new Israel remained, but the task of explaining what Jesus had taught and accomplished broke out of a purely Jewish context. At such centers as Antioch in Syria, Alexandria in Egypt, and Rome in Italy, the work of spreading the gospel and expanding the community went forward energetically. The destruction of Jerusalem in 70 C.E. was traumatic for the Christians as well as the Jews, but the vigor of the churches outside of Jerusalem shows that Christian universalism was well established. By the year 100, when the legacy of the eyewitness disciples had been worked over for several generations, the church was ready to take its somewhat countercultural message throughout the Roman Empire.

As we saw when dealing with Revelation, the imperial power of Rome struck some churches as a beastly ungodliness. As they tried to understand the promise that Christ would return, the Christians clung to ideals of poverty and purity that opposed the materialistic ideals of the Empire. In addition, they opposed the religious cult associated with the Emperor, professing ultimate allegiance only to God. This did not mean, however, that the majority of early Christians were revolutionaries or even prominent social critics. A strain of loyalty to the secular powers, good citizenship, and (increasingly) dedication to this-worldly tasks balanced the radical implications of the Sermon on the Mount or apocalyptic interpretations of the Kingdom of God. The ethical ideals of late Judaism, including care for widows and orphans, are prominent in the counsels of the early church fathers. Christians were not to take on the lusts and ambitions of the pagans. Their true home remained the heaven to which Christ had ascended. So from the second century the church was struggling to be in the world but not of the world. It tended to soften such imperial factors as slavery, by urging Christian masters to deal with their slaves kindly and Christian slaves to make obedience a religious service, rather than to condemn such factors outright.

W.H.C. Frend has described the "normative Christianity" that had developed by 100 C.E. as still situated within Hellenistic Judaism. Still, the church now had a body of authoritative teaching, the writings that became the New Testament, and a fairly secure sense of its legacy from the early apostles. As well, it had an ordered hierarchy of leaders, whom it regarded as a chain back to Peter and the twelve. In terms of geography, its greatest strength lay in the seaport towns of the eastern Mediterranean and the cities that lay along the principal roads. Messages traveled back and forth among the churches, and bishops were in regular contact. The main religious problems came from Pharisaic Jews, who sometimes vigorously opposed Christians as heretics, and from groups within the church who deviated from main-line faith. For example, the group that came to be known as Docetists downplayed the humanity of Jesus, saying that the Word had only seemed to take on flesh. In terms of ethical deviations, the greatest troubles came from libertines, who tended to argue that the gift of salvation or the Spirit freed them from ordinary moral restraints.[1]

The more general doctrinal problems that arose by the third century clustered in Gnosticism. Expanding on Docetic and libertine tendencies, the Gnostics claimed a secret knowledge of salvation that put them in opposition to the traditions and authorities of the mainline churches. Thus we find such leading early fathers as Irenaeus of Lyons criticizing the Gnostic teachings as fanciful speculations and urging Christians to hold fast to the solid traditions about Jesus' full humanity, the function of the community in salvation, the need for ethical uprightness, and the God-given power of church leaders to determine genuine faith.

The second century also brought enough persecution to make martyrdom a serious matter. Until the church won imperial approval early in the fourth century, both bishops such as Ignatius of Antioch and ordinary lay Christians had to contend with the possibility of dying for their faith. The Roman culture thought of religion as its most important source of unity. For the Christians to qualify their allegiance to the Emperor, and draw back from civic or personal ceremonies that venerated Graeco-Roman gods, branded them as unpatriotic, or even as potentially seditious.

Among the pagan intellectuals, the church could seem to threaten a revival of religious superstitions. We see, for example, in Origen's response to the pagan Celsus (we don't have Celsus' own writings) a defense of Christianity against charges of credulity and low emotionalism. Augustine, writing at the end of the fourth century, represents a later phase of this long-playing argument. In his day the charge was that Christian faith had led to the decay of the Roman Empire, so he felt obliged to describe the church as the City of God containing the highest of treasures.

Indeed, Augustine came to think of the church as the community of those whom God had predestined to salvation. This had a mysterious side, however, because external participation in the sacramental life of the church did not guarantee predestination to salvation. As Jaroslav Pelikan has summarized Augustine's very influential notions: "It was by no means self-evident that those who 'participated physically in the sacraments' were to be regarded as members of the body of Christ, the church. For 'in the ineffable prescience of God, many who seem to be on the outside are in fact on the inside, and many who seem to be on the inside are nevertheless in fact on the outside.' "[2]

In their battles with the Gnostics and such other heretical groups as the Marcionites (who wanted to sever ties with the Old Testament), the fathers increasingly relied on the apostolic character of church authority. It was the leaders who could trace their lineage back to the apostles who had the authority to settle doctrinal and moral disputes. Irenaeus stressed the dignity of the church of Rome, and later Rome became the principal referee in doctrinal disputes, because of its historic associations with Peter and Paul, and also because of its reputation for doctrinal purity.

Thus "apostolicity" became an important mark of the Christian community, by which one might distinguish it from unlawful pretenders. Other marks that the fathers stressed were unity, holiness, and catholicity. Their consensus was that all the local communities were part of something both larger and more basic: the one body of Christ or overall assembly of the Christian faithful. This body was holy because of the divine life given it in the Spirit, which it was to nourish through scripture and the sacraments. As well, the holiness of the church gave both the power and the imperative to live purely, forsaking the pagan vices that were incompatible with divine life. Finally, the catholicity of the church was what Vincent of Lerins, a fifth century father, had in mind when he described orthodox faith as what had been believed "everywhere, always, and by all." Catholicity meant wholeness and universality, opposition to any partialism or fragmentation. When the leaders of the church met in the great councils of the fourth and fifth centuries, they understood themselves to be declaring not just the traditions of their own particular communities but the faith of the church as a whole.

From the second century an ascetical instinct led increasing numbers of Christians to vow virginity or take themselves to the desert to pray. The life of the holy man Antony, as interpreted by the bishop Athanasius, became a powerful argument that desert solitude could dovetail with strict orthodoxy and communion with the local bishop. As the ascetical life became more popular, both for its intrinsic merits and as a protest against accommodations to the world, church leaders sought to bring it under clear discipline. The result was the ordered monastic life legislated by Basil in the East and Benedict in the West. Devotees were committed to celibacy, poverty, and obedience to the head of their community. The basic idea was that those setting out on the harsh paths of intense asceticism need the counsel of wise elders and the support of fellow seekers. Monasticism has continued to the present day, furnishing the Eastern church its bishops and the Western church a great corps of dedicated servants.

The ecumenical councils of Nicaea (325) and Chalcedon (451) were perhaps the most dramatic events of the patristic era, but all the councils that the Eastern church venerates, down to the Second Council of Nicaea (787), illustrate the sense of the church that grew under the fathers. This sense was collegial: the leaders of the different geographical areas would come together to discuss, pray, debate, and finally decide matters of faith and discipline. To be sure, the early councils had a political stamp, in that the emperors frequently intervened and sought a say in what would be considered orthodoxy. The first church historian of note, Eusebius of Caesarea, makes it clear that many in the church tended to think of the imperial office as including considerable authority over the church. Athanasius, the hero of the First Council of Nicaea, several times had to flee into exile, because he fell into disfavor with the imperial leadership. Yet the councils themselves spotlighted the assembly of the bishops, and by the time of Chalcedon the bishop of Rome had a certain preeminence among them. Thus the "Tome" of Leo I shaped the understanding of Christ's two natures that Chalcedon made the standard for later orthodoxy.

The fall of the Western Roman empire to the barbarians in the fifth century plunged the Western church into a dark era. The tribes who had not been conquered or assimilated into the empire were the force that attacked from without, but Roman culture had for some time been decaying from within, and Christianity played a part in this decay. Thus Frend accepts a portion of Edward Gibbon's judgment that the Western empire succumbed on account of "Christianity and barbarism." The Vandals, Alans, and Suebi who crossed the Rhine at the end of 406 to invade Gaul might have had a much harder time, except for the lack of will among the provincial members of the empire: "If one looks below the surface of the military events one may also detect some subtler changes of opinion that undermined the provincials' will to resist. These changes deprived the empire in the West of the popular support that had sustained it through the almost equally grave crisis of the mid-third century. Added to the feebleness of Honorius's government, protected by the marshes that made Ravenna almost inaccessible, was a breakdown of will among the natural leaders of the community. Estrangement (*alienatio*), turning one's back on the business of the world in order to assure one's own salvation without distraction, was the logic of the Western creed. Accepted as the Christian ideal for the times, it contributed to the fall of the empire that Christianity had conquered only a short while before."[3]

The Eastern empire continued for another thousand years, until the capture of Constantinople by the Turks in 1453. This further millennium gave Eastern Christian theology its markedly conservative character. So, for example, the residence of the Greek Orthodox patriarch in Istanbul is still called "the Roman patriarchate," and Greeks of Istanbul still call themselves "Romans." Their identification with the imperial structure of their Christianity has survived the fall of the Western empire, the alienation of Eastern and Western Christianity, and Muslim rule. Thus in the East the patristic sense of a collegial church, most fully expressed in its ecumenical gatherings to define faith and discipline, continued to the eve of what in the West was the Protestant Reformation. The Eastern church had no medieval period, as the West would understand such a phrase.[4]

If we were to single out one episode that might epitomize the story of the development of ecclesiology during the patristic period, Augustine's response to the Donatist controversy might be the best candidate. The Donatists felt strongly that members of the church ought to manifest their faith through external holiness and loyalty. Thus, they were loath to consider Christians who had made compromises during the persecutions of Diocletian (303) members in good standing. In particular, they considered clergy who had made compromises polluted and so unfit to administer the sacraments. Augustine and others countered that unity and universality are as important to the church as holiness, and that God is the primary administrator of the sacraments. Thus, they relativized the gravity of the compromises that had been made.

The unity of the church, in fact, is central to Augustine's ecclesiology. This unity (in Pauline fashion) comes from the organic relation between the church and its head. "The solidarity between the head and the members is maintained by the Spirit, and the manifestation of the Spirit is love. Love is therefore the essential characteristic of the Church, and although Augustine shares Cyprian's organizational definition of the Church's visible structure and boundaries he thinks of the inward operation of love as the real distinguishing mark of the Church which separates it from the rest of mankind."[5] Augustine then goes on to analyze schism, or rupture between different ecclesiastical bodies, as a lack of love.

The period 100–451 therefore witnessed a considerable development in the church's self-understanding. Its missionary ventures had succeeded beyond its first dreams, in that it had become the favored religious institution of the Empire. Yet it had suffered numerous heresies and schisms, and in the West it had suffered grievously from the victories of the barbarians. The bishop of Rome had consolidated great power in the West, putting himself in the position of being one of the few leaders who could fill the vacuum created by the fall of the Empire. In the East the leaders of the major churches (the patriarchs) had the greatest say. Doctrinally, the patristic church defined Christianity's central dogmas, which concerned the Trinity and Christ. Organizationally, it spotlighted the power of the bishop and showed itself most concerned about a proper administration of the sacraments.

The monastic movement served as a counterweight to this increased organization, offering people a sort of free zone in which they might pursue union with God apart from worldly distractions. The mainstream of the bishops and the monastic leaders alike wanted monks kept in close union with the hierarchy, but even when monasteries were completely loyal and orthodox they moved to a different spiritual measure. From the early persecutions the patristic church drew the conviction that the profession of faith ought to be a momentous undertaking. In their apologetic writings, the fathers sought to portray Christ and his community as the fulfillment of both Jewish and pagan ideals. This proved more complicated when Christianity became part of the imperial establishment, but the church remained confident that the salvation it offered was Christ's fulfillment of both Jewish and Gentile hopes. For the fathers, then, the church was the best place on earth to find God.

The Middle Ages

In his interesting book CHRISTIANITY IN EUROPEAN HISTORY, William A. Clebsch deals with the Middle Ages in two chapters. The first, covering the years 476–962, focuses on the Germanic kingdoms and has as its main themes theodicy (the justification of God's ways) and prelacy (the dominating role of bishops). The second chapter, covering the years 962–1556, deals with the (relatively) unified Holy Roman Empire and has as its main themes mystics and theologians. We can use this scheme to suggest the evolution of the medieval church.

Any era of church history of course is colored by the changes in the culture at large. In the case of the early portion of medieval church history in the West, the general cultural changes mainly stemmed from the replacement of Roman imperial rule by that of German tribes. More precisely, German barter replaced Roman gold coinage, giving the economic system a quite different look. Villages and farms became more important than cities and shops. Where Rome had kept a standing army, the Germanic tribes enlisted soldiers for particular campaigns. Where the Roman aqueduct had symbolized progressive engineering, the German wheeled plow symbolized the tribes' agrarian bent. Architecture reflected the woodland holdings of the Germans, which contrasted with the Mediterranean cast of the Roman properties. Learning shifted from elegance to practicality. In a word, the culture dominating early medieval Europe was rustic and rude, when compared to its urban and sophisticated predecessor.

Politically, the Germanic kingdoms moved by customary law rather than the explicit codes developed by the Romans. By the death of the barbarian Theodoric (526), who had gained rule of the entire prior Roman realm except Britain, parts of Gaul, and North Africa, the imperial context in which most of the Western church fathers had shaped their Christian communities was no more.

Such a dramatic cultural change, often worked through plunder and bloodshed, pushed to the fore the question of God's justice. To be sure, earlier Christian speculation, as we see from the book of Revelation, had tackled this question. How could it be that God would allow his people to suffer the assaults of impious pagans? What was the meaning of a history in which the saints were not the earthly victors but the persecuted? In the dark ages that followed the fall of (Christianized) Rome, thinkers such as Boethius kept Christian culture alive by searching out consolations that went below the troubled currents of worldly history. Even after the missionaries had converted many of the Germanic tribes and actually extended the church's influence, this search for a peace that the world could not take away stamped the medieval church. The quotation from W.H.C. Frend that we used earlier suggests that such other-worldliness was a strong factor in the Christian faith that preceded the fall of Rome. Nonetheless, the often savage rule of the Germanic tribes, which destroyed the urban culture of the Graeco-Roman European heritage, greatly increased this factor.

Paradoxically enough, a church which had faced the dissolution of the culture in which it had been born proved capable of forging the foremost institution of the Middle Ages. The clashes of the Germanic tribes broke the sense that God had blessed the Roman Empire and considered it the mirror on earth of the heavenly divine rule. Into this vacuum or disarray stepped the leading church power, the bishopric of Rome. Drawing on Augustine's speculations about the earthly dimensions of the City of God, churchmen built the papacy into a new kingdom, powerful in the measure that it seemed to be keeping the forces of chaos at bay. In the opinion of Clebsch, the theodicy of Boethius, as institutionalized by the Roman Catholic church, formed the next thousand years of European consciousness: "After the fall of Rome the questions had been, How could the divine-cosmic order be believed to outlive the crumbling of the imperium that had embodied and mediated it? How could social and historical chaos, visible to all, be reconciled with the ordering invisible deity's management of the universe? The theodicy of Boethius lodged itself at the center of European consciousness for a thousand years. It made the ultimate reason for all these changes the God of Christianity."[6]

The God of Christianity had delivered the rule of his people to the bishop of Rome. That was the gist of the institutional aspect of the Western medieval response to the threats of chaos. It took some time for this institutional aspect to achieve full form, of course, but by the death of Pope Gregory the Great in 604 the structure had been well laid. Gregory was a most able administrator, whose Roman family ties made it seem natural that the head of the church should also be the dominant force in secular affairs. Indeed, before entering Benedictine monastic life, Gregory had been one of the leading Roman politicians. His administration of the church greatly expanded its landholdings. As well, it brought Italy some recovery from the onslaughts of the Lombard tribes, against whom Gregory organized a successful resistance. The wealth of the church was made over to the poor. The office of the bishop gained a sharper pastoral edge, since the agricultural economy likened the people to flocks. If this brought bishops the aura of princes, distancing them from the people who worked the church's lands and filled the Sunday gatherings, it seemed a small price to pay for security.

The security offered by the church throughout the Middle Ages was temporal as well as spiritual. When the heads of the new and supposedly holy Roman Empire received their legitimacy from the bishop of Rome or his legate, the people at large could feel that their culture had been made whole. The power of the popes finally reposed in their mediation of grace and salvation, but their sacramental system bore quite directly on daily life. Excommunication and interdict, for example, undercut the political power of a king or tribal leader dramatically. Marriages that were not sanctioned by the church had no popular credibility, so political alliances had to be blessed by the local prelate. From its medieval period, the Western church gained a heady sense of the secular power it could wield. Ever after, it has been hard for the popes not to think of kings, presidents, and prime ministers as fellow heads of state. Indeed, it has been hard for popes not to seek to guide temporal affairs by their spiritual sanctions.

The Middle Ages therefore have contributed significantly to the institutional aspects of ecclesiology. Certainly one can see the seeds of institutionalism in the New Testament, in that even the first Christian communities had an organizational form and a sense of authoritative power. Because of the medieval struggles between popes and kings, princes and bishops, however, the institutional aspects of ecclesiology were greatly refined. In the eyes of Eastern Orthodox and Protestant critics, the Roman Catholic church became so institutionalized, so elaborate a this-worldly power structure, that it lost the spirit of Christ's original community. Such charges, with the Roman counter-charges, have plagued the last thousand years of church history. At the least, they have raised the practical question of what price the church pays when it attempts to exert this-worldly power.

On the one hand, the medieval period gave the church the experience of being the one institution able to provide cultural integrity. Without such thinkers as Boethius and such pastoral administrators as Gregory, the dark ages might well have snuffed European culture out. The church is bonded to an incarnate God, so this-worldly or historical matters are somewhat natural to it. It bears a responsibility for the well-being of its people (all people), so it has the right to take the practical steps and invent the practical, governmental forms necessary to fulfill its responsibilities.

On the other hand, the treasure of the church is the divine life at its center. This is the main good it has to offer people in any age, and the main source of its proper influence. If the church wanders away from this center, it loses its reason to be. As well, it loses its best source of influence. The problem for church leaders, therefore, is to make the Christian worldview sufficiently persuasive to shape the given age and culture in which they dwell. Only by the intrinsic authority of wisdom and holiness can the church be as incarnate and effective as it should.

The medieval heritage contains this lesson both positively and negatively. Positively, the periods in which Christian art, natural philosophy, political thought, social services, and spirituality clarified daily life and gave it a profoundly beautiful rationale are some of the church's most shining successes. Negatively, the periods of corruption, and the dissolution of church influence or credibility in the fourteenth century, suggest the dangers always stalking a princely or curial style of church leadership. Unless people perceive the power of the church as spiritual, given by holiness and expressed in a humble service, they will judge the ambitions of the medieval church an ongoing source of corruption.

Among the counterbalances to the corruptions of the medieval Western church, the mystics deserve a place of honor. Bernard of Clairvaux, Francis of Assisi, Catherine of Siena, and many more called the church back to its union with Christ in love. Moreover, their descriptions of the interior states that an intense pursuit of Christ can bring influenced the leading theologians. Thus one is hard pressed to decide whether the Victorines and the Rhineland contemplatives should be considered mystics or theologians. The ideal for both groups was an exegesis of faith that did justice to the experience of meeting God directly, in naked prayer. So influential a late medieval work as THE IMITATION OF CHRIST carried this ideal into an age depressed by the disgrace of the fourteenth century papacy (when three different "popes" claimed legitimacy) and the plague that the Crusaders had brought back from Constantinople. THE IMITATION speaks to the individual soul seen under the aspect of death and eternity. Its predecessors in mystical reflection had been absorbed by the presence of God to all creatures. Either way, the church at large received a sober yet ultimately vivifying recall to the heart of the Christian matter. Unless one felt grace and consolation, tasted their savor and knew their import experientially, all the official words meant little.

The theologians of the high middle ages, culminating in the thirteenth century era of Thomas Aquinas and Bonaventure, were well rooted in the mystical tradition. Thomas, whose work has received the most praise, thought of himself as a teacher charged to present traditional faith as clearly and coherently as possible. His use of Aristotle, whose works had become available through Arab translators, eventually produced a systematic theology that leaves an impression of exquisite balance. By turning away from Platonic and Augustinian theories of knowledge, Thomas was able to elaborate crucial distinctions between the natural and the supernatural orders that preserved the integrity of each. His critical realism helped Christians to view the world soberly and work in it wholeheartedly, without losing their sense that every hair of their heads was numbered by an otherworldly God. Thomas accepted the institutional church of his day, but precisely ecclesiastical concerns ranked rather low in his theology. The main authorities were Scripture, the fathers (as the leading sources of tradition), and reason. The sayings of popes or curial officials never determined Thomas' opinions.

In a useful survey of Christian doctrine between 604 and 1350, David Knowles has treated questions of canon law and the sacraments in his section dealing with the years 1050 to 1200. The twelfth century was a period when church law developed great influence. After that, inevitably, theologians and laity alike had to contend with a more impressive institution. Legal articulation, for better or worse, specifies what a body thinks of itself and its relations to other bodies or even the world as a whole. The papacy of the high middle ages used the developments of lawyers to sharpen its decisions in matters of church policy and discipline. These decisions, along with the papal interpretations of previous custom, greatly influenced the sense of faith in later years. As Knowles summarizes the process: "Historians of theology and canon law have not always appreciated the very considerable influence of the canonists in the development of doctrinal expression. In every field of Christian worship and discipline, practice, the outward manifestation of common conviction, has always run ahead of theory and definition. The established way of acting as well as the established form of prayer may create the established formulae of belief. If this had always been so, it became far more evident in an age when papal decisions, often based on a mixture of law and practice, became at once firm precedents and definitions of doctrine. The sacraments, for example, and in particular the discipline of penance and holy orders, had been constantly topics for legislation and papal decision, and the tradition thus established had been expressed or modified by canonists in their ordinary task of presenting and explaining the law."[7]

The canonists' concern with the sacraments of penance and holy orders came after the theologians' debates about eucharistic matters. In the ninth century the main question was the mode of Christ's presence in the eucharistic elements of bread and wine. In the eleventh century the term "transubstantiation" arose to settle this question, using a philosophical vocabulary derived from Boethius. Those deemed unorthodox in eucharistic theology could find themselves in jail, and the overall approach of church authorities in these disputes was more legalistic and logical than what a current sacramental theology finds fitting. Nonetheless, the disputes about the eucharist, like the legislation concerning penance and orders, shaped the tendency of the later church to consider sacramental matters one of its prime spheres of juridical authority. As it tried to imagine its competence in sacramental matters, the medieval church somewhat assimilated such matters to material questions of property.

Quite apart from the historians of doctrine, we find intriguing portraits of the medieval church in such literary masterpieces as Chaucer's CANTERBURY TALES and Dante's DIVINE COMEDY. The latter expresses well the hierarchical thinking that prevailed: circles upon circles. As well, it expresses the keen medieval psychology of virtues and vices, which in effect was a characteriology. One could interpret people in terms of the virtues or vices that dominated their souls. Dante takes harsh swipes at many clergymen, and his total view of the institutional church is rather negative. Yet one could no more cut away Christian faith, even ecclesial faith, from the DIVINE COMEDY than one could cut away its poetic form. For Dante assumed that the church mediated grace and salvation, so much so that the best of pagans, such as Vergil, waited outside heaven and divine glory because they had not received baptism and church membership.

Chaucer is similar to Dante in offering us a window upon the medieval world, but his typical characters are more concrete. Thus in THE CANTERBURY TALES one gets a better sense of how clergymen, nuns, and Christians went about their daily business. To be sure, the literary form of a pilgrimage offers Chaucer what today's anthropologists, influenced by Victor Turner, might call a "liminal" period. For Turner pilgrimage has been one of several occasions when people shed their workaday patterns, assumptions, and inhibitions.[8] Nonetheless, Chaucer's characters suggest not only the rich, several-sided significance of pilgrimage to the burial places of saints but also the pervasiveness of Christian faith and church life. The saints were venerated in the context of the church. The pilgrims felt bonded to them because they had been members of one Christian body. So their merits could help less holy folk, and their example was an edifying common property.

Eastern Christianity

The fall of the Western Roman empire, rise of the papacy, and crusades against the Muslims who had gained control in the Eastern empire were significant factors in the estrangement of the Eastern and Western wings of the church. Long before the formal separation of 1054, cultural and theological differences divided the churches. After the formal separation, the crusades brought a Latin presence to the East that proved more irritating than helpful. For the best part of fifteen hundred years, therefore, the Eastern and Western Christianities have lacked the union, love, and mutual support that Christ prayed for his church.

When Eastern Orthodox historians and theologians deal with ecclesiology, two themes are sounded from the beginning. The first is that Eastern Christianity becomes distinctive (perhaps to the point of de facto separation from Western Christianity) through the formation of Byzantium, the imperial configuration that continued in the East after the disintegration of the Western Roman Empire. The second theme is that ecclesiology came late to the table of Eastern theological concerns, and that the principal difference between the Eastern and Western ecclesiologies has been the papacy.

In Byzantium, the Hellenistic political viewpoint, as integrated with Christian faith, made the Emperor a representative of God. The "cosmological myth," as Eric Voegelin has called it, by which many peoples have pictured earthly life as a miniature of heavenly life (placing both within the all-inclusive orbit of nature), continued to form the popular mind. To be sure, Christian faith separated divinity from nature and made "Christ our God" a figure independent of creation. Yet the rights of the Emperor in church affairs reflected the Eastern sense that culture should be whole. Nature and grace, politics and faith, ought to combine into something harmonious or integral. Where the West developed the papacy into a force quite able to oppose the secular rulers, the East contained such opposition.

Francis Dvornik has summarized this interpretation as follows: "The differences that become clear both in Byzantium and the West in the conception of the Church and its earthly aspect, the differences which stand out also in the evolution of the organization of the two Churches, are due to the fact that the two portions of Christendom have developed under different political and social conditions. The only political philosophy which the Byzantines knew was founded on the Hellenistic political system which the first Christian ideologists, Clement of Alexandria and Eusebius, had adapted to Christian doctrine. This system, which one could call Christian Hellenism, saw in the Emperor a representative of God upon earth, almost the vicegerent of Christ. According to this political conception, the Christian Emperor not only had the right but also the duty to watch over the Church, to defend the Orthodox faith, and to lead his subjects to God. It is from this point of view that we must judge the development of Eastern Christianity and its ideas on the relation of the Church on earth to the civil power."[9]

The theology of the church came late to Byzantium because other doctrinal matters were more pressing. In the period of the great councils, from 325 to 787, trinitarian and Christological issues predominated. The iconoclastic controversy dominated the eighth and ninth centuries, so it was only at the end of the ninth century that the church became a clear focus of theological reflection. Naturally, the prior theological concerns had carried ecclesiological implications. The Byzantine theologians accepted the images of the church found in Scripture, and then their reflections on the trinity, the nature of Christ, and the processes of divinization inclined them to think of the church as the people bonded to Christ for the sake of living the life of the trinitarian God. The church accomplished its work of sanctifying believers in the divine life through its priesthood and sacramental system. Essentially, therefore, its nature was mystical or otherworldly. To balance this, the Eastern theologians elaborated a rationale for an ecclesiastical structure, pivoted on the bishops, that would allow the church to function in space and time. The liturgy quite elaborately played out the church's mystical focus on divine life, while the synods in which the bishops came together to deal with church affairs epitomized the Eastern approach to political life.

Because of its close ties to the emperor, the Byzantine church never fully understood the Western approach to political life. There the bishop of Rome predominated over his fellow bishops, and the church experimented with the thesis that spiritual power should prevail over temporal power. The bishop of Rome claimed jurisdiction over the whole church, which the patriarchs of the historic centers of Eastern Christianity, such as Constantinople, Jerusalem, Antioch, and Alexandria, found belittling. Western church law developed in papal hands, whereas Eastern church law developed under the influence of the emperor. Insofar as the emperor had a tendency to interest himself excessively in church matters, especially the definition of doctrine, the Eastern church leaders looked toward the Western papal model with some envy. They wished to enlist the power and prestige of the pope in their battles with intrusive emperors, yet they remained suspicious of the pope's universal claims and wanted to keep Byzantium free of Western dominance.

In the view of Western historians of Eastern Orthodoxy, the church was able, in such crises as the iconoclast controversy, to preserve the true faith, but it lost its proper independence of worldly authorities such as the emperor. Thus, a Western historian such as Adolf Von Harnack would think of the Eastern Christian "theocracy" (fusion of religion and politics) as a failure. In the view of Eastern historians, such as Alexander Schmemann, the monks who spearheaded the victory of orthodoxy in the iconoclast controversy emphatically did not cede the church's proper freedom to the imperial powers: "But what sort of freedom is in question here? The monks were not fighting for the separation of Church and state—still less for a clericalist subjection of the state to the Church—but only for that conception of theocracy which, since the days of Constantine's conversion, had opened the arms of the Church so broadly to the empire. In opposition to Harnack and all historians who measure Byzantium according to Western criteria (which in fact did not exist in the West itself until considerably later), it must be affirmed that the Church, not the empire, was victorious in this struggle."[10]

Schmemann goes on to support this thesis by referring to the theocratic conception that Orthodoxy had expressed in its EPANA-GOGE, an introduction to a code of laws published under Emperor Basil I the Macedonian at the end of the ninth century. This code remained the fundamental law concerning relations between church and state until the end of the empire in 1453, when the Turks conquered Constantinople. In the EPANAGOGE the emperor and the patriarch stand parallel. Together they are "the most exalted and most necessary members of the realm." The code describes the responsibilities of each leader, and while these responsibilities overlap, so that the emperor could be construed as having rights and duties regarding the preservation of orthodox doctrine, the patriarch clearly is the major custodian and interpreter of the maxims of the ancients, definitions of the fathers, and teachings of the church councils.

Despite this attention to practical matters of church organization, the main thrust of Byzantine ecclesiology has been sacramental. That is to say, the main conception of the church dominating the classical Eastern sources is of a community united to Christ and the Spirit. The historical actions of the church ought to build up this unity and embody it in the world, but the communion of the church reaches into heaven, where it includes the angels and the saints. The Roman influence assured that the Byzantine church would pay sufficient attention to canonical law, but the mystical bent of the Eastern theologians made such law subordinate to the conception of the church as the sacramental community of divine life.

In his fine book on Byzantine theology, John Meyendorff has enumerated the standard sources of Eastern church canons as follows. First have come the Apostolic Canons, a collection of eighty-five disciplinary rules that became the standard text in Syria from the first half of the fourth century. In the sixth century this collection became an integral part of the code of the church of Constantinople. Second, various ecumenical councils formulated canons, and the prestige of these councils made the canons important. Thus Nicaea formulated twenty canons, Constantinople formulated seven canons, Ephesus formulated eight canons, and Chalcedon formulated thirty canons. The Quinisex Council, also known as the Council *in Trullo,* collected and sanctioned one hundred and two canons developed by prior councils, and Nicaea II developed twenty-two canons. In this enumeration, by the end of the group of councils that have dominated Eastern theology, one hundred eighty-nine canons gave the church a rather full disciplinary code.

In addition to these primary materials, the Eastern church leaders venerated the canons of local church councils, from Ancyra in 314 to the Constantinopolitan assembly of 879–880. Although these ses-

sions were not "ecumenical," and so did not have the weight of a consensus of bishops of the whole church, they placed before all of
Byzantium the disciplinary wisdom of particular churches or areas. A
last source of canonical direction was the writings of venerable church
fathers, whose letters or answers to questions entered the treasury of
Eastern discipline. The standard Byzantine collection called the
Nomocanon, which dates from 883, included materials from before
265 (the death of Dionysius of Alexandria). Among the eminent fathers represented in this collection are Athanasius of Alexandria,
Basil of Caesarea, Gregory of Nyssa, Gregory of Nazianzus, and Cyril
of Alexandria. Basil was especially important, for his collection of
ninety-two canons was highly esteemed.[11]

As this veneration of the fathers and councils suggests, the Byzantine church was concerned to follow the tracks marked out by its
authoritative predecessors. Both the Greek and the Slavic branches of
Orthodoxy have maintained this tendency. "Tradition" has been both
weighty and living, while innovation has been suspect. Perhaps this
tendency, too, derives from the Hellenistic intellectual heritage. The
archetypes that Greek philosophy venerated, and its high regard for
theoria, meant an inclination to consider the church less than fully
historical. The church existed in heaven as much as it existed on
earth, perhaps even more. What the leaders of the church, under the
inspiration of the Spirit, decided in the centuries closest to Jesus had
more prestige than what the church had decided more recently. By
the end of the eighth century, the Byzantine church had the essentials
of the patrimony from which it has lived ever since. This patrimony
said (more implicitly than explicitly) that the church existed mainly
to preserve the wisdom of the past concerning salvation.

Salvation was no assured matter, so the two main streams of Byzantine spirituality, the sacramental and the ascetical, deeply influenced the church's daily practice. Writing of Russian Christianity in
the tenth to thirteenth centuries, George P. Fedotov describes the
theological foundation of Byzantine spirituality as follows: "The typical Byzantine icon of Christ is that of the Pantocrator, the Lord Om-
nipotent. It is the image of the glorified Christ regnant on His
heavenly throne . . . Sorrow and severity are written upon this divine
face as if it were forced, unwillingly, to contemplate men's crimes and
sins. Christ-Pantocrator is, indeed, the Christ of the Last Judgment
or of the 'Terrible Judgment' as it is called by the Greeks, not the Re-

deemer but the Judge—as He is expected by the faithful . . . A thousand years later, at the other pole of Christianity, the same Old Testament concept of God was revived by Calvin. It is curious to observe how many common features the radical form of Protestantism has with oriental monophysitism [stress on one—the divine—nature] or with some radical trends of oriental monasticism. In both a miserable man stands before the terrible God, finding no words strong enough for self-humiliation. The hope for salvation is small. Hell is the lot of the average, not only of the worst people. But there is a hope and a way of salvation."[12]

The way of salvation actually had two paths, monastic asceticism and the church's sacramental life. Eastern Christianity came to see monasticism as the peak of Christian life, so monastic ideals were passed on to the church as a whole. For example, the private confession to a spiritual director that Eastern monasticism had developed became part of the general church's discipline. Monastic rules for fasting became required of laity, and the monastic liturgical traditions became the standard for all churches' worship. (That is why the Eastern liturgy is so long: it was devised for monks who had no competing responsibilities.) The Eastern monasteries stressed manual labor and lengthy prayer, with little time for cultural development. Thus they did not play the educational and intellectual roles played by monastic centers in the West. In the opinion of Fedotov, the majority of the monasteries stressed only the lower levels of prayer, the path of purgation (examination of conscience, resolve to amend one's moral life), considering mystical contemplation something beyond the reach of the majority. So great was the prestige of this ascetical monastic life that the rite of tonsure (shaving one's head), by which one gained admission to a monastery, often was considered a sacrament that brought forgiveness of one's prior sins. Thus many laypeople on the verge of death received tonsure, as a way of ensuring their passage to heaven.

The sacramental life of the Eastern church as a whole derived from the "mysteries" celebrated in early Christianity. Thus the regular liturgy was solemn, lengthy, and enwrapped in prayer. Only in the seventeenth century did the Eastern church accept the Western notion (itself only stemming from the twelfth century) that there are seven official sacraments. This late acceptance was less than enthusiastic, too, because the Eastern tradition had placed no hard and fast distinction between sacraments and other holy rites (such as tonsure, the anointing of the emperor, the "great consecration" of water on the feast of the Epiphany, etc.). To be sure, baptism, "chrismation" (what the West calls confirmation), and above all the eucharist stood out as the most important sacramental actions. But blessings for the fields, children, and women who had recently given birth melded together with blessings for the sick and those to be married, all such rituals being considered sanctifying.

Moreover, the central importance of icons in Eastern Christian worship brought an expansive sense of sacramentality. Everything material had come from the good God of creation and had, in principle, been taken up by the Logos in the Incarnation. The images of the saints, and even more the images of Jesus and Mary, were powerful presences of divine grace. Orthodoxy had no problem distinguishing between reverencing icons and worshipping them. Its theology always knew that the true God is beyond all material representation. Yet its instinct was that the holy images are an inseparable part of Christian worship and faith. Without them the Word would not be fully worshipped as having taken flesh and sanctified all of life. Without them, too, the saints would not be fully appreciated as heavenly brothers and sisters able to help in times of distress. The Virgin Mary, reverenced throughout the East as the *theotokos* or "God-bearer," has graced the most beautiful Eastern icons, softening the terrors of God's justice.

The Reformation

The Protestant Reformation owed a great debt to Martin Luther's preoccupation with the terrors of God's justice. Out of the turmoil of the fourteenth and fifteenth centuries, when social chaos and laxity in the church moved thoughtful Christians to tears, the Reformers drew the conviction that something more reliable than the institutional catholic church was necessary if people were to live with high hopes of salvation. As is well known, Luther dissolved his own scruples about salvation by taking to heart the Pauline notion that justification comes through faith and grace. No human works can make a person right with God. Only God's own Spirit and the merits of Christ can give righteousness. So for Luther faith became the religious pivot, and the scriptural word that promised justification through faith became the central Christian authority. The sacramental works of the church fell under a Pauline cloud, while the individual conscience became the arena of the most crucial battles. In Luther's train, the Reformers opposed the authority of the bishop of Rome as having swollen beyond biblical proportions. They stressed the right of each individual to interpret scripture under the guidance of the Spirit, and they called for a reform of a church grown immoral and perverted by "works-righteousness" (including the peddling of indulgences and a view of the Mass as a meritorious sacrifice).

To be sure, neither Luther nor the other leading members of the first generations of Reformers sought schism. They preserved many features of the catholic tradition (indeed, probably they would have called themselves "Catholics"), and their main goal was to bring the church back to its scriptural charter. But rather quickly their opposition to Roman authority legitimized opposition within their own groups. The result was that authority became, in the phrase of Robert McAfee Brown, the "achilles heel" of Protestantism.[13] The Protestant tradition came so to respect individual conscience that it allowed groups to split off and form new churches whenever serious disagreements arose. The twentieth century Protestant movement to reunite the churches testifies to Protestant Christians' own realization that their divisive tendency had gotten out of hand.

Martin Luther's focus on scripture as the prime authority in Christian faith was not meant to deny the importance of tradition, but when disputes between Protestants and Catholics became polemical the effect was to diminish the significance of the church leaders who hitherto had been the leading interpreters of Christian tradition. Relatedly, Luther and the other leading Reformers attacked the distinction between clergy and laity that had grown quite sharp in medieval Christianity. For example, in his "Treatise on Christian Liberty" (1520), Luther argued that all Christians are priests: "Injustice is done those words 'priest,' 'cleric,' 'spiritual,' 'ecclesiastic,' when they are transferred from all Christians to those few who are now by a mischievous usage called 'ecclesiastics.' Holy Scripture makes no distinction between them, although it gives the name 'ministers,' 'servants,' 'stewards' to those who are now called popes, bishops and lords and who should according to the ministry of the Word serve others and teach them the faith of Christ and the freedom of believers. Although we are all equally priests, we cannot all publicly minister and teach. We ought not to do so even if we could."[14]

One sees, then, that Luther and the early Reformation had a new but not discontinuous view of church membership. Maintaining a functional distinction between those qualified to preach and minister officially and those not so qualified, they wanted to bring out the kinship between baptism and priestly existence. By having entered the church and been quickened with divine life, all Christians enjoyed a priestly existence. This was clear from such New Testament texts as 1 Peter 2:9. Priestly existence meant the right to offer praise and worship to God, and also the responsibility of ministering to others, as one's competence and situation allowed, the good news of the gospel.

John Calvin, who brought the Protestant Reformation to power in French-speaking Switzerland, was a talented biblical scholar and systematic theologian. His INSTITUTES furnished the Protestant world a clear and profound statement of faith. In treating the church, Calvin agreed with Luther that the terms "catholic church" and "communion of saints," which appear in the Apostles' Creed, refer to the entire body of the redeemed, regardless of their time or place. God alone knows the membership of the universal church. It is invisible to human eyes. To be charitable, we must regard those who confess faith in Christ and live the sacramental life of the church as members of the true, invisible church. The visible church makes the body of Christ available in space and time, but not all who claim membership in it are redeemed, since some are hypocritical. The notes of a true church are true preaching and reverent hearing of the gospel, along with the administration of the sacraments according to Christ's institution. These notes have become very significant for the Calvinist wing of the Protestant tradition. Calvin himself added a third note or mark, discipline, which has been important in churches that interpret his theology quite strictly. In John T. McNeill's view, discipline maintains "the tone of the visible Church, correcting the behavior of the members and excluding from communion scandalous and obdurate offenders. Discipline is described as the 'nerves' or ligaments of the Church. It is held necessary in order to maintain inviolate the sanctity of communion."[15]

The Puritan tradition, derived from Calvinism, laid great stress on such discipline. For the "saints" to be what they were supposed to be, even harsh punishment might be necessary. Churches from this Puritan tradition, along with other sectarian groups, have practiced "shunning" (cutting communications with members deemed sinful or in violation of church discipline) to carry out their obligation to keep the church holy. The severity of the Calvinist God (Calvin himself laid more stress on the divine mercy and desire to save human beings than many of his interpreters did) became razor sharp in the doctrine of "double predestination" (the idea, stimulated by Romans 8:29–30, that from eternity God foresees heaven for some people and hell for others). Churches with this Calvinist legacy could divide the world into elect and damned. When they coupled this division with the idea that this-worldly prosperity was a sign of election and this-worldly poverty was a sign of damnation, they raised strong questions about their fidelity to the biblical Christ.

The Church of England, which has seen itself as a middle road between Catholicism and Protestantism, retained a larger place for bishops and clergy than proved true in many of the continental Protestant bodies. As well, sacraments and tradition were less subordinated to scripture. The Anglican view of the church may be seen from the catechism appended to the most recent version of THE BOOK OF COMMON PRAYER: "What is the Church? The Church is the community of the New Covenant. How is the Church described in the Bible? The Church is described as the Body of which Christ is the Head and of which all baptized persons are members. It is called the People of God, the New Israel, a holy nation, a royal priesthood, and the pillar and ground of truth. How is the Church described in the creeds? The Church is described as one, holy, catholic and apostolic." After explaining each of these notes of the creedal church, the catechism deals with the mission of the church: "What is the mission of the Church? The mission of the Church is to restore all people to unity with God and each other in Christ. How does the Church pursue its mission? The Church pursues its mission as it prays and worships, proclaims the Gospel, and promotes justice, peace, and love. Through whom does the Church carry out its mission? The Church carries out its mission through the ministry of all its members."[16]

Although the catechism is a contemporary piece, reflecting today's sense that peace and justice should stand high on the church's missionary agenda, its recourse to biblical and creedal sources of ecclesiology, and its stress on the ministerial character of all members' faith, suggests the Church of England's own appropriation of the sixteenth century reformers' demands.

Anglicanism itself later brought forth cries for reform, however, and the Methodism that looks back to John and Charles Wesley stands as one of the most important results of these cries. In basic theology Methodism has been loath to accept the strict Calvinist notion of double predestination, according more freedom to human beings and a wider outreach to the saving work of Christ. From the late eighteenth century Methodist churches were organized according to principles developed by John Wesley. Their ecclesiology stressed the priesthood of all believers, and they welcomed to membership all who sincerely desired to be saved from their sins through faith in Jesus Christ. Such people had to evidence this sincerity in their life and conduct, but such a focus on salvation from sin easily led to the often emotional religion of revivals and personal confessions of faith in Jesus. Methodism has provided for superintendents or bishops, but lay influence has been strong. It has especially distinguished itself for social services, ministering to the poor, itinerant seamen, alcoholics, and wayward women. From the nineteenth century it has also had a strong missionary outreach to non-European lands.

Albert C. Outler, the editor of a fine selection of John Wesley's writings, sees Wesley's ecclesiology as varying little from that of the Anglicanism in which he was educated. The nineteenth and twentieth of the Thirty-nine Articles of Religion prominent in that education stressed the preaching of the Word and administration of the sacraments that we saw when dealing with Calvin. Wesley himself, using this text, went on to stress the phrase "a congregation of faithful men," seeing in it a bridge to the lively faith prominent in the New Testament descriptions of the church. Ephesians 4:1–6, which speaks of "one Lord, one faith, one baptism, one God and father of all," is especially important in his reflections. When he comes to summarize his sense of the church, as it has been chartered by the New Testament, Wesley writes: "Here, then, is a clear, unexceptionable answer to that question, 'What is the Church?' The catholic or universal church is all the persons in the universe whom God had so called out of the world as to entitle them to the preceding character—as to be 'one body,' united by 'one Spirit,' having 'one faith, one hope, one baptism; one God and Father of all, who is above all, and through all, and in them all.' "[17]

The so-called "Radical Reformation" went beyond the beginnings of Luther, Calvin, and the Church of England, especially in its demand for a church restored to the holiness implied in the scriptural accounts of God's people. Indeed, the Anabaptists ("rebaptizers") wanted to restore the pattern of the early church as much as possible. They regarded the time of the martyrs as more representative of what the church ought to be than the later periods when Christianity had become the established imperial religion. Roland Bainton has characterized the Anabaptist position as resting on a pessimistic view of the world and an optimistic view of the church: "The world—that is, society at large—will always be the partner of the flesh and the devil, but the Church must walk another road and must exemplify within its fellowship the living and the dying of Jesus Christ. It must be a community of the saints whose members, though not perfect, yet aspire to perfection and strive mightily. The complaint against the Lutherans and Zwinglians [German speaking Swiss Protestants] was that they had not produced a sufficient improvement in life. Promptly came the retort that the Anabaptists were reverting to monasticism and seeking again to win heaven by their good deeds, to which the answer was that they were not seeking to fulfill the law in order to be saved but rather to give proof of their faith by exhibiting its fruits. The kernel of Anabaptism was an ethical urge. If the Catholic Church had improved its morals they might not have found it too hard to return to its fold, whereas Luther said that his objection to the Catholic Church centered not on the life but on the teaching."[18]

In the United States this moralistic viewpoint has to some extent been represented by the Baptists, whose lineage is complex but owes an important debt to the more radical arm of the Puritan movement. Roger Williams, who founded Rhode Island in an effort to make an area of religious freedom in which his followers could live out their faith, stressed the experience of conversion and the importance of baptism by immersion. He thought that the church had lost authority through the corruption of the Middle Ages, and this in turn led him to deny that any church body had the right to form governments (the colonies were in effect theocracies) that would restrict anyone's freedom of conscience. Williams thought that scripture was the only source of saving knowledge, and his demand for religious freedom, although very differently based than that of a John Locke or a Thomas Jefferson (the main sources of what became the American tradition of separating church and state), became typical of American baptists.

While denying that Williams' own extreme theology had great influence in subsequent American religious life, Sydney Ahlstrom has

accorded Rhode Island the distinction of being the first commonwealth in modern history to make religious liberty a cardinal principle
of its incorporation. Both Baptists and Quakers there provided a welcome relief from the general pattern of intolerance that dominated seventeenth century America. Still, this religiously based tolerance did
not become the inspiration for the constitutional guarantees worked
out a century later. As mentioned, Locke and Jefferson had more to
do with that than Williams. So Ahlstrom concludes his description of
the experiment in Rhode Island rather whimsically: "Yet in view of
the pragmatic way in which Americans have in fact resolved the problems of democracy, liberty, and order, Rhode Island seems to illustrate
in an almost tragic way the political corollary of a dictum often voiced
by historians of science, that premature discoveries are uninfluen-
tial."[19]

We have perhaps crossed the rather vague border between the
Reformation and Modernity, but legitimately so, since the Reformation, along with the Renaissance, contributed much of the momentum
that begot Modernity. For our ecclesiological concerns, the history of
the church through the sixteenth and seventeenth centuries stands
out for spotlighting the rights of individual conscience. In practical
terms, the upshot of the Reformers' revisions of Catholic doctrine was
to transfer ecclesiastical authority to the bible as interpreted by the
individual believer. Certainly, the majority of Protestant groups themselves stumbled over this principle. Often, in fact, the leadership of
reformed churches (perhaps especially the leadership of left-wing and
Puritan churches) was as overbearing as the popes ever had been. But
a new model of Christian existence had arisen.

In its counter-reform, Roman Catholicism more hardened its traditions than acceded to Protestant demands or insights, yet the Council of Trent set in motion a renovation of seminary studies that before
long had begotten a better pastoral care. The most influential Roman
Catholic spirituality, that of Ignatius Loyola and the Jesuits, was emphatically anti-Protestant in professing special loyalty to the pope, but
its concern for the experience of the individual Christian brought it
quite close to Protestant interests in conversion and spiritual affec-
tions.

The sorriest result of the whole Reformation, clearly, was the
further split of the church. The separation of East and West had been
tragic, but the further split of Western Christianity paved the way for

the modern ridicule of church authority. When Protestant and Catholics went to war and slaughtered hundreds of thousands, moderns
had good grounds for asking who needed Christianity. Before long,
many were asking who needed God.

Modernity

Modernity has many definitions, but the majority of them stress
the autonomy that science, philosophy, and political change made the
ideal. Perhaps the strongest intellectual expression of modernity came
from the eighteenth century Enlightenment, for which autonomy was
a watchword. The success of Galileo, Copernicus, Newton, and the
other giants who changed the West's notion of the physical world
seemed to stem from their independence of traditional patterns of
thought. Insofar as these traditional patterns wove into Christian
faith, both Catholic and Protestant, the scientists' advances seemed
to strike a hearty blow against the churches' claims to authority.
Rather quickly the heliocentric view of the planets challenged traditional biblical notions, while the confidence in the power of reason
that the new science bred made dogmatic traditions appear passé.

Immanuel Kant, the greatest philosopher of the Enlightenment,
did not deny the existence of God. His critiques of human reason did,
however, diminish the medieval confidence that any person of sound
mind and good morals would find God the obvious source and end of
the world. Prior philosophers, such as Descartes and Hume, had prepared Kant's ground, while philosophers who worked in Kant's wake,
such as Hegel and Marx, could take his break with traditional forms
of authority for granted. Throughout modernity, therefore, human
reason has paraded as the supreme judge. What could not pass muster
before the bar of critical reflection was to be relegated to the bin of
myth, superstition, mere custom, or mindless faith. Obviously, much
of traditional religion fell into this category.

In political affairs the great events were the American and
French revolutions. Modern thought had prepared the way for each
of these tumultuous happenings, especially by its near-dogma that
each individual has the right to freedom from an alien political rule.
In the United States the leading thinkers had been influenced by such

continental philosophers as John Locke and the French *philosophes*. As well, Americans were trying to overcome a colonial history in which established churches had dictated the political tunes. From both sources Americans such as Franklin and Jefferson drew an ideal of tolerance and reason. No dogmatic revelation, church, or God was to have the determining word.

The French Revolution put these convictions into more violent form. There the leading forces of change combined hatred of the crown with hatred of the church. Indeed, anticlericalism was the fashion of the day, and a new humanistic religion bid to replace traditional Christianity. One can criticize this revolutionary hatred of traditional Christianity as unfair and self-serving, but the very intensity of the French anticlericalism shows the bind into which the church had gotten itself. Intellectuals looked on it as a source of repression, backwardness, bigotry, and superstition, while enough commoners found it part of an ineffective old order to support the destructive assaults.

When the scientists, philosophers, and politicians had done their work, historians and cultural analysts began to bring forward more perceptive analyses of the modern changeover. As they applied the ideals of critical reasoning to traditional texts, including the bible, these cultural analysts realized that meaning is always evolving. The findings of geologists and biologists that led to an evolutionary perspective on the physical world found a parallel in the rise of historical consciousness. It would be some while before the social sciences would arrive at their current autonomy and great influence, but Auguste Comte (1798–1857) anticipated this arrival, seeing it as the climax of an evolution from religion through philosophy to a science of humanity.

When twentieth century Christian theologians reflected on the rise of historical consciousness, they found many of its roots in the bible. The Israelite sense of time was linear, in contrast to the cyclical sense of time among Israel's neighbors. More recent studies have added nuance to this description, but much in it remains popular. One could say, therefore, that the origins of Christianity planted the seeds of Western historical consciousness. Nonetheless, the classical (Graeco-Roman) culture of the Empire in which Christianity came to dominance had rather ahistorical ideals. As a result, Christian theology and church life tended to speak as though one faith and practice could hold true and good for all times and places. Because of this tendency, "tradition" easily could become stagnant and repressive.

There are other important aspects to the modern period of church history, of course, but what we have described to this point was very significant. The modern aspiration for autonomy and freedom, coupled with the church's ahistorical sense of tradition (stronger in Orthodoxy and Catholicism than in Protestantism, but influential in Protestantism as well), made the Christian church seem the enemy of progress, enlightenment, and human ideals.

By the nineteenth century this adversarial relationship had become quite extreme. Such far-reaching theories as Darwinian evolution, Marxist economics, and (early in the twentieth century) Freudian psychoanalysis all got a cold shoulder from church authorities. For example, only in the mid-twentieth century did the Roman Catholic church allow modern (historical and literary) methods for studying the bible. The encyclical HUMANI GENERIS of Pope Pius XII (1950) still opposed *polygenism,* the notion (ingredient in modern evolutionary anthropology) that humanity arose from several different gene pools (rather than from a single "Adam"). From the pontificate of Pope Leo XIII a stream of "social encyclicals" tried to apply Christian faith to the manifest political and economic problems of the modern age, but they completely rejected Marxist analyses, because of their ties to a doctrinaire atheism. It would not be hard to find parallels in the reactions of other churches.

Psychology, too, has been late in coming into Christian favor. The rule of biblical and metaphysical models of the self meant a retarded appreciation of what the philosophers called "subjectivity" and then "intentionality analysis," while the interest of the depth psychologists in unconscious motivations horrified churchpeople by focusing on sexuality. No doubt all of these modern insights and movements had their aberrations and excesses. In hindsight, a fair-minded evaluation can say that many of the churchpeople's negative reactions had considerable basis. But the wholesale rejection of modernity, the regularly negative reflex, wrote the churches out of the central plot-line. Today's post-modern culture, heir to the horrors of two world wars and beset by a half-dozen global crises (nuclear, ecological, economic, political, sexual, and racial), looks at religion more favorably than modernity could. The churches have to realize, however, that a considerable part of today's cultural detritus lies on their consciences. If they had responded to modernity with more intelligence and less self-serving, modernity might not have been so warped by a viciously atheistic humanism.

Two quite different studies of modernity bear out this analysis. Marshall Berman's ALL THAT IS SOLID MELTS INTO AIR presents its interpretation in its title. For Berman the modern appreciation of complexity, contradiction, groundlessness, and the like is simply realistic, and the way out of our frightening chaos is to embrace such representative moderns as Karl Marx more deeply: "I have been arguing that those of us who are most critical of modern life need modernism most, to show us where we are and where we can begin to change our circumstances and ourselves. In search of a place to begin, I have gone back to one of the first and greatest of modernists, Karl Marx. I have gone to him not so much for his answers as for his questions. The great gift he can give us today, it seems to me, is not a way out of the contradictions of modern life but a surer and deeper way into those contradictions. He knew that the way beyond the contradictions would have to lead through modernity, not out of it. He knew we must start where we are: physically naked, stripped of all religious, aesthetic, moral haloes and sentimental veils, thrown back on our individual will and energy, forced to exploit each other and ourselves in order to survive; and yet, in spite of all, thrown together by the same forces that pull us apart, dimly aware of all we might be together, ready to stretch ourselves to grasp new human possibilities, to develop identities and mutual bonds that can help us hold together as the fierce modern air blows hot and cold through us all."[20]

In this analysis, alienation is simply the way things are. We may use it to come together and forge defensive meanings (what these might be the quotation doesn't say), but no salvation or divinization can rescue us from the alienation itself. The analysis of modernity available in Eric Voegelin's FROM ENLIGHTENMENT TO REVOLUTION[21] would see this conclusion as utterly logical. For Voegelin the deification of humanity wrought by Hegel, Marx, and other leading moderns was bound to shipwreck in alienation. The great grief of modernity, in fact, has been its loss of the transcendence clarified by Israelite revelation and Greek philosophy. And while the churches contributed to this grief, by losing the experiences that their doctrinal symbols were supposed to represent, the atheistic revolt of modernity was an even more reprehensible failure. Because of it Hitler, Stalin, and the other great butchers of recent times had an easy path.

Through all the periods of its history, the church of course has striven to mediate meaning and salvation. Much of its success in the early centuries of the Christian era stemmed precisely from the cogency Hellenism found in its message. Through the Middle Ages the church offered a haven against an oppressive sense of mortality. In the Reformation it broke through to new resources for coping with guilt. This is not to deny that the church also contributed to Western guilt, fear of God's judgment, and bodily unease. On the whole, however, the gospel proved sufficiently fertile in assurances of God's love to give any patient reader many grounds for hope.

It remains to be seen what verdict historians will pronounce on the services of the modern and post-modern church. If modernity assaulted God, and then found humanity without God well-nigh meaningless, the church was slow to develop a creative response. Indeed, it was more the sufferings brought by the twentieth century than any creative response by the church that broke modernity's confident assertion of autonomy. Nowadays theologians have good responses to the defective visions of Marx and Nietzsche, but in their day such thinkers were far more imaginative than the theologians.

In our day, as we hope to show in the chapters that follow, the church is abrim with appropriations of the positive aspects of Marxist, Freudian, Nietzschean, and other modern visions. Before the Protestant churches' move toward reunion early in the twentieth century, however, Protestantism had few effective counters to modernist alienation. Roman Catholicism delayed its full response to modernity until the second half of the twentieth century, when the Second Vatican Council tried to bring Catholicism up to date, and Orthodoxy has yet to make its full response. The story of the seventeenth, eighteenth, and nineteenth centuries therefore is rather depressing. Of course there were brave individuals and proud moments, but the main initiatives were too few and too slow.

One exception to this judgment might be the church's foreign missions. Priests and ministers followed hard on the heels of the explorers and traders who opened up the New World, as they did in Asia and Africa. This connection with Western exploration and trade proved a mixed blessing, especially when Western conquests begot a colonial rule, but many of the missionaries displayed a wonderful zeal.

To the mind of a Francis Xavier, for instance, Indians and Asians were languishing outside the pale of salvation. In his eagerness to draw them into the riches of Christ, Xavier wore himself out. The missionary creativity of his fellow Jesuits Matteo Ricci and Roberto de Nobili, which stressed adapting Christian faith and customs to, respectively, Chinese and Indian traditions, might have won great swathes of Asia for the church. But bureaucrats back in Rome insisted on trying to impose Latinate models, so the work of the pioneers went virtually for naught.

The Protestant missionary story was less marred by the ineptitude of a central church authority. In its case the fragmentation of the Christian community proved the embarrassment and stumbling block. In effect the churches were transporting their differences onto foreign soil, confusing Africans and Asians considerably. In addition, many who accepted the offer of Christian faith did so for less than purely religious reasons. When the colonial power was nominally Christian, and the missionary schools seemed the best way to advancement, native peoples faced a complex set of opportunities.

The venture of Christianizing Latin America, which mainly fell to Roman Catholicism because of the Spanish and Portuguese predominance, was like the Protestant (and Catholic) ventures in Asia and Africa in presenting the native peoples a complicated option. The greater apparent success of the Latin American missionaries covered over the native peoples' dividedness concerning their pre-Christian traditions, and recently this dividedness has come home to roost. As well, the alliance of the church with the wealthy and powerful gave Latin American Christianity an authoritarian if not oppressive countenance. That, too, has come home to roost in recent years, but lately many Latin American Christians have been distinguishing themselves for bravery in facing down brutal military regimes.

In Karl Rahner's analysis of the ecclesiological implications of Vatican II, a new schematization of church history appears.[22] Rahner sees the very long stretch from the admission of Gentiles into (Jewish) Christianity to the twentieth century as an era when the church culturally was much less than catholic. Only in this century (for Roman Catholics only at Vatican II) did a truly world-wide church come into focus. The European assumptions that dominated for nineteen hundred years began to give way, in face of the strength of the African, Asian, and Latin American churches. Whether Christianity will prove able to diversify sufficiently to let the non-European cultures have their proper say remains to be seen. If it does, modernity may after all have done the church a favor.

If Christianity does not open itself to the global culture that started to dawn in the modern era, it will have its own performance in the period from sixteen hundred to nineteen hundred to blame. The First Vatican Council (1869–70) summarized many of the Roman Catholic tendencies through those years by stressing the preeminence of the pope and capping an ecclesiology signal for its ahistoricism. In that spirit, the "Oath Against Modernism" prescribed for seminary teachers and students by Pope Pius X in 1910 was a last gasp of official negativism. For while some of the proposals of the modernists did not do justice to the importance of either Christian tradition or the teaching authority of the church, many other proposals were honest efforts to take historical criticism and an evolutionary perspective to heart.

The Oath did not succeed in closing the Catholic church to modern intellectual influences. Virtually nothing other than intellectual suicide could have done that. But it furnished one last sorry example of the lack of sympathy and ghettoed mentality that vitiated the church's mission throughout the modern era. Proudly claiming to possess a truth that did not operate outside its borders, and refusing to be part of God's obviously evolving and historical world, the modern church, Catholic-Protestant-Orthodox, had little to say to the best and the brightest. Again and again it forced those who wanted to overthrow the corrupt systems that were responsible for poverty and suffering to choose between faith and intellectualism or between faith and fellow-feeling. No wonder faith lost so many.

Summary

We began our survey of church history with the patristic era. In the first centuries after the death of Jesus' immediate disciples, the presbyter-bishops predominated. Christianity had to shift from expecting the parousia, and so considering itself alien to the Roman Empire, to settling down for citizenship. Periods of persecution made martyrdom a prime interpretation of faith. Doctrinal deviance, above all that of the Gnostics, pushed apostolicity—connection to the first generation of church leaders—to the fore. Unity, catholicity, and holiness were the other marks of the church important to the fathers. Monasticism provided a counterbalance to over-immersion in imperial affairs, especially after the approval of Christianity early in the fourth century. The great councils that hammered out trinitarian and Christological doctrine show the fathers at their most influential.

The Middle Ages began for the Western church when Rome fell early in the fifth century. The changeover from imperial to German tribal rule wrought many cultural changes, and as Christian missionaries converted the pagan tribes the church emerged as the prime healer of the cultural breakdown. By the early seventh century, when Pope Gregory I died, the bishop of Rome was the most important European leader. Ecclesiologically, this period launched the papacy on its career of trying to deal with this-worldly powers as at least an equal. The medieval mystics and theologians balanced this secularism, Thomas Aquinas capping their work with a brilliant synthesis. Work in canon law and sacramental theology buttressed the theological centrality of the papacy, while the later medieval spirituality of THE IMITATION OF CHRIST shows the church's resources for dealing with plague and moral breakdown. Dante and Chaucer are perhaps the best authors to study if one wants a rounded view of medieval Christian culture.

Eastern Christianity had no such discontinuity as that caused by the fall of Rome. In the East the reign of the fathers continued until the fall of Constantinople in 1453. The Byzantine theopolity gave the emperor specifically Christian rights, while a sacramental view of the church stressed its heavenly dimension. Western scholars tend to think that the Eastern church lost its proper autonomy, but many Eastern scholars believe that Eastern Christian culture was properly holistic. The crusades distanced the East from Western sympathies, and the Eastern iconographic tradition reveals a spirituality that increasingly focused on Christ as the Pantocrator. Monasticism had a heavy influence, although the sacramental system continued to be the major church feature. The split of East and West in 1054 was more political than doctrinal.

The Protestant Reformation brought a second great division to the Christian community. Luther and the early Reformers were seeking both security of salvation and institutional renewal. They focused on faith and biblical authority. Calvin gave Protestantism a systematic statement of faith. In ecclesiology, his insistence on true preaching and proper administration of the sacraments was very influential. The Church of England accepted this viewpoint, as did such Anglican reforms as Methodism. However, they tended to disregard Calvin's double predestination. The radical reformation stressed moral reform, while in the United States religious liberty advanced to the forefront. The Baptist tradition has kept both of these concerns paramount.

In our opinion, modernity was not a good time for the church. On the whole, thinkers outside the church called the cultural tunes and the church reacted negatively. Autonomy was the watchword in the Enlightenment, and the American and French revolutions strove to work out more autonomous political arrangements. A new science undergirt a great confidence in human reason, while historical consciousness ousted the classical cultural ideals of stability and universality. The church's ahistorical ideals stiffened, and by the turn of the twentieth century it seemed a bastion of backwardness. However, the alienation in which godless modernity ended, and then the sufferings of the twentieth century, gave the church and religion a reprieve. Foreign missions were an exception to the stagnation of the modern church, and today postmodernity asks the church to follow through on the pluralism implied in missionizing the non-European peoples.

STUDY QUESTIONS

1. Explain Augustine's views on membership in the true church.
2. What is the "collegiality" exhibited by the ecumenical councils?
3. Why did theodicy arise after the fall of Rome?
4. Should the pope act as a politician?
5. Explain the Christian Hellenism predominant in the East.
6. How did iconography contribute to the Eastern way of salvation?
7. Explain the place of "the priesthood of all Christians" in Protestant ecclesiology.
8. How does Wesley's ecclesiology exemplify a Protestant theological instinct?
9. What in the ahistoricism of the modern church was healthy?
10. What is the truth in the modernist conviction that we should be stripped of "all religious, aesthetic, moral haloes and sentimental veils"?

NOTES

1. W.H.C. Frend, THE RISE OF CHRISTIANITY. Philadelphia: Fortress, 1984, p. 137.

2. Jaroslav Pelikan, THE CHRISTIAN TRADITION, Vol. 1. Chicago: University of Chicago Press, 1971, pp. 302–303.

3. Frend, THE RISE OF CHRISTIANITY, p. 701.

4. Kallistos Ware, "Christian Theology in the East 600–1453," in A HISTORY OF CHRISTIAN DOCTRINE, ed. Hubert Cunliffe-Jones. Philadelphia: Fortress, 1980, p. 183.

5. G.W.H. Lampe, "Christian Theology in the Patristic Period," in A HISTORY OF CHRISTIAN DOCTRINE, p. 175.

6. William A. Clebsch, CHRISTIANITY IN EUROPEAN HISTORY. New York: Oxford University Press, 1979, p. 93.

7. David Knowles, "The Middle Ages 604–1350," in A HISTORY OF CHRISTIAN DOCTRINE, p. 211.

8. See Victor Turner, PROCESS, PERFORMANCE & PILGRIMAGE. New Delhi: Concept Publishing Co., 1979.

9. Francis Dvornik, BYZANTIUM AND THE ROMAN PRIMACY. New York: Fordham University Press, 1979, p. 18.

10. Alexander Schmemann, THE HISTORICAL ROAD OF EASTERN ORTHODOXY. Crestwood, NY: St. Vladimir's Seminary Press, 1977, p. 214.

11. John Meyendorff, BYZANTINE THEOLOGY, Second Edition. New York: Fordham University Press, 1979, pp. 80–81.

12. George P. Fedotov, THE RUSSIAN RELIGIOUS MIND (I). Belmont, MA: Nordland Publishing Co., 1975, pp. 30–31.

13. Robert McAfee Brown, THE SPIRIT OF PROTESTANTISM. New York: Oxford University Press, 1965, pp. 171–185.

14. Lewis W. Spitz, ed., THE PROTESTANT REFORMATION. Englewood Cliffs, NJ: Prentice-Hall, 1966, p. 64.

15. John T. McNeill, THE HISTORY AND CHARACTER OF CALVINISM. New York: Oxford University Press, 1967, p. 214.

16. THE BOOK OF COMMON PRAYER. New York: Seabury, 1977, pp. 854–855.

17. Albert C. Outler, ed., JOHN WESLEY. New York: Oxford University Press, 1980, p. 313.

18. Roland H. Bainton, "The Radical Reformation," in PROTESTANTISM, ed. Hugh T. Kerr. Woodbury, NY: Barron's Educational Series, 1979, p. 34.

19. Sydney E. Ahlstrom, A RELIGIOUS HISTORY OF THE AMERICAN PEOPLE. New Haven: Yale University Press, 1972, p. 183.

20. Marshall Berman, ALL THAT IS SOLID MELTS INTO AIR. New York: Simon and Schuster, 1982, pp. 128–129.

21. Eric Voegelin, FROM ENLIGHTENMENT TO REVOLUTION. Durham, NC: Duke University Press, 1975.

22. Karl Rahner, "Basic Theological Interpretation of the Second Vatican Council," in his CONCERN FOR THE CHURCH (Theological Investigations XX). New York: Crossroad, 1981, pp. 77–89.

Chapter 4

Theological Models

Sacramentality ♦ Institutionalism ♦ Discipleship ♦ Summary,
Study Questions, Notes

Sacramentality

We have spent two chapters reviewing the foundation that a contemporary ecclesiology can seek in the data of the New Testament and
church history. From this point on, our task becomes more construc-
tive. On the basis of the contemporary questions that we sketched in
Chapter 1 and the background that we have seen in Chapters 2 and
3, what understanding of the church best fits an ecclesiology for the
year 2000? What are the models, understandings of the key tasks of
the church (worship, mission, and governance), and essential answers
that past experience and present grace tend to promote? These are the
matters we shall pursue in the rest of the book.

Probably people have always used models to organize their experience, but only in recent times, when scientific and then humanistic methodologies have become self-conscious, have theologians
focused on the models by which we best conceive the church. The
general sense of "model" that prevails in such work is perhaps less
precise than what Bernard Lonergan has described, but his description can serve our purposes: "Models, then, stand to the human sciences, to philosophies, to theologies, much as mathematics stands to
the natural sciences. For models purport to be, not descriptions of
reality, not hypotheses about reality, but simply interlocking sets of
terms and relations. Such sets, in fact, turn out to be useful in guiding
investigations, in framing hypotheses, and in writing descriptions."[1]

The ecclesiological model that makes the church the basic sac-

rament of salvation can point to data of the New Testament and
church history as strong warrants, but only rather recently has it come
into clear focus. For while the New Testament certainly gives considerable importance to the eucharist and baptism, and certainly
makes the Christian community the axis of the salvation revealed and
brought by Christ, it does not develop the notions of "sign," "plan,"
and the rest so as to make the church the primal manifestation of God's
revealing and saving love. Church history is similarly rich in implying
that the Christian community is the prime embodiment of God's purposes for human beings, yet it too does not yield a thorough-going
interpretation of the church as the prime sacrament of salvation.

Probably the contemporary theologian most closely associated
with a sacramental ecclesiology is Karl Rahner. In a series of studies
published in the early 1960s Rahner dealt with various ecclesiological
problems—the inspiration of Scripture, the dynamic element in the
church, and sacramentality itself—from the viewpoint of one interested in basic symbolism. Rahner's studies in cognitional theory, both
that of Thomas Aquinas and that of such modern phenomenologists
as Martin Heidegger, had convinced him that the matter-spirit composition of the human person forces all of our meaning to be symbolic
and historical. If we wish to communicate even to ourselves as individuals, let alone to others in our social groups, we have to embody the
insights, feelings, and choices that we are making. We use speech,
gesture, and dozens of other carriers that are condemned to ambiguity
and suggestion. Very seldom can we express ourselves univocally or
immediately. Indeed, the more holistic our communication, the more
it would carry our integral selves, the more we must allude, evoke,
and then stand silent, offering our irreducible selves as both the to-
kens and the substance of the love or faith we finally want to receive
and give.

Linking this understanding of human consciousness with his
faith in the Incarnation of God's Word (God's symbolic self-expres-
sion), Rahner reconsidered all the Christian mysteries and doctrines.
To both particular problems, such as the role of bishops in the church,
and general problems, such as the meaning of grace, his incarnation-
alism or sacramentalism brought a rounding out and a simplification.
Almost always, the mystery of God that is the constant backdrop and
foundation for human knowing and loving became more pregnant and
present. Almost always, the poetic, symbolic character of religious

teachings and actions became more plain. The church itself, in Rahner's reflections, stood midway between the enveloping grace of the mysterious God and the needy openness of all human beings. The church itself, in other words, became a basic sign or sacrament of salvation.

The church has this nature or character, of course, only by virtue of its connection with Jesus Christ. The people who form the Christian community can embody and suggest salvation only because Christ has joined them to himself as his "body." Yet in the light of Christ's resurrection and the church's faith that in him grace triumphed once and for all, the church becomes what Rahner calls the "eschatological" sign of salvation: the definitive, never-failing reminder, embodiment, and invitation of salvation. For Rahner "salvation" is a union with God brought about by God's own self-giving love. The church then becomes the "place" in the world where God's purposes for all of humankind can be discovered. Rahner's last comprehensive work, FOUNDATIONS OF CHRISTIAN FAITH, puts all this as follows: "In the period before the resurrection Jesus Christ knew himself to be the 'absolute mediator of salvation,' the inauguration of God's kingdom, and the eschatological climax of salvation history. The historical continuation of Christ in and through the community of those who believe in him, and who recognize him explicitly as the mediator of salvation in a profession of faith, is what we call church. And if the period before Christ was already encompassed by God's salvific will and by his self-communication, and hence if it was a history of hope, although it was hope in a future which was open and ambivalent from the perspective of man's freedom and mankind's freedom, then the period after Christ is all the more encompassed by and bears the stamp of an explicit profession and knowledge of the fact that this Jesus Christ is the salvation of the world, and that in him God has offered himself to the world *irrevocably*."[2]

Rahner's model of the church, it follows, is that the people who stand in the world as believers in Christ symbolize the decisive moment in the history of salvation. (Since salvation is the main issue in human history—whether or not humanity will attain healing and complete fulfillment—the history of salvation is the inmost drama of all human time.) They do this in many ways: through their worship, ministries, teachings, and other formal, institutionalized activities. The crucial issue, though, is their love of God and their love of neighbor. Indeed, insofar as radical love of neighbor implies a faith-filled love of God, the crucial issue of the church's existence becomes its treatment, its service, of humankind.

This is all rather abstract and theoretical, however. Appealing as it may be on the level of generalization, it only homes in on the actual church and the real world when we translate it into daily experiences. One of the intriguing aspects of Rahner's ecclesiology, in fact, is its sobriety. After developing the most exalted appreciations of the church's subsistence in the love of God, Rahner regularly swings back to the daily experiences that show the sloth, stupidity, and general sinfulness of the church, as well as its acts of love.

No doubt this sobriety has deep roots in the years Rahner spent under Nazi rule, working as a parish priest. The church did many good things to counteract the naked evil of Nazism, but it was too deeply enmeshed in German and European culture as a whole for it not to have to bear some rightful criticism. The anti-Semitism on which Nazism depended, for example, went back a thousand supposedly Christian years. The tradition of compromise between church and state went back even further.

Even after the end of the Second World War, Rahner found the Catholic church in which he worked authoritarian and repressive. He and such other progressive theologians as Henri de Lubac and Yves Congar found themselves harassed if not silenced by the Roman authorities. Vatican II represented a considerable triumph for the progressives, but Rahner never ceased to remind churchpeople that their sinfulness obscured the proclamation of Christ. Even after one made proper provision for human weaknesses, the sinfulness of the church, leaders and laity, remained an ugly blot.

This sinfulness may stand out dramatically in the historical scandals of the papacy, in the religious wars, and in the divisions of the Christian churches, but its more vicious face is the undramatic, commonplace pride, covetousness, lust, envy, gluttony, anger, and sloth that mottle most neighborhoods. It is what Christians do or don't do in their homes, at their jobs, in their social interactions that determines the efficacy of the church's sacramentality. It is the love shown or withheld that gives the world a shining witness to a good God or a witness greatly dulled. Let Christian parents sacrifice for their children wisely and lovingly and the children will be forced in all honest moments to admit that God just might be parental. Let Christian workers do their jobs competently and kindly and the marketplace will be forced to admit that God is not just an excuse for the worthless or the weak. The formal teaching, worship, and ministry of the church is of secondary importance, compared to the daily practice of faith by the Christian community as a whole. The sacramental model developed by Rahner and others would have official church acts express and enable unofficial, utterly ordinary good living of faith, hope, and love.

A further advantage of the model that describes the church as the sacrament of salvation is its efficacy for non-Christians. Salvation concerns everybody, not just the official members of the Christian community (let alone just the leaders of the different churches). The God who has left no place without grace "uses" the church to embody the powers and rituals that might mediate salvation to all people torn and tried. Christ on the cross is the suffering servant not just for those fortunate enough to have heard his historical words or been born into his long-lived community. Christ on the cross has been lifted up to illumine the lives of all people whom the Father desires to love to health and fulfillment. By any generous reading, this is all people who ever have been born.

As a result, the sacramental model easily leads to stressing the universally human qualities that would make the existence of so good a God credible. These certainly include honesty, hopefulness, resistance to evil, and love of every decent sort. The light that shines and is honored when children tell the truth, parents do not lie, spouses do not cheat, workers give solid labor, elected officials serve the common good, and the like is a powerful presence of a God, a creative mystery, at work to repair human brokenness. The stamina and forgetfulness of self that enable people to raise children, make sober pledges, pursue an education, take on demanding projects, and even bother to vote in national elections tell the world that the future is worth pursuing, posterity does have rights. When freedom-fighters, consumer advocates, peace-marchers, teachers, nurses, and doctors say no to oppression, legalized theft, war-making, ignorance, and disease, a God creative and redemptive hovers at the corners, implied in each denial that corruption should hold sway. And, lastly, in every act of decent love the source of creation and salvation comes back into view. Those who form friendships, marriages, prayer-compacts with the Spirit, and other forms of warm commitment update the biblical covenant. Indeed, they show that God continues to be with human beings, neither more nor less mysterious than God was for Abraham, Moses, and Jesus.

In Robert Kress' recent and solid work THE CHURCH: COMMUNION, SACRAMENT, COMMUNICATION,[3] sacramentality mediates between the communion or social sharing that people have with God and one another and the expression or communication of faith through preaching, teaching, and ministry. In less scholarly ruminations on the church, sacramentality tends to focus on the seven traditional rites—baptism, confirmation, penance, eucharist, holy orders, matrimony, and anointing—that "apply" to different serious moments in life the faith and grace which the church would mediate. Our own reflections have emphasized the orientation of what Christians do and are to humanity as a whole, thinking that whenever Christians clarify the powers that heal human existence or make it godly they are sacramental in the most crucial sense. Whatever the stress one places, however, the main point is plain. Christians, following an incarnate divinity, believe that salvation deals in matters of space and time. The church, existing in space and time, has as its main task being sufficiently genuine—sufficiently filled with God's light, love, and life—to keep before the world God's purposes for the world. As the principal treatment of the church at Vatican II, the dogmatic constitution LUMEN GENTIUM, implied in its very title, the church ought above all to be a light, a sacrament, to the Gentiles.

For people aware of how diverse, and frequently well-developed, the Gentile world can be, the sacramental model has both pluses and minuses. The minuses include the tendency to subordinate all other religious traditions to Christianity and, in a too liturgical or spiritualized interpretation of sacramentality, the tendency to keep Christian life apart from politics and secular culture. The pluses include the chance to relate the church more intimately to general history than often seemed possible in the past, and the chance to discuss crucial issues with Buddhists and Hindus, Muslims and Jews, whose traditions a sacramental church ought to be clarifying. Let us concentrate on the pluses.

General history is the movement of time and events around the world. Nowadays we are more aware of general history than was true even two generations ago, because of recent advances in global communication and travel. So nowadays the sacramental church begs correlation with tribal wars in Africa, a billion Communist Chinese, endemic poverty in India, the labor camps of the Soviet Union. It begs correlation also with the artistic treasures of ancient civilizations, as they travel the circuit of our leading museums, the athletic feats of our international athletes, as they go on display at the Olympics, the new vistas unveiled by our leading scientists, as the Nobel prizes honor them each year. In tragedy and triumph, at home and abroad, the sacramental church would be relevant. What it celebrates at the eucharist, reads in Scripture, and tries to be through ministerial service must illumine both the worst and the best of the news that dominates our headlines. Indeed, it must oppose the sources of the worst news and abet the sources of the best news, if it is to be a light to the Gentiles of today's world.

The unwavering conviction of the Christian believer, of course, is that the church can indeed be such a light. Equally, mature believers are convinced that the church will only learn more about its God-given potential and its God-given ministerial mandates by engaging in sincere conversation with other religious traditions. The Buddhist-Christian dialogue that has gotten under way, for example, shows solid signs of enriching both partners. Each tradition has a rich spiritual heritage, full of wisdom about meditation, self-discipline, and the experience of ultimate reality. Each tradition has a profound philosophical or theological interpretation of ultimate reality, as well as a demanding ethical code. If it takes to heart the wisdom of a high tradition such as Buddhism, the church is bound to see ways that its sacramentality could be more comprehensive. The same would be true for taking to heart the wisdom of post-biblical Judaism, which Christianity has tended to ignore. In both instances, people outside the church would be suggesting what human and religious traits Christians ought to develop and support. In analogous instances—for example, discussions with unbelieving scientists or Marxist political analysts—the church would be meeting fellow-children of God on a basis of equality and potential friendship, to learn how the divine love has been making its presence felt in new or initially surprising channels.

Institutionalism

Sacramentalism is one of the models that Avery Dulles, perhaps the leading American Catholic ecclesiologist, has stressed in his recent writings. Another model that he has stressed depicts the church as an institution. This model makes sense, granted the fact that Christ singled out the twelve. It builds on both the organization we can find by the end of the New Testament period and the regularities of human sociology. (What tribe does not have institutions?) Realistically, we should not expect or even want no Christian institutions. Realistically, we are not going to have a non-institutional church, so we'd best provide for institutionalism in all our ecclesiological modeling.

Still, when our ecclesiological modeling focuses too closely on the large bureaucracy that the church has developed, it can blur and so sap our enthusiasm, self-confidence, and purpose. Dulles is a careful ecclesiologist, given to balancing pluses and minuses with a scrupulous fairness. Nonetheless, one senses that his description of the institutionalism that prevails in the popular conception of the Catholic church is not meant as praise: "In the minds of most Americans, Catholic or non-Catholic, the prevailing image of the Catholic church is highly institutional. The Church is understood in terms of dogmas, laws, and hierarchical agencies which impose heavy demands of conformity. To be a good Catholic, according to the popular view, is simply to adhere to the beliefs and practices demanded by the officeholders. At the risk of caricature, one may say that many think of the Church as a huge, impersonal machine set over against its own members. The top officers are regarded as servants of the institution, bound by a rigid party line, and therefore inattentive to the impulses of the Holy Spirit and unresponsive to the legitimate religious concerns of the faithful. The hierarchy themselves, according to this view, are prisoners of the system they impose on others. Following the inbuilt logic of all large institutions, they do what makes for law and order in the Church rather than what Jesus himself would be likely to do."[4]

Dulles goes on to make the point that this institutionalism runs aground on contemporary personalism. People simply won't give their hearts and souls to a church that cannot treat them warmly as individuals. Whatever validity the notions of a church bureaucracy, canon law, uniform dogmatic system, and multinational set of agencies may have, they make the church seem too much like a business corporation. One may show a business corporation loyalty and give it solid work, but one will not love it as a teacher and mother, let alone as a community of salvation.

The model of discipleship, which we shall develop in the next section and connect with the phenomenal rise in many parts of the world of "basic communities," offers an attractive alternative to church institutionalism. Before turning to it, however, we should ponder the tension between charismatic power and institutional power that seems an inevitable part of any ecclesiology. Charismatic power is the force and authority that comes through gifts of the Holy Spirit. People who are wise, insightful, prophetic, good at counseling or preaching or healing, have a direct, immediate authority. So do people who are saintly: blessed with close union with God. Their gifts certainly bring them personal progress, but Christian tradition, from as early as Paul's discussion of various charismata in 1 Corinthians 12–13, holds that all spiritual talents are for the community as well.

This means that the church depends, generation after generation, on the fresh inspirations that the Spirit gives to various individuals. The saints are the clearest example of how charismatic power has worked through church history, but many humbler folk have contributed gifts of prayer, good counsel, healing, or simply steady hard work. Indeed, generation after generation the church has depended on the docility and generosity of the membership as a whole, without whom it could never have built its schools, staffed its hospitals, or sent out its missionaries. Both the people who played the prominent roles in these works—the teachers, nurses, and missionary preachers—and the people who played the back-up roles exhibited gifts of the Spirit. Both leadership and loyal membership depended on a nuture of faith, hope, and love that went well beyond what the institutional side of ecclesiology alone can account for.

The institutional side, of course, also can claim historic rights. The Pastoral Epistles, as we saw, provided for presbyter-bishops to oversee church affairs, and from shortly after the apostolic era a hierarchy of church leaders was in place. This hierarchy proved its value in the early struggles against heretics, and the fate of many purely charismatic movements that died without leaving historical issue suggests that Christianity owes much of its survival to its ongoing institutional forms.

These two sides of church life and authority come together, of

course, insofar as the best church leaders show gifts of prayer, teaching, and wisdom. Many ecclesiologists go out of their way to defend
the structures of the church as gifts of God, and almost all the people
who write about church matters sketch an ideal state in which institutional authority encourages, guides, and facilitates the gifts or inspirations that the Spirit seems to be lavishing on any given time.
Things only get out of hand or become imbalanced when charismatic
power and institutional power do not complement one another. Unfortunately, in too many eras of church history the institutional power
has been slow or unwilling to accredit and guide the charismatic
power that the Spirit was bestowing.

It would be naive and irresponsible not to bring this description
into our own era of the 1980s, for as we write the tension between
authorities of the institutional Catholic church centered in Rome and
various local charismatic personalities has reached nearly critical proportions. The general profile of this conflict has the Roman authorities stressing conservative doctrine and traditional discipline and the
charismatic local authorities asking for innovation, adaptation, and
greater freedom.

The most publicized cases in recent times have concerned
clashes between theologians and the Roman authorities responsible
for safeguarding sound doctrine. In the news as well have been many
American feminists, male and female, who have been opposing a traditional exclusion of women from church leadership. In their view
this exclusion is sexism, pure and simple. In the view of the institutional authorities who continue to hold that women may not be ordained to the Catholic priesthood, the feminists are proposing changes
that run contrary to the structures with which God endowed his
church.

The most celebrated theologians who have clashed with Rome no
doubt are Hans Küng, Edward Schillebeeckx, Gustavo Gutierrez, and
Leonardo Boff. In the cases of Küng, Schillebeeckx, and Boff, a major
factor seems to have been their criticism of the church's recent interpretation of its institutional authority. Thus Küng has questioned the
recent understanding of papal infallibility, Schillebeeckx has questioned the recent understanding of ordination and ministry, and Boff
has criticized the church's institutional authority for violating human
rights. Gutierrez is under a cloud for having fathered liberation the-

ology, which in Roman interpretation takes official church ministers too deeply into politics.

By the standards of the modern Western democracies, the way these theologians have been treated is shameful. The proceedings against them have been secretive, heavy-handed, and prejudicial. One example, from Boff's recent book CHURCH: CHARISM & POWER, shows the inquisitorial style of the Roman authorities at its worst: "The procedure against Ivan Illich became famous for its ideological violence to all rights. The interrogation began thus: 'My name is Illich.' 'I know that.' 'Monsignor, what is your name?' 'I am the judge.' 'I thought I might know your name!' 'That is not important. My name is Casoira.' They wanted to obligate Illich under oath to maintain absolute secrecy as to what was to take place in the halls of the Sacred Congregation, something Illich did not accept. The interrogation mixed trivial questions about his institute with questions about some fifty people, questions of faith, disputed subjects in theology, and 'subversive interpretations.' These included questions such as 'Is it true that you want women to go to confession without the separation of a curtain?' "[5]

This sort of dialogue would be comic, were it not conducted in all seriousness by Roman authorities who have considerable power to shape religious lives around the world. The best face one can put on it is that such authorities sincerely believe the church to be principally an institution governed by canon law and bound to treat its members with all legal rectitude. They do not, of course, believe that such rectitude need conflict with Christian charity, but they see their primary responsibility as upholding the codes by which their institution runs.

This understanding of the church has not been confined to officials in Roman bureaus. Until very recently institutionalism has been the dominant model in the consciousnesses of the American clergy, above all in the consciousnesses of the American bishops. The recent pastoral letters of the American bishops on peace-making and economics, which we shall consider later, suggest that institutionalism is on the wane. But certainly it retains a powerful influence, and certainly it shaped most official interactions with local American bishops in the 1970s and early 1980s.

Consider, for example, the letter from Joseph T. McGucken, Archbishop of San Francisco, that John S. Duryea includes in his au-

tobiography, ALIVE INTO THE WILDERNESS. Duryea had been a priest
for over twenty-five years when he decided to marry. He had an in-
terview with McGucken, his superior, but when he persisted in his
desire both to marry and to continue his priestly ministry he received
swift notice that he was excommunicated. McGucken's letter is not
uncharitable. Granted the assumptions of the institutional model it
may even seem kindly. But the bottom line is that Duryea has broken
a (sacral?) rule and so must be cast outside the community of Christ.
Duryea's own sense of the Spirit's guidance, the support he was re-
ceiving from many members of his parish, and the experience of married ministers in other churches are all irrelevant. McGucken feels
he must treat Duryea as a layman (quite a demotion, in the institutional scheme of things), and his major concern is that Duryea not give
scandal (publicly contest the rules by which the institution runs). It
is hard to imagine the biblical Christ writing such a letter:

"Dear Mr. Duryea:
    "It is with deep sorrow that I am obliged to notify you that by
attempting marriage [in the institutional scheme of things one under
vows of celibacy cannot accomplish marriage] you have incurred the
automatic excommunication provided in Canon 2244 of the Code of
Canon Law. In addition to the suspension which you have already received, under Canon 2244 you will be automatically excommunicated.
Consequently, you are forbidden to celebrate holy Mass or to receive
Holy Communion.
    "We have been saddened by the fact that many people are scan-
dalized at St. Ann's Chapel when they see you approach the holy table.
I hope that you will respect the provisions of the law of the Church
and not place any priest who is celebrating holy Mass under the dis-
agreeable obligation of refusing you Holy Communion.
    "Despite our sorrow over this situation, I assure you that we will
keep you in our prayers, with the hope that through the grace of God
you may be restored to full membership in the Church and priestly
activities, through your obedience to the laws of the Church."[6]

The royal "we" that runs through the letter perhaps is the tipoff
to the whole. The archbishop might well have been a humble man in
his personal piety, but he conceived of his station within the church
as princely. Nonetheless, he presents himself as helpless in face of the

Canons of church law, which appear to operate automatically. There is no room for him to negotiate seriously with Duryea or make exceptions to the general laws because Duryea has a special situation. The Canons, in fact, determine the sacramental life of his church, good legal standing being the main requisite for admission to Holy Communion. Thus the final line of the letter, with its hope that the grace of God may restore Duryea to full membership in the church, sounds almost ironic. It reads as though God required Duryea's obedience to the laws of the church, if God were to gift Duryea with his grace.

The feminists who have been agitating for a church freed of sexism have run into a similarly legalistic mentality. Where theologians on the whole find little scriptural or doctrinal need to restrict ministry in the church to males, the Roman Catholic and Eastern Orthodox church leaders have stood adamant in claiming that tradition and church law render female ministers impossible. This is contradicted, of course, by the practice of many Protestant churches, and it seems to depend upon a sense of "tradition" considerably more static than what has actually obtained throughout church history. For example, Elisabeth Schüssler-Fiorenza has shown that many New Testament churches were quite egalitarian, and that women may well have led several local churches.[7] Other theologians, such as Karl Rahner, have pointed out the holes in the logic offered by official statements against women's ordination and reminded their readers that the magisterium of the church has erred on not a few occasions in the past.[8]

One could argue, of course, that an institution may be more flexible and open to change than what we have seen in these two examples of clerical celibacy and reserving ordination to men. When it is, however, almost always it has opened itself to charismatic inspirations, letting the signs of the times convince it that change is quite in order. The leading example of such an enlightened institutionalism in recent times was Pope John XXIII. Certainly he served the institutional church throughout his long ministerial career, and certainly he never contested the centuries-old design of the Roman power structure. Yet John XXIII was able to see that the church had to update itself, if it were not to fail in its obligations to God and humankind. The church described by Vatican I in 1869 seemed unable to serve the twentieth and twenty-first centuries as God desired. So John XXIII called the fateful Vatican Council II, and the Roman Catholic church opened its windows to change.

Precisely how the Catholic church ought to continue to change remains highly debated, of course, and one would not be wrong to view the conflicts between curial officials and progressive theologians or feminists as excellent examples of this debate. The only problem with such a view is that "debate" seldom occurs. To the present the institutional model of the church so prevails that there is no equality between the parties who disagree about the church's best future. A theologian such as Leonardo Boff stands very much below a doctrinal judge such as Joseph Cardinal Ratzinger, even when Boff goes to Rome accompanied by his own Brazilian cardinal. When Ratzinger decides that Boff's views are inappropriate or dangerous, he can order him to desist from all preaching, teaching, and writing for an indeterminate period. At the least this gives the appearance of a church unconcerned about such basic human rights as the right to free expression of one's responsible opinions. At the worst it flies in the face of the church's own needs as a community of free people engaged in an on-going discernment of the Spirit's inspirations. The people at the top are telling the people at the bottom (as they see it) that Rome knows better than Brazil what Brazil should be thinking and doing in Brazil. Similarly, the male leaders of the hierarchy are telling the female members of the church everywhere that they know better than the women what the Spirit is inspiring women of the late twentieth century to want to be and do. The great danger of the institutional model, clearly enough, is that people in bureaucratic power easily can come to think they can predetermine what the Spirit of God can inspire or provoke.

Discipleship

Avery Dulles has discussed other models of the church that complement sacramentality and institutionalism. Primary among these other models have been the biblical images of "the Body of Christ" and "the People of God." In addition, he has reflected on the classically Protestant model that makes the church first of all the community that heralds the Word of God.[9] More recently, however, discipleship has become central in his ecclesiological thinking, in part because Pope John Paul II's first encyclical spoke of "the community of the disciples" and the personal "call" that each church member has from

God.[10] Let us expand upon this model, considering first its refreshing proximity to the primitive Christian focus on the humanity of Christ and then, second, its correlation with the basic or grassroots communities that have been springing up like wildflowers.

The sacramental and institutional models of the church, for all their value and influence, occur at some distance from the ecclesiological picture we get in the synoptic gospels and the Acts of the Apostles. There the church appears, respectively, as the people who follow Jesus of Nazareth, become by his death and resurrection the Christ, and the people who, under the inspiration of Christ's Spirit, move out into the Gentile world to proclaim salvation in Christ's name. Despite the slight differences in shading, both pictures connect Christians very closely with Jesus as Master (Teacher) and Christ (Messiah). The synoptics, especially, consider the twelve leading followers of Jesus as (flawed) models of discipleship. Jesus himself is the leading disciple (of God), but the twelve, despite all their frailty, show Christian life to be a following of Jesus. Indeed, the early church's self-designation as "the Way" implies that Christian existence is primarily walking as Jesus did, trying to fit oneself to Jesus' salvific journey.

The pope does well to stress the personal aspects of such a church membership, because it has always moved the saints and now, in a personalist time, it begs reaffirmation and updating. Furthermore, the personal vocation that each Christian has in God's sight gives the lie to the vicious, depersonalizing possibilities latent in untoward interpretations of institutionalism. Far from being an ant hill or a bee hive, the church must become the freest of human societies, the grouping that most honors and depends upon the individual charismata of its members.

The basic communities that have become the leading ecclesiological feature of the Latin American landscape stress politics more than personalism but, as we shall soon see, they certainly include personal liberation on their agendas. Influenced more by European political theologians such as J.B. Metz, and by the Canadian philosophical theologian Bernard Lonergan, Fred Lawrence recently has analyzed basic Christian communities precisely as social entities that make individual authenticity central, speaking of how they should foster life "according to the immanent norms of intelligence, reasonableness, and responsibility."[11] Lawrence is quite willing to grant communities a priority over individuals, insofar as individuals only come to maturity within the communities—domestic, neighbor-hood, ecclesial—in which they grow up, but he certainly is unwilling to support institutionalism. The conversational quality of the basic Christian community, its constitutive relation to an ongoing dialogue about divine truth, love, and current inspiration, quite undercuts any attempt to limit the church to the external or depersonalized relation-ships that nearly always predominate in large institutions. Rosemary Haughton and many others have described the exodus of large num-bers of Christians from such an understanding of Christian commu-nity. In place after place, little groups are springing up because people want to discuss their faith, share their joy, collaborate in attacking local problems. The faceless institutions they grew up in don't allow this as they require. So they are forming freer ad hoc communities, and frequently for the first time they are finding what following Jesus might mean.[12]

By the internal logic of these things, it is not surprising to find a theologian such as Edward Schillebeeckx, who has met the institu-tional model "up close and impersonal," plumping for smaller-scale and more personal alternatives. Schillebeeckx's term for such alter-natives is "critical communities," because he wants to stress their po-litical dimension. "Critical" does not necessarily mean negative. Rather it stresses the need that all Christians, indeed all mature hu-man beings, have to discern the spirits, test the signs of the time, and decide which expressions of faith are liberating and which are en-slaving. Our global technological society has become so complex that all of our vocational choices have become political. The education we members of Northern nations choose, the theology we espouse, the work we accept, and even the way that we recreate has an impact on our economies and cultures that waves out to the third and fourth worlds.

In his wonderfully personal conversations with Huub Oosterhuis entitled GOD IS NEW EACH MOMENT, Schillebeeckx has discussed criticism and office in the church quite frankly. The beginning of the chapter dealing with "Critical Communities and Office in the Church" runs as follows:

"O. You say you once compared the Church to a decrepit old woman, but you would never make that comparison again [because of feminist objections]. It's obvious, of course, what you meant by it.

How is it possible for anyone still to accept an office in that Church? Do you think there is still any justification for encouraging men to become priests?

"S. If becoming a priest were to mean that a man would simply become a moving part in a hierarchical machine and act as a functionary, unquestioningly carrying out the orders of those in authority in that Church, then I would certainly ask that man: Could you take that step?

"O. But that is what usually happens, isn't it?

"S. That is what often happens, yes, but I think it's also possible to be in the Church and even to hold office in the Church, as a priest, that is, and be constantly aware of the prophetic task and the need to criticize the Church again and again in the light of the gospel. That is one of the tasks of the person holding office, after all.

"O. So you think you can choose to hold office in the Church to maintain a counter-movement in that Church?

"S. If you hold office, you have the prophetic function of proclaiming the Gospel of Jesus, in other words, of proclaiming justice. So, wherever there is injustice, you have to oppose it and that means you have to oppose it first of all in the Church itself. If criticism of the Church were only to come from outside the Church . . . Well, the Church is generally speaking not particularly troubled by that sort of criticism."[13]

The further discussions in the book make it plain that Schillebeeckx takes his own phrase "wherever there is injustice" quite seriously. His interest in church office therefore definitely is not inbred or clerical. He is much concerned with secular politics and culture, yet he will not limit the prophetic task of Christian ministers (indeed, of all who have been baptized) to criticizing the Gentiles outside the gates. Like the prophets of Israel, who continue to set the background for Jesus' prophetic ministry, Schillebeeckx's ministers would turn the sometimes harsh light of the Word of God onto the people of God themselves, asking for conversion and new beginnings wherever that light turns up injustice, dishonesty, or a lack of liberating love.

The basic communities that now are such a powerful factor in the religious life of Latin America essentially swing between Christian faith, as it is vigorous and original in the New Testament, and the social circumstances in which the common people find themselves.

The usual celebration of a small community includes a group reflection on a given scriptural text, with a self-conscious effort to link the text to what the members of the community are experiencing and trying to understand. Thus an interpretational circle is drawn, such that the political experiences of the people color their meditations on the New Testament and their meditations on the New Testament color their interpretations of their political experiences.

The three volumes of such communal reflections that Ernesto Cardenal has collected under the title, THE GOSPEL IN SOLENTINAME, display these dynamics in very winning fashion. The simple people of the Solentiname community (which was destroyed by the soldiers of Anastasio Somoza) prove amazingly aware of the liberating implications that Jesus' words and example can carry. For example, here is a portion of their reflections on John 8:31–47, where the central motif is "The truth will make you free":

"Alejandro: 'He says the truth will make us free, because the oppressors have concealed reality from us. The truth that Christ talks about is to uncover the injustice there is in our society, to show that there are social classes. Our eyes are opened and we see these things. With lies we're deceived; we believe it's proper to have rich and poor. When we understand reality, we liberate ourselves.'

"Laureano: 'I believe the truth makes us free because the truth is equality. If we're all equal, we're free; if there's nobody who's bigger than the others, then we're free. Deceit is what enslaves us. They oppress us with deceit, and we free ourselves with truth, unmasking the deceit.'

"Felipe: 'Truth teaches us that we're all equal, as Laureano says, and that all of us human beings must live a single reality, the reality that we're brothers and sisters. Not to look on anybody as master or slave, that seems to me the truth. The truth makes us brothers and sisters and therefore it frees us.'

"Gloria: 'I think it's clear. That's why they keep the poor in ignorance, because without ignorance you can't have exploitation.' "[14]

There is a danger in this sort of biblical interpretation, of course, and consequently in this sort of ecclesiastical orientation. People could come to distort the message of Jesus by bending it too much to the needs of their own times. But all communities run such a risk, even when many communities don't explicitate their point of view or political situation as clearly as the Nicaraguans of Solentiname were explicitating it in the mid-1970s. The people who sit in heavy oaken pews in wealthy North American churches bring to the gospel a different social outlook, but in the measure that their faith is lively they too are passionately seeking to correlate the words and deeds of the biblical Christ with their own daily experiences.

It is no accident, however, that Latin America is the site of tens of thousands of basic communities while in North America the institutional model continues to prevail. Things are too successful, in material terms, for the majority of North Americans to want to become deeply critical of their current political and cultural arrangements. To be sure, one can find large zones where things are deeply uncomfortable. The number of North Americans who are poor and unhappy must reach the tens of millions. But on the whole we do not suffer the dramatic poverty and abuse suffered by our neighbors to the South. On the whole they are closer to the people whom Jesus beatified, the marginals and oppressed to whom Jesus' Kingdom was such especially good news.

Discipleship on the model of Jesus' earliest followers ran counter to the religious establishment, just as the Solentiname Christians found it running counter to the values of the political establishment under Somoza. If anything, the clash is stronger in present-day Latin America, because the ruling authorities show less shame about trying to keep the majority of the population poor, ignorant, and compliant. The moving film EL NORTE depicts well the violent repression regularly visited upon the *campesinos* of Guatemala, whenever they would dare to challenge the combination of landlords and military leaders who run that country. Phillip Berryman's comprehensive study, THE RELIGIOUS ROOTS OF REBELLION: CHRISTIANS IN CENTRAL AMERICAN REVOLUTIONS, documents in close detail the causes of the basic communities' resistance to the prevailing power-structures.[15]

Precisely what forms of basic Christian community best suit other parts of the globe is not immediately clear. If Africans, Asians, Australians, North Americans, and Europeans are to follow the Latin American lead, they will have to do so carefully, making full provision for the local traditions that might dictate different emphases. But the political orientation of the Latin American basic communities should surface in some proper modality, if the gospel is indeed being read with an eye to liberation. The truth that sets us free concerns the whole of human life, politics and culture as much as personal health and peace of mind.

Discipleship of this holistic type probably better imitates what Jesus himself had in mind than does any disjunctive option for a faith or church life that would stress any one facet to the exclusion of the others. Jesus had relations with God, his fellow human beings, himself, and nature that all begged and received clarification from the revelation and mission God was giving him. The parental nature of God that he stressed, the sacrificial love of other people that he displayed, the integrity of personal life that he manifested once he had set his face for Jerusalem, and the gratitude he showed God for the gifts of creation rounded out to compose a rich interpretation of what fulfilled life in the Kingdom would mean.

The basic communities that would foster a holistic discipleship in our day do well to keep all of these primary foci in view. If we relate badly to either God or other people or ourselves or nature, we are alienated and perhaps deeply sinful. To miss so primal a mark as our connection to nature, for example, is both to endanger the ecosphere near and far, as we are vividly doing, and to show ourselves practical atheists—people unaware that every gift and good thing comes down to us from above, from the Father of Lights. Were we rightly related to the Father of Lights, we could not continue to live as wastefully as we in the Northern technological nations do, nor could we continue to prepare the destruction of the majority of our fellow creatures, sub-human as well as human, future as well as present.

The more usual focus of the Latin American basic communities on politics, economics, and the dialectial relations between very rich and very poor yields much the same lesson. To choose to structure social relationships as we have, so that a relative few (in global perspective) indulge in the pursuit of gilded luxuries while the vast majority lack bare necessities, is to convict ourselves of a radical irreligion. How can we claim to love the God we cannot see when we so abuse the siblings we can see? This Johannine theology offered the early church a large portion of a potentially very critical basis for its communal life. Discipleship tutored by such a theology could sponsor an equally critical ecclesiology today. The practical crux of our claim to love God is how we treat our neighbors. Unless we are part of the systems that are working to free, succor, and build up our neighbors, we are on the side of Satan. It complicates matters today, of course, that so much of everybody's life is shaped if not determined by impersonal structures or systems that seem to rumble forward on their own, through little conscious decision by any controllers. All the more reason, then, for the disciples of Christ to insist on models of the church that resolutely target a deeply liberating personal care.

Summary

We have been considering three important theological models of the church. The first, sacramentality, flows from the incarnational character of Christian faith. As developed by Karl Rahner, it stresses how the church, as the community witnessing to the eschatological salvation that Jesus worked, should display the humanity for which all people are hungering. The official teachings and public doings of the church are important in this regard, but more important is the quality of faith among the general church membership. Properly understood, therefore, the sacramental model could encourage Christians to bring out the best potential of current culture and converse with people of other religious traditions very openly.

The model of an institution has had great influence, some of it beneficial but more of it harmful. By and large, the harmful effects have come from an imbalance between official (hierarchical) church power and charismatic church power. We used the examples of theologians and feminists conflicting with central doctrinal authorities in Rome to illustrate how this imbalance has been occurring recently. To analyze it further and show the distance from the New Testament that institutionalism can take the church, we reflected on the legalism that has obtained in many recent efforts to discipline dissidents.

Our third model, discipleship, could claim sponsorship by such diverse authorities as Pope John Paul II, the synoptic gospels, and the popular movements of Latin America. We used Edward Schillebeeckx's notion of critical communities to bridge the way from a personalist stress on authenticity to the political stress of the Latin Americans. The community formed at Solentiname stood for the groups that organize around an interaction between the Scriptures and current political circumstances. We then concluded by reflecting on the holistic outlook that basic Christian communities ideally would foster.

STUDY QUESTIONS

1. Why does the sacramental model of the church spotlight the quality of all members' faith?
2. How does the sacramental model set the church in dialogue with general history and other religious traditions?
3. What are the main warrants and defenses that the institutional model can muster?
4. How legitimate is the authority being exercised in the dialogue between Illich and Casoira or in the letter of Archbishop McGucken?
5. What is the main focus of a disciple's faith?
6. How legitimate is the political focus that many of the Latin American basic Christian communities have assumed?

NOTES

1. Bernard J. Lonergan, METHOD IN THEOLOGY. New York: Herder and Herder, 1972, pp. 284–285.

2. Karl Rahner, FOUNDATIONS OF CHRISTIAN FAITH. New York: Seabury, 1978, p. 322.

3. See Robert Kress, THE CHURCH: COMMUNION, SACRAMENT, COMMUNICATION. New York: Paulist, 1985.

4. Avery Dulles, A CHURCH TO BELIEVE IN. New York: Crossroad, 1983, p. 3.

5. Leonardo Boff, CHURCH: CHARISM & POWER. New York: Crossroad, 1985, p. 168.

6. John S. Duryea, ALIVE INTO THE WILDERNESS. Palo Alto, CA: Coastlight Press, 1985, p. 200.

7. See Elisabeth Schüssler-Fiorenza, IN MEMORY OF HER. New York: Crossroad, 1984.

8. See Karl Rahner, CONCERN FOR THE CHURCH. New York: Crossroad, 1981, pp. 35–47.

9. See Avery Dulles, MODELS OF THE CHURCH. Garden City, NY: Doubleday, 1974.

10. See John Paul II, REDEMPTOR HOMINIS. Washington, D.C.: U.S. Catholic Conference, 1979, no. 21, pp. 89–90.

11. Fred Lawrence, "Basic Christian Community: An Issue of 'Mind' and the Mystery of Christ," in LONERGAN WORKSHOP, vol. 5, ed. Fred Lawrence. Chico, CA: Scholars Press, 1985, p. 269.

12. Lawrence quotes from Haughton's unpublished paper, "Spirituality for the '80s." See also her book, THE PASSIONATE GOD. New York: Paulist, 1981.

13. Edward Schillebeeckx, GOD IS NEW EACH MOMENT. New York: Seabury, 1983, p. 79.

14. Ernesto Cardenal, THE GOSPEL IN SOLENTINAME, vol. 3. Maryknoll, NY: Orbis, 1979, pp. 84–85.

15. See Phillip Berryman, THE RELIGIOUS ROOTS OF REBELLION: CHRISTIANS IN CENTRAL AMERICAN REVOLUTIONS. Maryknoll, NY: Orbis, 1984.

Chapter 5

Worship

Eucharistia ♦ The Word of God ♦ Mystagogy ♦ Summary, Study
Questions, Notes

Eucharistia

From the beginning of the church's existence, the disciples of
Christ have gathered regularly to celebrate their faith. The center of
their communal existence has been their *anamnesis* or memorial of
Jesus' life, death, resurrection, and promised return in glory for judgment. On the Lord's Day, the sabbath-become-Sunday that Christians designated their day for special worship, the church has felt
itself most real or fully actualized. The Sunday liturgy has been like
a regular recall to Easter, when Christ secured salvation definitively.
As Rahner has put it, the church is the community that witnesses to
the definitive or eschatological salvation of Christ. It does this through
all the aspects of its being—preaching, teaching, healing, suffering
for peace and justice—but nowhere more centrally than in its formal
worship. There, at the eucharist or Lord's Supper, the church man-
ifests the fundamental dispositions that living faith in Christ's salvation should arouse. There the church expresses the *eucharistia* or
thanksgiving that the Spirit is ever active to inspire.

Salvation restores people to right order, a proper perspective on
what is truly important, how creation actually coheres. The pillar of
right order, for biblical faith, is confession and praise of God. The
Psalms, for example, praise God even more than they petition God's
help. At sunrise and sunset, the solace and joy of the Psalmist is to
admire the mighty works of the Lord, appreciate the splendors of the
divine beauty and steadfastness. Like the everlasting hills, which

128

seemed a constant source of hope, the biblical God was stable and wonderful. Merely to gaze on creation could restore the Psalmist's sense that God ran the world, and nothing could be too far awry.

The church took over this Jewish inclination to praise God, forming most of its prayer and Sunday liturgy on the pattern of Jewish ceremonies. It read the Hebrew Bible or the Septuagint as its own Scripture, and it took to heart the convictions and emotions of the Jewish sabbath meal. Where Christian worship became distinctive, of course, was in referring all of its thanksgiving and hope to Jesus, its Messiah and Lord. By the end of the first century, as we can see from such canonical materials as the Gospel of John and such extracanonical texts as the Didache, the Christian eucharist had become a rich, full, and incarnational symbolism. The people gathered to remember God's mighty acts and bedrock promises, yes, but they read them through the lens of Christ's death and resurrection. They repeated the venerable blessings of bread and wine, yes, but these now focused on a nourishing communion with Jesus. Where the Creation and the Exodus had structured Jewish faith, the death and resurrection of Jesus riveted Christians to a new creation and a new exodus or passover. Where Jewish faith had longed for the day of the Messiah, Christian faith longed for the Messiah's return to consummate history.

The worship of the Christian community down through the centuries has moved in the tracks of these New Testament beginnings. Now well, now poorly, it has adapted the basic pattern of memorial and thanksgiving to the needs and cultural styles of different times. So the Christian liturgy has varied significantly from geographical area to geographical area and from one historical period to another. The Roman rite which has dominated the Western church owes a great deal to the imperial style of the era in which the church became a favored religion, but even it remains heavily indebted to Jewish forbears. Thus throughout all the variations of Christian worship, the instinct to praise God has remained primary. In the beginning God made the heavens and the earth, purely because of God's goodness. When things had reached a very low ebb, and the children of Adam and Eve seemed impossibly mired in sin, God sent the only-begotten Son to work salvation and a new creation. With such foundations, any day could be a time to give thanks to God and expect to experience the divine mercy.

In principle there seems no reason why this conviction shouldn't continue to structure Christians' lives today, but our secular cultures often render it problematic. Consequently, the eucharistic center of the Christian community is less luminous than it ought to be. People are confused about the role of God in their lives, since nature seems to run quite autonomously and human technology shapes both nature and society as (certain interpretations of) our own goals dictate. Thus worship in older styles, which presumed God's obvious lordship, seems inappropriate or even inauthentic. Louis Weil recently has expressed the problem thus: "I am suggesting that beneath the problem of [liturgical] prayer is the problem of God. Liturgists cannot keep their heads in the sand on this issue. The traditional doctrine of God as imaged in the classical liturgies (and conditioned, I believe, by political images of the period in which those liturgies developed) cannot be maintained. It can only breed among Christians a type of liturgical schizophrenia which is probably more prevalent than we would want to admit. If God were simply the most important resident in heaven, we would not have the problem. The Romans knew how to act toward the emperor as the most important resident on earth, and that might continue as our model. But that model has disintegrated, and the real challenge which faces all of us is that the disintegration reveals the deeper problem of faith again."[1]

If the model of the church as a community of disciples were to supplement and reset the institutional model, much of the sociological misfit between our current liturgical forms and our present sense of reality (including the reality of God) probably would vanish. Let us try a little thought-experiment along this line, musing about what a liberational model suggests for the relation between worship and politics. Other theologians, of course, rightly could pitch such a thought-experiment differently. Even if they would not agree with our liberational slant, however, they would have to deal with the sobering thesis of 1 John 4:20: "If anyone says, 'I love God,' and hates his brother, he is a liar; for he who does not love his brother whom he has seen, cannot love God whom he has not seen."

In a liberationally oriented worship, people gathering in the memory of Jesus, recalling the life and words of Jesus, and trying to position themselves socially and politically as Jesus positioned himself, would take a more anthropological and soteriological slant than is now often the case. Now the remnants of the old cosmological myth, according to which human societies, including the church, derive their legitimacy from heavenly archetypes in whose pattern they are thought to move, impede a truly contemporary or post-modern sense of gratitude and worshipful thanksgiving. Liberation is not so central as it needs to be, if basic communities passionately concerned about liberation are to find the God of the biblical exoduses (both that of Moses and that of Christ) who seems the deity most reponsive to their concerns.

Such a liberational focus need not, of course, deny the truths in the older cosmological outlooks. God can continue to be the creator from nothingness who is the inmost explanation of our truly mind-boggling contemporary cosmology. Just as the Psalmist found no conflict in both recalling God's saving acts on Israel's behalf and praising God for the orderly flow of the seasons, so today's believer need find no conflict between worshiping a God who can free societies from dead-ends and praising a God of sunrise and sunset. It is merely a question of where a given age best begins, most appropriately finds entry into the inexhaustible riches of the divine mystery. Today the best entry-point seems to be the sufferings of the poor that move genuine religion to a constant cry for liberation and justice. Today the best tone in which to sing songs of thanksgiving and praise seems like that of the ancient song of Deborah: "That the leaders took the lead in Israel, that the people offered themselves willingly, bless the Lord! Hear, O kings; give ear, O princes; to the Lord I will sing, I will make melody to the Lord, the God of Israel" (Judges 5:2–3). The rest of the song details various military triumphs that divine providence oversaw on Israel's behalf. Those, presumably, were the crucial national events of the prophetess' day. The analogous events in recent Nicaraguan history might be the overthrow of the oppressive dictator Somoza. One can easily picture a remnant of the fractured community of Solentiname praising God for such liberation. Only imagination (and some proper restraint on political partisanship) limits the extensions of such a liberational worship to other parts of the contemporary church.

When people praise God, they consciously place themselves within the orbit of the divine power. Quickly indeed, this leads them to realize and confess their own sinfulness: they are not worthy to stand before the holy God. So much are praise and confession of sin linked together, in fact, that liturgists debate which of the two ought to begin the eucharistic celebration. Massey Shepherd has described the debate in these terms: "Reduced to its simplest issue, the question is whether Eucharist should begin with praise or with confession of sin, or, if both, in what sequential order. Strong arguments can be made for either position. Certainly, we are not worthy to come before God's presence. But can we make adequate confession without first acknowledging God's glory and grace? South India [an ecumenically significant new church, formed in 1947 of Episcopal, Presbyterian, and Congregationist churches, that found itself required to fashion a new eucharistic liturgy] opted for the sequence of Isaiah's vision [Isaiah 6:1–8]: the glory of the Holy, confession and absolution, and then the call to mission and response of dedication. This may or may not be the best pattern of making Eucharist. The ancient liturgies of the East and West began with praise and adoration but reserved penitence for a place after the hearing of the word or in devotional preparation for communion."[2]

A liturgy sparked by the liberational interests characteristic of the Latin American basic communities could both praise God and confess human sin with significantly political overtones. To praise God in genuine worship is to set a limit to the allegiance one offers all this-worldly powers. Any this-worldly power runs the risk of soliciting a devotion that is idolatrous because it forgets the priority of the One God, who alone deserves human worship. In fact, it is impossible to worship God sincerely and not submit one's whole life—political behavior quite included—to God's standards. If either individual citizens or political leaders refuse such a submission, they reveal themselves to be practical atheists. For example, the Latin American leaders who refuse justice to the peasantry, or who even kill them at will, cannot be considered authentic Christians. They may show up at all the church ceremonies. They may receive the blessing of coopted church authorities. But their worship is proclaimed null and void by their murderous actions. They have never lifted their minds and hearts to God unreservedly, never confessed the Lord of the Universe with the willingness to repent and follow the standards of the Christ that true worship requires.

The confession of sin runs to much the same conclusion. A little community concerned about local injustices and the plight of the poor knows sin in the marrow of its faith. Indeed, as the reflections of communities like that at Solentiname clearly show, the regular interplay between Scripture and local experience leads people to appreciate their own personal sinfulness. It is not merely the oppressors "out there" who fail to live up to Christ's standards. It is also we "right here" who must admit that we have been unjust, or violent, or filled with hatred rather than love. This does not mean the members of a basic Christian community have to gloss over the sinfulness of their oppressors. It does not mean they must lessen their criticism of the economic, educational, or medical systems that may be denying help and justice to millions of their fellow-citizens. It just means they have to include themselves among the masses of sinful people for whom Christ died. This alone protects them against the fanaticism and self-righteousness that afflict most irreligious revolutionaries. Confessing that they too have sinned and fallen short of the glory of God, members of basic Christian communities sense that all utopian schemes are illusory, especially those that would sacrifice or slaughter people today for the sake of a supposedly pure tomorrow.

The worship of God that has some of its purest moments in eucharistic thanksgiving is not, therefore, politically neutral. It definitely sets people on the side of light and love, forcing them to name lying and hatred the ungodly enemy. This consequence of genuine Christian worship is as inevitable as the exercise of fundamental conscience. Bad people hate the light that worship sheds, because it shows their deeds to be evil. Good people delight in praising God and confessing their own wrongdoing, because their hearts are set on the one thing necessary: the lightsome love that is our best index of the divine nature.

When Christian worship knows the God to whom it should bow, there is no valid opposition between prayer and politics. When Christian worship shunts itself away from the radical mystery of light and love that should be its center, it can become an esthetic enterprise trying to shield people from the ugly social realities that cry out to be changed. A lively, engaged worship and a radical, clear-eyed commitment to social change therefore go hand in hand. A worship that is merely beautiful, well-spoken and well-sung, is not the praise of God and the confession of sin that the Son of Man had in mind.

The different Christian churches have developed different senses of how worship and political action ought to combine. Churches of the left wing of the Reformation, for example, often have combined a very spare worship service, pivoted on a bare reading and preaching of the Word of God, with a pacificist and critical stance toward secular culture. Churches with solemn liturgies that leave little room for personal discussion of the Word of God probably tend to support the status quo uncritically. That does not mean such churches have no ethical codes forbidding the gross injustices which the status quo too often includes. It does mean that members of such churches have to find places other than the formal liturgy in which to forge the links between their worship and their ethics, between their love of God and their love of neighbor as themselves.

Consider, for example, the following paragraph from a book by a leading Russian Orthodox liturgist: "The Orthodox liturgy begins with the solemn doxology: 'Blessed is the Kingdom of the Father, the Son and the Holy Spirit, now and ever, unto ages of ages.' From the beginning the destination is announced: the journey is to the Kingdom. This is where we are going—and not symbolically but really."[3]

This doxology is both beautiful and brimming with the sort of political implications (for example, anti-idolatry) that we mused about above. However, unless the people who pray with such solemn doxologies have the chance to discuss what their prayer means for their very concrete political and cultural circumstances, they are likely to remain politically naive and so be abused by their secular leaders. Without discussion of the truth that makes them free, they are not likely to realize that their abusive secular leaders want them to stay ignorant of the conversions that the Kingdom of God entails. So while the doxology and the theologian's commentary are beautiful, considerably more remains to be said. If that more in fact never occurs, Christian worship leaves itself open to the charge of being merely an opiate that keeps people's consciences deadened to the social changes, even the revolutions, that justice requires.

The gratitude to God that flows out in worship cannot be separated from the gratitude that prompts people to take up their crosses and follow Jesus in trying to reset human relationships so that they produce a fuller justice. In the freedom of his relationship with his Father, Jesus saw the radical equality of human beings that would obtain in the Father's Kingdom. The Christians who today try to live out a preferential option for the poor keep alive this link between the free, honest worship of God and the radical equality of all human beings. A contemporary martyr such as Oscar Romero, the Central American bishop who was slain at the altar for his defense of the poor, becomes an icon of this linkage. That makes him very much a saint for our times, a worshiper in spirit and truth who shows us what our thanksgiving can entail.

The Word of God

The Catholic and Eastern Orthodox traditions have stressed the eucharistic banquet. At the center of their liturgies has stood the meal that Jesus celebrated with his disciples in anticipation of both his own death and the messianic feasting that would prevail in the full coming of the Kingdom. The Protestant churches have formed themselves around a different focus. For them the Scriptural Word of God has been the key. Thus their services have led up to Scriptural readings and a well-worked preaching that was to expose the meaning of the readings for the audience at hand. Some Protestant churches occasionally have celebrated the Lord's Supper, but the majority have considered the proclamation of God's Word sufficient to provoke full thanksgiving and confession of sin.

The "Word of God" obviously has a rich set of connotations throughout Christian history.[4] It depends on the prophetic tradition of Israel, which saw the prophets as mouthpieces of a God intent on addressing his people for both their correction and their consolation. Thus the classical prophets Isaiah, Jeremiah, and Ezekiel are all presented as dominated by the *Dabar* or Word that comes to them. The Torah that Israel associated with Moses interpreted the Word of God more legislatively. The teaching God had given to Moses was a sort of constitution. By obedience to this constitution Israel would keep faith with its Lord and so could expect to receive the divine favor. Toward the end of the Old Testament period, the Wisdom literature that constitutes the third portion of the Hebrew Bible made the divine Word more speculative and ontological. God's expressions—Wisdom, Torah, Spirit—were hypostasized or given a semi-independent status. Thus they could be pictured as existing before the divine throne at the beginnings of creation.

The Pauline and Johannine Christologies both drew on this wisdom literature. Perhaps the clearest example is the Prologue of John's Gospel, according to which the divine Word was with God at the beginning and indeed was God. For the author of John the Word plays the role that Wisdom played in Proverbs and other Jewish sapiential writings. For the author of Colossians (1:15–20) the Word was that in which creation occurred and it continues to be that in which creation coheres. Both authors therefore give the divine Word cosmic overtones. It is not simply the ethical imperative issuing from the mouth of God. It is also the expression of divine intelligence that makes exist whatever comes to occur in nature and that stands behind human creations as the ultimate source which they imitate.

The evangelists are more prophetic than sapiential, although recent New Testament research has found more influences of Hebrew Wisdom than past generations had. Nonetheless, it is Jesus the bringer of salvation or eschatological prophet who intrigues Mark, while Matthew portrays Jesus as the great new teacher of Torah. Luke stresses how Jesus moved under the inspiration of the Holy Spirit, and he sees the time of Jesus' ministry as the central panel of salvation history. Overall, then, the synoptics make the preaching of Jesus, and his personal example of faith, the central modalities of the revelation (the expression of the divine Word) that the Father worked through him.

Last, we should note again that by the time of the Pastoral Epistles the Word of God had become something to safeguard, a treasury of faith easily doctrinalized. The presbyter-bishop who dominates the ecclesiology of the Pastorals has a heavy responsibility to protect the tradition he has received, and one gets the impression that the divine Word is something less than the active two-edged sword depicted so famously in Hebrews 4:12. The images of Revelation make it plain that "Word of God" was prominent among the titles of the risen Christ, and in that literary framework the term bears heavy overtones of justice or vengeance: the Word is the agent through whom God's suffering people will receive redress.

Even this hasty survey of some of the biblical overtones of the term "Word of God" suggests the richness that the post-apostolic church inherited. As the institutional model took hold, however, in practice the term frequently narrowed to the connotations of the biblical text and the authoritative teaching of the church's leaders. Theologians developed the notion that Jesus, as the divine Son, proceeded from the heavenly Father the way that an inner word or concept proceeds from an act of understanding, but the Protestant Reformers felt it necessary to reset the proclamatory context of the Word. Only when Scripture again became the privileged locus of divine truth, and only when this truth again became more existential (geared to piercing hearts to stir repentance and salvation) than doctrinal, would the Western church regain its spiritual health. The Eastern church continued to venerate the Scriptural Word in the highly ceremonial context of its luxurious liturgy, but the sorry political fortunes of the Eastern church after the rise of Islam truncated the cultural implications that the Word might have borne.

For all its familiarity, then, the Word of God is a notion whose potential has never been fully realized. Indeed, it offers current ecclesiologists quite new angles for considering the divine life that makes the church the people of God. If the eucharistic modality that is clearest in the Lord's Supper ought to stamp the people of God through and through, making them above all creatures who delight in using their minds and hearts to praise the goodness and beauty of their Lord, the sapiential modality that is clearest in the biblical recall to hear God's voice and harden not one's heart (Hebrews 4:7) ought similarly to stamp Christians through and through. The followers of Christ have as their birthright, and as a key portion of what they should be sharing with the world, a symbolization of reality, an understanding of human prosperity, that their worship ideally would make compellingly beautiful.

What, then, ought one to say about the Liturgy of the Word, as ecclesiologists would be apt to call it, that should have the people "work over" the wisdom their God has given them for salvation? How ought Christians to retrieve, revive, and take to heart the "Word that breathes forth love," as some of the fathers and scholastics described the divine Logos? Slowly, contemplatively, sparely, and simply, we believe.

First, we must distinguish the Word of God from the glut of words that bombard the people of the developed nations every day. Many of our people are verbally incontinent, unable to control their tongues and possessed of ears that either itch for the latest bit of gossip or have grown deaf from abuse by the tongues of others. Any teacher knows how hard it is to extend students' span of attention beyond twenty minutes or so. Any practitioner of meditation knows that the first step toward inner peace is shutting the doors, blocking out the noise and babble that steal away most people's tranquillity. So the liturgy of the Word has to clear itself some space, grab itself some attention. Unless celebrants put borders of space and time around the divine Word, it will just meld into the verbiage that profanes the rest of the day. If they would simply slow things down, put pauses between the key scriptural verses, make it plain that what they are going to say in their sermons comes from the center of themselves rather than from the top of their heads, celebrants would already have moved themselves to the upper percentiles.

Second, this slow, contemplative, spare approach to the liturgy of the Word ought to have simple results in mind. The only thing necessary is the renewal or revivification of the people's faith. The key to such a renewal is the representation of the divine love, as Jesus once and for all gave it flesh both lovely and crucified. So the steady drumbeat of the churches' preaching ought to be the love of God from which nothing can separate us (Romans 8:39), the love of God poured forth in our hearts by the Holy Spirit (Romans 5:5). This love is ever ancient and ever new. It lays the foundations of all our hopes, and it is relevant to all our needs. If we are beset by moral failures, they reduce to a lack of love. If we need to give or receive healing, the surest conduit is love. Paul surveyed the various charismata of the church in 1 Corinthians 12 and then gave all of 1 Corinthians 13 over to charity, the more excellent way and greatest of charismata. The Johannine school had only one new commandment, which really was the old commandment: love one another. Why? Because God is love, and those who abide in love abide in God and God in them.

In season and out of season, preachers of the divine Word must keep their flocks riveted to this center. For sentimental times, they must show that divine *agape* is nothing easy or cheaply emotional. Indeed, God so loved world he gave his only begotten Son, who mounted the cross with no cheap emotions. For arid, rationalistic times, they must have the masculine self-confidence, the feminine self-knowledge, to propose the subversive doctrine enunciated by Pascal: the heart has its reasons, which the mind cannot know. God cares more for the reasons of the heart, the deep commitments we make at the center of ourselves, where intellect and emotion merge, than for our petty little balance sheets or self-justifications. The parable of the Pharisee and the publican (Luke 18:9–14) makes that absolutely clear. Against its own catechisms and canon laws, the preaching church has to show the primacy of charity, the foundational character of the love that is the divine life. Otherwise it is a collection of worse than profitless servants.

One implication of this simple interpretation of preaching, of course, is that preachers have to know the God they would proclaim. If preachers are not themselves steeped in the love of God, convinced of the primacy of charity, they will sound like tinkling brass and clanging cymbals. They will not be steeped in the love of God, certainly, unless they pray, regularly and sincerely. Equally, they will know little about the realism of the love of God unless they have tried to carry it into the political arena, tried to let it inspire them to help heal the pathologies of the local economy or school system or hospital arrangements that are keeping people from fully flourishing. Preachers do not have to be mystics or saints. Both mysticism and sainthood are special graces of God that God distributes as God finds best. But all ministers of the divine Word do have to strive to be authentic. If they are willing to approve a big gap between the Word they celebrate and the life they live, their proclamation will lead more to their condemnation than to their heavenly reward.

In all the Christian churches, however, the clergy have reserved the proclamation of the Word to themselves excessively, as they have reserved the eucharistic celebration to themselves excessively. The essentially lay orientation of the Latin American grass roots communities challenges this reservation, and theoreticians of the grass roots communities, such as Leonardo Boff, have not hesitated to analyze the pathology behind such a clericalism in Marxist terms. Just as the Marxist analysis of economics faults capitalists for reserving the means of production to themselves excessively, so a Marxist analysis of the patterns that have prevailed throughout church history faults church leaders for reserving the (spiritual) means of production to themselves excessively. The New Testament, to be sure, gives some grounds for distinguishing different roles in the Christian community. In no way, however, does it justify a two-level church with a great gap in power and prestige between a few clergy at the top and the hordes of laity at the bottom. Christians are far more equal than unequal in their standing before God. Their roles as clergy or laity are quite secondary to their common graces of baptism and divine life.

The practical significance of this more lay ecclesiology is that the Word of God should be pried from the hands of any small coterie that would attempt to control it. In all its major significances—divine Logos, Scripture, Truth, prophetic inspiration—the Word of God is the birthright and burden of all the "saints" (all the faithful, according to

New Testament usage). One way to capitalize on this theological conviction is to engage all the members of the community in listening to the divine Word and trying to discern what the Spirit would have the traditional Scriptural passages mean here and now. The common reflection that we saw the community of Solentiname practicing makes all the members ministers of the Word. A basic democracy invites each person to open wide and let the Spirit reveal how God's love might be more fully enfleshed. This basic democracy need not deny the special talents or responsibilities of particular members. It doesn't have to fire broadsides at the distinction between clergy and laity, ordained and unordained. But it does have to fight to preserve the church's call upon all members to contribute their insights, stir up their graces. Otherwise, the church is trying to do a demanding job with only a fraction of its available resources.

That finally is the bottom line that any serious reflection on the Word of God as the church's sapiential patrimony reaches. The church has not been given God's wisdom or God's life mainly for itself. It has been given God's wisdom and God's life, the Word and the flesh of Christ, for the life of the world. As the sacramental ecclesiological model best makes clear, Christians have as their main missionary imperative manifesting to the world the vocation that God offers all people. This is a calling to divine life, to a share in a divine nature that is best indicated by love. The wisdom of the Word of God is inseparable from the twofold commandment of Christ. If the church makes present in the world the love of God, with whole mind, heart, soul, and strength, and the love of neighbor as self, it will be the great sign lifted up for the nations, the city shining from the hilltop. It cannot make these loves present in the world, cannot be the great sign God asks it to be, if only its leaders feel responsible for the Word of God. All have the vocation to show the world God's love, so all have the right and responsibility to discern what Wisdom presently is asking, what Torah ought now to mean.

Some may say that this seems fine theory but they cannot see how to put it into practice. The reply is as near and obvious as the actual operation of the basic communities of Latin America or the critical communities of Europe. Let a given parish actively support smaller units, organized either by geographical ties or by spontaneous affinities, and it will be able to give the more democratic theology of proclamation that we have been pushing a fair test. Perhaps many parishes will fail this test, the people as a whole saying they are quite content with the Word they receive en masse each Sunday morning. Others, though, are quite likely to come alive for the first time in decades.

As one travels the country, again and again one hears almost despairing complaints about the poor quality of worship and political involvement in the local parishes. Our North American problem is not laity running amok with enthusiasm, charismata flying out of control, disregard for the gifts of bishops and theologians. Our problem is apathy, conservatism, closure to the Word that is like a two-edged sword, the Spirit that is like a refining fire. The more intelligent the people in our pews, the more disgusted they are by the impersonal structures of official leadership and worship, by the superficial character of the majority of sermons and eucharistic celebrations. Life actually is a lot simpler and more vibrant than what our establishmentarian churches deal in each Sunday morning. People of any spiritual substance know this instinctively and holistically—so instinctively and holistically they refuse their obedience and enthusiasm to leaders, rules, liturgies, churches that haven't earned it by manifest wisdom and love. One can't cheat in the religious life. Below all the docile words and expected smiles, the only real issue is whether the true God of light and love is being served.

Mystagogy

This brings us to our third category for reflecting on the worship so central to the church's being and flourishing. By mystagogy we mean evoking, stirring up, helping to make present the living God who is always mysterious, fuller than what our little minds and hearts can contain. The traditional Greek word for "sacrament" was *mysterion*. Each of the rituals by which the church initiated and nourished its members was supposed to bring them face to face with the divine majesty and love. The early catechumens underwent a quite rigorous training, to prepare them for the mysteries they would celebrate as Christians. The *disciplina arcani* of the early church was an effort to keep Christians from tossing their mysterious pearls before swine who could only profane them.

How does one make worship mystagogic? There is no trick or gimmick. A eucharist slowly and beautifully celebrated, a Word lovingly and prophetically proclaimed, is bound to summon the mystery of beginning and beyond, certain to carry something of the Christ who has promised to be with any two or three who gather in his name. For centuries Christians have read the Scriptures devoutly, giving the sacred words a privileged place in the interpretation of reality. They need only do this together, in their little groups, for the Word of God to swell into its proper proportions. Similarly, they need only confess their sins in a well-wrought penitential ritual, or baptize their children in the spirit of Easter, or anoint their dead in a sincere hope of their rising again for the mystery of God to show itself what it always is: the foundation, height, end, and inmost pulse of all that lives and moves, of anything that has ever existed. Unbelieving astronomers, if there are any, probably would dismiss Christian mystagogy as so much galactic dust. Common people, and astronomers still able to gape at the wonders of the universe, will realize they have been on the verge, if not indeed in the midst, of mystagogy again and again.

The worship of the Christian church either intends a real, mysterious God, or it is all the pernicious, debilitating things that positivistic and Marxist sociologists have ever accused it of being. A real, mysterious God is the quickest leveler of our human pretensions, the straightest way out of our human deadends, that saints or sinners have ever found. In medieval times, when the black death forced the European population at large to meditate on life's fragility, the distinctions between commoner and royalty, pope and peasant, ebbed away as lightly as the measures of a macabre dance. For the medieval artists, we all go round and round the same human core: our certainty of death. The God who conquers death does nothing to remove the radical equality that mortality forces upon us. We are all saved from death into divine life only by grace, God's free gift of the love that is imperishable. The mystery of God, wherever found, is a great revealer of truth. The truth the church's theology has wonderfully preserved but the church's organization structure has horribly obscured is the root similarity we all have as mortal, sinful, finite creatures who owe everything to the goodness of God.

This should be a liberating truth, of course, and if people are allowed to chew it over together it quickly becomes such. Take the parable of the Pharisee and the publican mentioned earlier. It obviously says that one's external place in a society, one's assigned measures of status and prestige, mean nothing to the God who descries all human hearts. This is painfully clear for the Pharisee, whose sense of ethical propriety and self-worth keeps him from being justified in God's sight. It is more subtly clear in the case of the publican or tax-collector, who is justified not because he works in a despised profession but because he is humble at heart. When the Kingdom of God, the mystery of God, comes into our midst it does indeed overturn many of our human assignments of virtue and blame, success and failure. But it does not do this doctrinairely, as though ignorance and failure, dirt and down-troddenness, immediately made one beatified. No, the poor are blessed because God cares for them and their poverty may well have freed them to attend to God's care, respond to God's offer of justice and love. In itself material poverty is no blessing. It tends to grind people down, to erode their hopes and stunt their cultural growth. But the mercy of God is such that even when our hearts or our poverty condemns us, God is greater.

This God who is always greater is most obvious when we feel immersed in the divine mystery. The function of mystagogy is simply to aid such an immersion. Lighting its many candles, raising its clouds of incense, singing its moving chants, the Christian church has long tried to create a physical atmosphere that would open the spirit to the mysterious implications all creatures bear. The water with which to baptize, the oil with which to anoint, even the bread to be consumed—none has been univocal or flat or two-dimensional. Each has been sacramental: a matter that could become holy, were the Spirit to breathe but the slightest bit of inspiration. So too with the words of Scripture and the liturgical sermon. Granted the atmosphere of recollection that well-designed churches and ceremonies could create, both easily became carriers of God, channels of the pure "isness" that blankly explains every bit of existence and beauty we know.

The Christian mysteries therefore have had the tendency to bring the natural world aglow with further significances. Water could no longer be simply water, after it had washed people clean of sin and waved them into the divine life. Wine could no longer be simply wine, after it had become the blood of Christ poured out for the salvation of many. Speech and silence, music and costume, icons and incense all were changed similarly. The incarnation of the divine Mystery, the enfleshment of the Word that from eternity had proceeded from the Father, laid a very thorough foundation. Once people accepted Jesus Christ as the key to their meaning, all the elements of Jesus' earthly habitat could become fellow enjoyers of God's gracious Kingdom. Any time that the bridegroom came to celebrate liturgically the presence of the Kingdom, all creatures great and small could be moved to cry out in rejoicing.

It has taken the Christian church many centuries to extend this sense of a gracious creation outside its own cultural boundaries, but nowadays most theologians are looking at the non-Christian religious traditions positively, admitting that the Father of Christ may well have been working in traditional India and China, Africa and native America, to save and beatify many. When worship and faith are mystagogic, the pregnancy of all decent, artistic, wise, or generous actions becomes clear. Then what Paul told the Philippians rings as a call to reconsider the outreach of the divine grace. Paul's stress was goodness wherever found: "Finally, brethren, whatever is true, whatever is honorable, whatever is just, whatever is pure, whatever is lovely, whatever is gracious, if there is any excellence, if there is anything worthy of praise, think about these things. What you have learned and received and heard and seen in me, do; and the God of peace will be with you" (Philippians 4:8–9). One need only expand the world beyond Paul's Mediterranean horizons to find a universal mystery of salvation.[5]

For example, Hinduism and Buddhism, the most significant religious traditions that originated in India, both speak of an ultimacy that a mature Christian faith can associate with its saving God. The Brahman that Advaita Vedanta, which is probably the most sophisticated Hindu philosophy, makes the inmost reality of everything that exists seem quite like the Christian Creator in its utter primordiality. Just as Christian theologians came to see that the divine mystery of love had to be present to each creature every moment, if the creature were not to fall back into nothingness, so Hindu philosophers saw (usually in meditative visions) that there is only one mystery of existence which applies to each and all. So the Upanishads, upon which Vedanta builds, tell religious inquirers that their own inmost identity coincides with that which is the foundation of the world. Christian theologians would want to add a few paragraphs to protect themselves against pantheism (the view that God is everything and only God exists), but they could affirm most of what Vedanta has been saying. And in both cases, for both traditions, this sort of inquiry into the ultimate foundations of the self and the world has not been merely academic or speculative. The *rishis* (seers) to whom Hindus credit their scriptures, like the great Christian doctors, have been people passionately searching for a God who could reset the bones of broken humanity and give desperately parched human spirits the water of everlasting life.

Dialogue between Christians aware of their mystagogic heritage and Buddhists ardently pursuing enlightenment frequently reaches a similar sort of rapprochement. The Buddhanature that Mahayana Buddhists try to understand, the nirvana that Mahayana Buddhists come to find in the midst of the samsaric ordinary world, and the appreciation of the integrity of the world that Buddhist enlightenment brings all are reminiscent of what Christian contemplatives such as the medieval Rhineland mystics have described. Everywhere there is the dependence of both the contemplative and what is contemplated on the foundational mystery that Christians call God and Buddhists call the Buddhanature. Everywhere the mystic's unitive vision shows reality to be connected and dynamic. What the Buddhists call the chain or circuit of conditioned coproduction finds parallels in the cosmological reflections of Christian process theologians or in the profound reflections of the Lonergan school on the "emergent probability" by which evolution unfolds. The mystery in which we have been placed is ecological, historical, on the move. It links us each and all. So, each and all, we find ourselves realizing that our lives are more a passion than a self-determining action. Without taking away our liberty or responsibility, the ultimate foundations of our world have placed us in the midst of a dynamic plan whose beginning, end, and final pattern we are too small to descry.

One could find soteriological parallels to these positive correlations between Christian views of ultimate reality and the views of major non-Christian religious traditions. Where Christians look to Jesus and the grace flowing from Jesus' cross and resurrection for their hopes of healing and fulfillment, Taoists look to the Way described by Lao Tzu and Chuang Tzu, Muslims look to the Qur'an revealed to Muhammad, and Jews look to the Torah given to Moses and developed by the Talmudic masters. Each reference is much more than the flicker of the mind to the intellectual place where the tradition has localized healing. In all four cases, millions of people have clung to the mystery symbolized by the referents as the central pillar of their hopes. So the Tao has defended millions of Chinese and East Asians against despair, taking them back to the primordial strength of nature, reminding them again and again that the force ultimately most significant is more like water than rock, more like an infant than a king, more like a woman than a man. It goes gently, patiently, and indirectly, but it finally is irresistible.

The saving mystery does of course emerge quite differently in the Qur'an, where the Lord of the Worlds stands far apart from nature and brooks no identification with any creature. Yet this Allah is as near as the pulse of one's jugular vein and is more concerned with mercy than with judgment. So one need only refer any happening or being to its sovereign source to find the world again falling into place, the depradations and stupidities of human beings again becoming secondary. The parallels between the stories of the Sufi masters who have pursued the creative mystery to its paradoxical depths and the stories of the Christian desert fathers is quite striking. In the desert, whether that of the fathers or that undergirding the Qur'an, things overturn; what initially seems obvious soon becomes puzzling and profitable. The overwhelming primacy of the divine creative force brings any sane hearers to their knees, bending their backs low and eliciting the most profound submission.

We could continue almost without limit, suggesting how the divine mystery experienced by the Hasidic masters is even closer to the covenanted God that the Christian masters have hymned. We could venture apart from the literate traditions, showing how the high God of many African tribes, like the Great Spirit of many native American tribes, is mysterious and sovereign. And in the measure that Christian patterns of worship had prepared ordinary believers, we would be able to elicit an instinctive praise and appreciation for all these signs that the Father of Christ has indeed not left himself without witness anywhere. Indeed, Christians versed in their Scriptures immediately would recall Paul's speech in Acts 17 about the unknown God: "Men of Athens, I perceive that in every way you are very religious. For as I passed along, and observed the objects of your worship, I found also an altar with this inscription, 'To an unknown god.' What therefore you worship as unknown, this I proclaim to you. The God who made the world and everything in it, being Lord of heaven and earth, does not live in shrines made by man, nor is he served by human hands, as though he needed anything, since he himself gives to all men life and breath and everything. And he made from one every nation of men to live on the face of the earth, having determined allotted periods and the boundaries of their habitation, that they should seek God, in the hope that they might feel after him and find him. Yet he is not far from each one of us, for 'In him we live and move and have our being'; as even some of your poets have said, 'For we are indeed his offspring' " (Acts 17:22–28).

The divine mystery, universal in outreach, nudging all consciences as the one perspective that can give them proportion and rest, immediately breaks apart any provincialism that an unmystagogic, overly literal or doctrinal approach to worship and faith might create. One cannot experience the living, truly mysterious God and be dogmatic in the prejudicial sense. For the living, truly mysterious God obviously has all the priority in creation and salvation. Let people but meet that God in their regular worship and they will grow humble indeed in their pronouncements about what can and what cannot serve as ways of salvation. The charges of "paganism" leveled by the early Christian visitors to non-Christian cultures said as much about the underdevelopment of their own faith as it said about the deficiencies of the non-Christian cultures. To be sure, those cultures had real and frightening evils, as supposedly Christian cultures frequently have had. But the wiser and more saintly attitude, displayed by missionaries such as Francis Xavier, sought out the positive elements in foreign cultures and tried to consider them as but further signs of the divine pedagogy. Thus Xavier was able to call the Japanese the most refined people he had ever encountered, realizing that in Japan the esthetic and the religious often had achieved a superbly polished union.

We shall draw upon this mystagogic dimension of Christian worship and faith later, when we deal with Christian mission and governance. Right now, however, we should secure its centrality to all ethical matters. The mystery of the living God levels human pretensions to dogmatic certainty and inclines any honest observer to home in on the heart of the ethical matter. This is the love and honesty that is present or absent. As Plato saw long ago, things are not good because some supposed authority says that they are godly or revealed. Things are godly or revealed because they are good: brimming with the life, light, and love that is our best index of the holy ultimacy that could make a world such as ours. So Jesus did not thump down a set of documents that supposedly served as his credentials. He let the works that the Father empowered him to do testify to who and what he was.

Jesus met the Father regularly in prayer, so the parental mystery was like his wellspring. One could hardly better describe the ends of Christian worship than by saying that it succeeds to the degree it makes the parental mystery our wellspring.

Summary

We have been studying the church at worship, certainly one of its most central tasks or modalities, and our study has proceeded under three headings. Under eucharistia we have noted the thanksgiving which ought to be a prime characteristic of the Christian religious life. This thanksgiving is most explicitly sacramental in the memorial of Jesus' last supper, death, resurrection, and parousia which the Christian eucharist enacts. Developed from Jewish liturgical patterns, the Christian eucharist celebrates the mighty, saving acts of God (the most extraordinary of which was the Christ-event) that set reality in proper proportions. The obstacles to such a celebration today include the secularization that has rendered the traditional doctrine of God problematic and the institutionalization of the church. A liberational model would tie both liturgy and theology more closely to the great crises of public life, and it would also show the intimate ties between confessing God's grandeur and confessing one's own sinfulness. Both confessions, when genuine, reveal Christian worship to be far from neutral politically. Both suggest the fittingness of a contemporary martyr such as Oscar Romero having been slain at the altar because he championed the plight of the oppressed.

The Word of God is a second all-important focus of the church that we find gathered for worship. This focus has a rich biblical background, and it has been especially significant in Protestant churches. Today we need to free the Liturgy of the Word from the glut of profane words that burden most church-goers. We need as well to show the simple goal that all live preaching intends, which is the renovation of people's faith in the divine love. Probably the best way to effect the proper ends of the Liturgy of the Word today is to follow the lead of the basic communities and invite all the participants to help work out the contemporary implications of the pregnant scriptural passages. Ours is not a time when anything less than a solid proclamation of a genuine Christian wisdom will carry conviction or win enthusiastic adherents.

Our third topic was mystagogy, the evocation of the real God who is always mysterious. We showed the link between mystagogy and sacramentality, and then we examined how a mysterious God challenges the assumptions of all pharisaic or superficial religion. As well, a mysterious God quite easily may be seen at work outside the boundaries of Christian cultures, inspiring whatever is honest and noble in the other great religious traditions. So the ultimate reality discussed by Hinduism and Buddhism, and the source of salvation praised by Taoism, Islam, and Judaism, share many of the characteristics of the Christian God, when the mysteriousness of the Christian God is properly appreciated. Paul's speech in Acts 17 seems to have anticipated this conclusion, and generous missionaries have often been led to it. Finally, we suggested the ethical simplifications that Christian mystagogy can bring—how it helps us zero in on the heart of the moral matter.

STUDY QUESTIONS

1. What are Christians' prime warrants for welcoming each day with deep gratitude?
2. What are the political implications of confessing oneself a sinner and completely dependent upon God?
3. How might "the Word of God" summarize the Christian sapiential heritage?
4. Suggest two ways to improve the impact of the Christian Liturgy of the Word.
5. What is the main tie between Christian mystagogy and Christian sacramentality?
6. How does a genuinely mysterious God simplify both one's view of the world religions and one's sense of the ethical crux?

NOTES

1. Louis Weil, "Liturgy in a Disintegrating World," WORSHIP 54/4 (July 1980), p. 301.

2. Massey H. Shepherd Jr., "The Berakah Award: Response," WOR-SHIP 52/4 (July 1978), p. 308.

3. Alexander Schmemann, FOR THE LIFE OF THE WORLD. Crestwood, NY: St. Vladimir's Seminary Press, 1973, p. 29.

4. See Frederick E. Crowe, S.J., THEOLOGY OF THE CHRISTIAN WORD: A STUDY IN HISTORY. New York: Paulist Press, 1978.

5. See Paul F. Knitter, NO OTHER NAME? Maryknoll, NY: Orbis, 1985.

Chapter 6

Mission

Proclaiming the Gospel ♦ Helping the Poor ♦ Building the Earth
♦ Summary, Study Questions, Notes

Proclaiming the Gospel

The church that is gathered by the call to worship God receives
an impetus to proclaim this God to the whole world. Specifically, the
Christian church receives an impetus to proclaim the good news of the
salvation that God worked in Jesus of Nazareth, raised to be the Messiah and Lord of creation. Just as Jesus came with good news for the
poor, healing for the sick, encouragement for all who had felt broken-
hearted, the disciples of Jesus have a commission to go into every ham-
let of the earth with the message that the time has come, the Kingdom
has arrived, grace is available to all who truly want it.

The "mission" of the disciples of Christ is their "sending" by God
to herald this gospel or glad tidings. Christian theologians have long
thought of the Incarnation of the Word and the work of Jesus of Nazareth as a mission. They have conceived of the work of the Holy Spirit
in the same way. It was in the train of Jesus and the Spirit, then, that
the earliest missionaries and preachers set out. The Epistles of Paul
occur in this missionary context, while the Acts of the Apostles is
Luke's interpretation of the missions of both Peter and Paul. In the
synoptic tradition, the risen Christ commissions the eleven to spread
the gospel to the whole earth: "And he said to them, 'Go into all the
world and preach the gospel to the whole of creation . . . And they
went forth and preached everywhere, while the Lord worked with
them and confirmed the message by the signs that attended it" (Mark
16:15,20).

Proclaiming the good news therefore is of the church's essence.
Just as it would not be the community of Christ without a regular and
mystagogic worship, so it would not be the community of Christ without its mission to preach the gospel. Through all ages, the church has
felt it imperative to keep faith with this mission. As new lands became
known, Christian missionaries quickly followed those who explored
them, convinced that they were but further fields ripe for the harvest.
Sometimes the missionaries met with resounding success. Other
times their work seemed to bear little fruit. Either way they felt it
necessary to carry on, because the Lord himself had laid on the church
the responsibility of bringing the gospel to the ends of the earth. If
certain peoples would not hear or embrace the good news, that was
their problem. The disciples' charge was to give all peoples the option,
to let no inhabited realm not have heard of the mighty acts of salvation
God had wrought in Jesus Christ.

Today Christian missionaries appear to be in a posture of re-
grouping, as they try to assess both the ambiguous aftermath of the
church's involvement in the European colonialism of the nineteenth
century and the counter-missionary surge of such established non-
Christian traditions as Buddhism and Islam. The demographic projections suggest that Christians will become a diminishing fraction of
the world population, while the upsurge of nationalism and ethnicity
suggests that areas traditionally dominated by non-Christian religious
traditions will not be fertile missionary ground. In the past decades
missionaries from the United States and other Northern powers have
been expelled from lands such as Iraq, while in Communist countries
they have regularly suffered persecution. So while the news that
Christian have to preach continues to be surpassingly good, many theologians of church mission have begun to ponder the formidable barriers to spreading this news in today's world.

As one might expect, different missionary ventures have responded with different tactics. Many evangelicals have taken up the
modern means of communication, using television, radio, and print to
beam their message to large parts of the world. More subtle groups,
such as the Little Brothers and Sisters of Jesus inspired by Charles de
Foucauld, have worked out a tactics of simple presence. Like the
"worker-priests" who arose in Europe after the Second World War,
when Christianity seemed on the wane and the Cardinal Archbishop
of Paris could seriously write on the theme, "France: A Missionary

Country?", the Little Brothers and Sisters have striven simply to be-with the common people, living and working alongside them in their often depressing circumstances.

Rosemary Haughton, reflecting on God's passion to break through our barriers and give us the love for which we are starving, finds the divine Wisdom often taking the lowly form of simply being-with ordinary people in their daily sufferings. Such a form of procla-mation and encounter took over the life of a Dutch worker-priest named Egide van Broeckhoven, making his prayer and his sharing with his ordinary friends but two criss-crossing modalities of his one love of God: "In that place where he was one with God he found those who were his friends, and in his friends he encountered God. And by that discovery he liberated, in them, the Wisdom who before had been imprisoned and dumb. He is, before the time when it was recogniz-able, the prophet of the new Church which 'turns the structure of the Church on its head', in the words of another worker-priest. Around Egide such a Church formed itself, for Wisdom found a home among those who loved her in him. She lived in and between them, she was their exchanges, of fumbling words, of sudden smiles, of awkward acts of kindness or gestures of solidarity. She it was who put on the coffee-pot late at night; she it was who exhausted herself in over-driven and unjustly rewarded labour; it was she into whose arms came the small son of an Arab labourer, rushing to be kissed by his friend; Wisdom in him suffered when unsafe machinery caused an injury, made worse by careless treatment, and she made that pain redemp-tive."[1]

The hard part of this interpretation of Christian mission is the way that it forces us to make ordinary daily life, with all its lack of glamor and all its grinding toil, the medium and crux of salvation. The encouraging part is its realism: proclaiming the gospel, or helping any other creature toward salvation, is as simple and possible as being kindly, caring, compassionate (in the root sense of suffering-with). All human beings serve or fail the purposes of God by the quality of their daily lives. Those of us who burden other people, showing them just another impersonal face or loading upon them just another dosage of couldn't-care-less, are the main impediments to the rise of faith and the spread of the gospel. Those of us who ease other people's burdens, shedding a little light into their minds or infusing a little hope into their hearts, are missionaries unawares. It is necessary and well, of course, for this light and hope to occur in explicitly Christian terms. Were the gospel never to be preached or exemplified in terms of Jesus, sin, grace, divine life, communal mission, heaven, and the like, the deepest import of human interactions might well be missed. But the explicit forms of the gospel and Christian mission always occur in the context of a wider theater of salvation. The grace of God is being offered and accepted or rejected everywhere, even when no Christian categories, words, or workers are there to refer it to Jesus of Nazareth, illumine it with the paradigmatic example of God's first missionary.

The gospel to be proclaimed therefore emerges as the real possibility of making human life good. Christians who take pains to distinguish the gospel from "humanism" have little penetrated the significance of the Incarnation that their faith says is at the center of God's salvational plan. They are right, of course, to point out the dangers of a secularist reading of human nature that would make no place for God or confess no human sin begging for redemption. But they are wrong to jump back in antiseptic horror from the dirt and moral failure in which most of God's children have to deal. Equally, they are wrong to disparage the art, science, and healing that occur outside the Christian camp, as though God had to find evangelical words on people's lips to use them for the divine purposes. No, far more Christian, and far more encouraging to Christian missionary activity, is the attitude of Paul that we found in Philippians 4. Whatever is true or honorable deserves Christians' support and forwards Christians' mission. Whatever brings light to the blind, hearing to the deaf, hope to the desperate is a sacramental carrier of God.

In this context, the disciples of Christ are missionaries of a church on the sacramental model that we discussed in Chapter 4. They should of course express themselves in biblical or traditionally Christian language to all who can hear it, but they should not be loath to translate this language into other interpretational systems. So the dialogues with atheists, Marxists, Buddhists, Jews, and any other people living in non-Christian language (and so interpretational) systems are central missionary work. Even more, the efforts of Christians to embody their faith, give flesh to the good news, in their offices and places of recreation place before people who perhaps would not darken a church door the essential message that all the churches have always been preaching.

One who lives mainly inside a Christian culture may take for granted the many bases for hope that the gospel affords and so not appreciate how much hopelessness afflicts the secularized or non-Christian world. To be sure, the non-Christian religious traditions are great reservoirs of hope, and some apparently anti-religious traditions, such as Marxism, have rallied millions to serve visions of a much-bettered humanity. Yet the advance of modern technology, and the concomitant break-up of many traditional cultures, has afflicted more and more of the world with what one might call "religious atrophy." Indeed, we would be naive not to admit that many nominal Christians have little feel for the truly mysterious God and cannot confidently say that they know what the hallowed symbols of "salvation" actually mean. So we should not despise the missions that merely bring the message of the gospels alive. In Jesus' day people assumed the existence of God and the warfare between God and Satan as they assumed the earth they walked upon and the air they breathed. We, their supposedly great evolutionary betters, have lost these elementary assumptions.

We authors, for example, have been somewhat stunned to see how tenuous a hold apparently solid Christians often have on such central matters as "resurrection" and "grace." The majority of devout Christians are poorly educated in theology. They may know some of the terms. They may even have passed some of the courses. But the words illumine little of their daily experience. So they don't direct the batterings they receive at work to the cross of Christ, and "resurrection" does not serve them as a complete reorientation, a whole new angle of vision in which to reset their batterings. Similarly, they don't think of the things that most gladden their hearts—the love of their children, the times of creativity at work, the hallowed moments of deep communion with their friends—as overflows of the divine life of grace. They live most of their lives interacting, spirit to spirit, with the divine fullness of light and love, but they virtually never realize it.

What does this suggest for proclaiming the gospel? First, that all missionary proclaimers come on the scene as but secondary agents, backup personnel. The primary agent of salvation and herald of the good news that life is more than food, the body is more than clothing, is the divine mystery itself. It is the one who gives whatever increase in faith, hope, and love actually occurs. We should try to plant and water, but all our efforts are ancillary and instrumental. Indeed, our efforts are liable to bear even visible fruit in the measure that we think of them as uncovering the good news already operative in the given situation.

This "already operative" may have several modalities, of course. If the situation is prosperous—healthy in minds that are honest and creative, rich in hearts that want to care and heal—we need only lightly recall that this sort of prosperity was what Jesus brought in fulfillment of the Isaiahan prophecy: "The Spirit is upon me, because he has anointed me to preach good news to the poor. He has sent me to proclaim release to the captives and the recovering of sight to the blind, to set at liberty those who are oppressed, and to proclaim the acceptable year of the Lord" (Luke 4:18–19; Isaiah 61:1–2; 58:6).

More frequently, the situation into which the missionary comes will not be brimming with prosperity, with humanistic health, but will be shot through with groans and suffering. The grace of God seems absent, the care of God seems long-gone. The delicate work of the missionary in such situations is to reveal the genuine longing for God that suffering carries. For while pain and disorder in themselves are negative realities, they automatically point to the positive realities of health and order which we "know" ought to obtain. Similarly, the lack of meaning and hope that genuine irreligion produces points to the meaning and hope that ought to obtain. The "ought," of course, is curious, since it does not occur on the level of statistical probability or the average commonsensical set of expectations driving the mental machine of John Doe or Sarah Lee. It is a moral ought, an instinctive sense of fittingness. Just as it would take considerable mental gymnastics to try to make the case that physical sickness is the standard or normal state of affairs—the bodily situation that we instinctively feel "ought" to obtain—so it would take considerable mental gymnastics to make the case that meaninglessness and hopelessness are normal, standard, what we all realistically should expect. The body rejects the idea that sickness is the way that somatic business ought to go. The spirit equally rejects the idea that senselessness and despair are the way that psychological business ought to go.

If all this is so, then the brokenness of human spirits, like the brokenness of human bodies, is a sort of accusation against the makers of our world. At the limit, it is a sort of accusation against "God," whom even non-believers can comfortably use as the traditional symbol for the final Maker of the world. But to be accusing God, as Job found out, is to be entering on a process which, if pursued honestly, takes one farther than one may have intended to go. For the silence into which we hurl our accusations, the midnight mood of blackness, can surprisingly turn over and force us to consider sources of meaning and hope that we have been overlooking, perhaps semi-willfully. It just may be that the people who claim to have found meaning and hope are not all self-deluders or psychologically infantile. On close examination, quite a few of them may be doing better, by the Freudian index of the ability to work and the ability to love, than we are. Among these people will be quite a few religious believers, not a few of them Christian. Obviously the percentages will not force us to correlate Christian faith with hopefulness, meaningfulness, and psychological health, but neither will the percentages allow us to pass over Christian faith as certainly insignificant. And if we start to ponder the central symbols of Christian faith we may, like Chaim Potok's Asher Lev, come to realize that no other symbol has the power of Christ's crucifixion to express the agony latent in the human condition.[2] The other side of such a realization, of course, is that the resurrection of Christ, the Easter Event, may be equally expressive of the enormous potential that the human condition bears.

The gospel that Christian missionaries proclaim is nothing more nor less than the death and resurrection of Jesus Christ. He is God's power and wisdom, the font of all Christian meaning and hope. One may preach him or take him on a dozen different levels. Myriad historical, philosophical, poetic, and mystical inquiries can remain. But as long as the world is having placed before it, by word and example both, the passover of Jesus from innocent suffering and death to unexpectable resurrection and life, the Christian mission will be in fine fettle.

Helping the Poor

As with our other considerations, the considerations that we use to ruminate about Christian mission overlap and flow together. We may try to parcel out the mystery of salvation into neat little tracts, but the mystery itself soon shows that all of our tidy abstracts fail to do justice to the simple holism of the divine reality. So preaching the good news of Christ's death and resurrection already is a major help to the poor, who are strongly tempted to think that human existence is only downtroddenness. Indeed, all of us are "poor" in the sense of morally weak, intellectually dim, hardly ever fit for the assaults that suffering or failure can make upon our faith. Consequently, all of us need to have good news preached to us, lived out in front of us, pressed into our flesh by the embraces of lovers and friends.

In this section, however, we want to concentrate on the quite physical poverty that afflicts "the wretched of the earth." These, the people living under the oppressions of hunger, sickness, illiteracy, indebtedness, lack of control over their own lives, and too many other evils, probably constitute a majority of the citizens of the planet. Certainly they do, if one extrapolates the indexes used in the developed nations to determine financial, educational, medical, and other sorts of poverty or disadvantage. In country after country, for instance, a single digit percent of people at the top of the economic pyramid controls more of the wealth than all the other classes or financial sectors at the middle and the bottom. On continent after continent, women and children are a clear majority of those not getting a fair, egalitarian slice of the material or cultural pie. Jesus seems to have directed his good news to such marginalized people, thinking that the materially and culturally "healthy" people in his society had little need of his ministrations. To be sure, Jesus connected the plight of the poor with the sin that he was trying to oust, the Satanic regime opposed to the Father's light and love. In the holistic culture of his day, all sorts of waywardness and dysfunction ran together. There are occasions on which we do well to distinguish different sorts of dysfunction, not immediately intruding moral evaluations into our analyses of economic patterns or civil rights. But we also do well to return more than occasionally to a holism like that of Jesus, for there certainly continues to be a level at which the mass of people damned to much less than a fair chance at a decent material and cultural life suffer from humanity's moral failures, humanity's stubborn immersion in the ignorance and wrong-doing called sin.

Among the happier fruits of the missionary activities of the American Catholic church in recent years is the first draft of the bishops' pastoral letter on "Social Teachings and the U.S. Economy," which appeared late in 1984. As we write the final draft has yet to appear, but the first draft, taken in the context of the bishops' previous letter on peacemaking and nuclear arms, gives considerable basis for thinking that the poor are to the forefront of the bishops' ruminations on the moral state of the country, and that the bishops are trying to provide for both the analytical viewpoint that treats economic matters on their own terms and the holistic viewpoint that sees how economics, politics, and ethics all finally interact. The American Catholic bishops have not yet quite come to the point that the Latin American bishops reached at Medellín in 1968, when they made a preferential option for the poor, making the poor the first object of their pastoral care, but our U.S. bishops are coming closer. At least, the day when the American Catholic hierarchy took little part in the nation's debates about public policies appears long-gone, and both the poor and the peacemakers should be feeling more blessed in consequence.

For example, the American bishops endorsed the Latin American bishops' "option for the poor," both on their own and on the authority of Pope John Paul II. The Pope had interpreted this option as "a call to have a special openness with the small and the weak, those that suffer and weep, those that are humiliated and left on the margin of society, so as to help them win their dignity as human persons and children of God."[3] The bishops took this papal interpretation to mean that opting for the poor, making them the primary target of pastoral care and economic reform, is a valid interpretation of the biblical witness. They saw it as entailing a responsibility on the part of the contemporary church to speak for the people who have no one to present their case, to defend those who are defenseless. These people, in biblical terminology, are the "poor," the *anawim* of God. Just as the biblical prophets, from Amos on, took the poor as their special constituency, so the contemporary church, in the exercise of a prophetic ministry suitable for our day, ought to take the poor as its special constituency.

The letter on the U.S. economy, to its great credit, goes on to suggest many of the far-reaching implications that such an option for the poor would seem to entail. Connected with the traditional social teachings of Christianity (especially those of the stream of papal encyclicals that began with Leo XIII's *Rerum Novarum* in 1891), and with Pope John Paul II's views on labor, the option for the poor quickly leads to a view of economic life in which the profits of stock-holders is far from the first consideration. Rather, the fruition of all the people of the society that an economy should serve is the first consideration, and an economy in which people are subordinated to financial profit stands condemned as inordinate, out of joint, disharmonious with the values of the biblical God. A properly ordered economy should "enable persons to find a significant measure of self-realization in their labor; it should permit persons to fulfill their material needs through adequate remuneration; and it should make possible the enhancement of unity and solidarity within the family, the nation and the world economy."[4]

Critics of the first draft were quick to mount their counter-attacks. Many of them had been stung by the bishops' pastoral letter on the challenge of peace and the dangers of the nuclear arms race. So they leaped to the defense of the American capitalist system, heralding it as the best hope of the world's poor people for an improvement in their standard of living and as the system most compatible with basic human freedoms and rights. What is one to make of the debate that the bishops' draft and their critics' counter-proposals have created?

For our focus on the mission of the church to help the poor, the criterion to keep in mind would seem to be both pragmatic and religious. An economic system, like a whole culture, is as good or as bad as the extent to which it helps people live a good life. A "good life," of course, immediately begs definition and concrete description. For Christians, though, much of the definition and description seems quite obvious. A good life entails a share in the goods of the earth, the material provision of the Creator, sufficient to keep people healthy and able to contribute to the several-sided cultural life of their society. Thus an economic arrangement that regularly kept significant fractions of the population or large actual numbers of people badly fed, housed, clothed, educated, and integrated into the labor force would be liable to serious criticism. Similarly, an arrangement that consigned significant fractions or large actual numbers to second-rate economic, political, or cultural status would receive less than laudatory grades. The Christian dicta that the goods of the earth are for all the earth's people, that no one has the right to luxuries while other people lack necessities, and that we are all equal before God in basic dignity in fact would seem to call for an economic arrangement in some significant sense socialistic or even communistic. The sense that these words have picked up in recent history probably renders them unfit to describe the goals of a genuinely Christian economic arrangement. But before rejecting them outright we should realize that the historical socialisms and communisms, including even those of the Marxist-

Leninist Soviet Union and Marxist-Leninist-Maoist China, have had a partial overlap with many Christian instincts about the primacy of the need to ameliorate the condition of the poor and enfranchise them in general society. That the most dramatic experiments in socialism have felt it necessary to consider traditional Christianity their enemy is a woeful condemnation of traditional Christianity. On the other hand, that such experiments also have become horribly oppressive regimes under which the blood of peasants and dissidents has flowed like water condemns the leaders who perverted their original hopes and practically forces one to conclude that when God is dead everything indeed will seem permitted, no atrocity in fact will not occur.

Thus, a Christian program to better the plight of the poor, honor the dignity of all citizens, and keep God clearly superior to mammon will turn out to be a quite different socialism or communism from those that have stained so much of recent history. This does not mean, however, that the Latin American bishops are wrong for having espoused Marxist tools of sociological and economic analysis, nor that the bishops of the United States do not have considerably farther to go if their service of the poor is to become politically effective. The Latin American bishops differ from the bishops of the United States in that they have come closer to identifying themselves with the poor and considering the poor to be the church's central constituency. As the quote from Pope John Paul II and the statement of the United States bishops suggests, the draft letter has yet to overcome the classist mentality that has so long afflicted the institutional model of the church. The American bishops certainly are making progress and moving away from this model, for which we would want to offer them considerable praise and support. The method of fairly wide consultation that they employed in preparing both the letter on the United States economy and the letter on the challenge of peace was a major break-through. Yet something a bit patronizing clings to the draft letter, as though the poor were unfortunates "down there" whom truly successful Christians ought to help by the principle of *noblesse oblige*. Perhaps because in Latin America the poor are the manifest majority, the Latin American liberation theologians have better closed the gap (originally perhaps even greater on their continent) between upper and lower classes. As well, they have taken bolder political stands on behalf of the poor, in the process incurring many martyrdoms. The bishops of the United States are right to be modest about their economic and political pronouncements, as they were right to be modest about their pronouncements about military strategy, when discussing technical matters. However, in our opinion they need to be bolder when discussing the political implications of the evangelical vision that motivates them to write.

For example, the bishops could do considerably more to wither the specious claims to Christian inspiration emanating from critics who are outraged that anyone would attack capitalism. Capitalism certainly has some good aspects—for example, its stimuli to creativity and enterprise—and certainly it has produced some cultural progress. But at its center is a powerful motivation nearly diametrically opposed to biblical religion. This motivation is greed. Easily indeed does the desire to heap up stores in one's barns and gather creature-comforts in fine measure become untoward and foolish. Moreover, where the New Testament God labels the person who succumbs to such a desire a fool (Luke 12:20), today's Christian analysts have forthrightly to label such a *system* foolish. More even than the decisions of individuals, the systematic arrangements through which we do most of our buying and selling determine the importance we are according to mammon. One has only to cast a critical eye at mainstream television or mainstream journalism to encounter an enormously powerful mammon driving the advertising and so much of the culture.

The bottom line of such a Christian criticism, we would say, is that an economy has first of all to target the fair and equitable prospering of all its citizenry, rather than the success of those with the most advantages and hustle. One ought of course to supply inducements for intelligence and hard work, but not to the point where the intelligent and hard-working can ride roughshod over the majority or wax fat while millions are crushed down. The well-fed critics of the bishops' pastoral letters, prospering greatly from the current economic and military arrangements, ought to be exposed as quite bogus in their claims to represent anything Christian. The quickest way to accomplish such an exposure is to place their arguments alongside the preaching of the New Testament Christ.

So doing, one finds ludicrous the notion that Christ could approve of a system that creates poverty, unemployment, and wholesale indignity for huge numbers of people, just as one finds ludicrous the notion that Christ could approve of building up nuclear arms. The entire cast of Christ's life placed him on the side of light and healing.

The Pharisees who opposed this cast in his day received the swift and stinging rough side of his tongue. The bishops come closest to this prophetic courage and candor when they call the plight of the American poor a scandal. They deserve considerable support for their stand, and considerable encouragement to extend it into an overhaul of the images of "success" that fill too many minds in today's world, not a few of them Christians'. Such an extension would take dead aim at the gilded life pushed by influential advertisers. It would say forthrightly to yuppies and guppies that they are being sold a bill of trash, being counseled to sell their birthrights for bowls of porridge. It would dash some cold water on the paeans to business being sung in the alumni magazines of Catholic colleges. It would explicitly deny the image of the bishop-prince that has prevailed throughout long portions of Western Christian history.

To be sure, this very frank analysis of cultural ideals ought to be cautious about backing particular parties and policies. Only when it has made it clear that the key is serving justice and peace, honesty and love, should an endorsement be given (as seeming to support the most likely means of bringing justice and peace a little closer). Theologians and pastors do have to guard against getting burned and so discrediting the gospel. On the other hand, they have equally to guard against tacitly supporting unjust establishments, and even more against cozying up to the affluent. All of this guarding or prudence would be made easier, of course, if the church's solidarity with the poor were obvious to one and all.

The best help for the poor, in the final analysis, is the beatitudes so central to the preaching of the synoptic Christ. Reflected upon even slightly, the beatitudes show a religious horizon intrinsically critical of all the variants of our perennial human tendency to squat down in this-worldly success. The Kingdom of God is not built of bricks of this-worldly success. The Kingdom of God is built of spirit and truth, justice and righteous suffering. Wearing a ragged coat and eating an inadequate diet do not guarantee an inclination to justice and righteous suffering. Poverty can coarsen people and set them at the edge of violence. On the other hand, poverty or suffering from injustice burns into one's soul as utterly obvious the difference between any God worthy of the name and success by worldly standards. If a given social system is tilted toward injustice, then success within that system is likely to bring one into conflict with divine standards. That is why it is easier for a camel to pass through the eye of a needle than for a rich person to enter the Kingdom of God. That is why money is the seat of so many problems. The Epistle of James, usually read as an antidote to imbalanced interpretations of "justification by faith," attacks riches forthrightly: "Let the lowly brother boast in his exaltation, and the rich in his humiliation, because like the flower of the grass he will pass away. For the sun rises with its scorching heat and withers the grass; its flower falls, and its beauty perishes. So will the rich man fade away in the midst of his pursuits" (James 1:9–11). In the background is Isaiah 40:6–8, one of the Bible's most trenchant statements of proper order, healthy spirituality. It makes a fine conclusion for any reflection on the conversions necessary if American Christians are to join Jesus in identifying themselves with the poor: "A voice says, 'Cry!' And I said, 'What shall I cry?' All flesh is grass, and all its beauty is like the flower of the field. The grass withers, the flower fades, when the breath of the Lord blows upon it; surely the people is grass. The grass withers, the flower fades; but the word of our God will stand for ever."

Building the Earth

The mission of the Christian community to proclaim the gospel and help the poor has gone forward (admittedly with varying degrees of success) throughout all the Christian centuries. The church's responsibility to help build up the earth has also gone forward, although with less clarity and enthusiasm. For while its Jewish heritage and the Incarnation gave the early church considerable impetus toward a humanism that would support all peoples' decent efforts to improve nature's flourishing and their own cultural development, an otherworldly orientation often detracted from this impetus. As we saw when considering the fall of Rome and the dark ages of the early medieval period, Christian faith often has been interpreted as having little to do with building up the earth. On the whole the fathers of the church, led by the Alexandrians, answered the supposed dilemma between Athens and Jerusalem (this-worldly faith or other-worldly faith) by coming down on the side of Athens and striving to make a Christian intellectualism. Yet the negative regard of the world evident in Tertullian, Jerome, and other fathers took its toll. For example,

Christian sexuality came under a cloud and women suffered vituperative attacks from Tertullian, Jerome, Augustine, Chrysostom, and many of the medieval and Reformation theologians. So it has not been as obvious as it might have been that Christian faith involves a strong responsibility to treasure the earth, preserve the ecosphere, and contribute to all peoples' cultural prosperity.

Today, however, the signs of the times, including most prominently the data on world poverty and global ecological disturbances, make the church's responsibilities to the earth quite apparent. Thus Pierre Teilhard de Chardin, the foremost Christian futurologist of the past generation, spontaneously constructed his spirituality in cosmological and historical terms. Teilhard would not allow the Christian to shun the realities of evolution or shirk the responsibilities that a thoroughly historical faith implies. Christians believe that the divine Word took flesh and dwelt among humanity. They believe that all creation is in labor toward an omega point where God will be all in all. The consequences they ought to draw from these aspects of their faith include a spirituality—a vibrant personal religion—that takes human work and play as crucial theaters of God's saving action.

What, though, "builds the earth" as Teilhard and other Christian futurologists understand it? Certainly proclaiming the gospel that is so radically hopeful about the world's divinely assured future. And certainly helping the poor, who otherwise may be swept aside by an uncaring, purely biological or political understanding of evolution. (One thinks of the "triage" and "lifeboat ethics" proposed by some ecologists, who think that the starvation of billions may be nature's way of keeping its systems homeostatic.) But in addition to these staples of Christian mission we seem to need a new commitment to the sanctity of life and a new dedication to helping evolution develop species more beautiful and moral.

Once again, the recent writings of the American Catholic bishops give considerable grounds for confidence. The pastoral letter on the challenges of making peace in a nuclear age directly targets the biggest threat to both the preservation and the flourishing of creation. Along with humanistic critics such as Jonathan Schell, the bishops have seen that nuclear peril dwarfs all other moral problems. Unless we avoid this peril, solve this problem, the global future hangs under a dark cloud of destructive winter. And if we are to avoid it securely, we shall have to overhaul our present ways of defending ourselves, doing business, conducting international diplomacy, and thinking about our place in evolutionary nature. In other words, not destroying the world is not enough. We have to take to heart the revelations (about our disordered current policies and self-images) latent in the nuclear peril and move to more positive commitments to build up the earth.

The church has not had a bad record in the area of war and peace, but its record in the area of ecology has been spotty at best. The traditional Christian teachings about the stringent conditions under which war may be justified, when combined with the pacifist strains in both the Bible and classical Christian theology, were a strong hindrance to destructive warfare whenever lords and military leaders had ears with which to hear. Today the question is whether nuclear weapons, so awesomely destructive, haven't rendered the just war theory obsolete. If scientists' recent speculations about nuclear winter are valid, there probably is no circumstance in which any strong use of nuclear weapons, for first or second strike, is justified, because any strong use would actually threaten most of the life of the planet. The American bishops, somewhat in advance of their fellow-bishops around the world, have tiptoed up to the threshold of condemning any use of nuclear weapons, and then by consequence any building of nuclear weapons, as grievously immoral. They have reluctantly left in place the currently dominant strategies of deterrence, which are based upon all partners to a prospective nuclear war having mutual assurance of their destruction at the hands of their opponents who are completely capable of retaliating. But these strategies are so manifestly irrational that they quickly pose the ethical question, "May one threaten what one may never legitimately do?" With a negative answer to that question there comes, of course, a veto of the current strategies and policies of deterrence. Building the earth then becomes in good part finding ways to get the nations to live together other than by threatening destruction for breaches of law, convention, or supposed national interests.

In the area of ecology the Christian populace has suffered from a certain anthropocentrism that afflicts the biblical and traditional theologies. Both have centered reality around human needs and interests, much the way that the geocentric models of the universe centered reality around the habitat of human beings. It has taken the pollution of the air, the waters, and the earth, along with the destruction of numerous species of non-human life, to shock human beings into realizing the toll that anthropocentrism can take. As a matter of fact human beings are the crucial species, the one most likely to determine the evolutionary fate of the earth, but not in a flattering way. It is rather as what ecologist Loren Eiseley called "the lethal factor" that we human beings hold the trump cards that will determine the evolutionary future. We are the species with the power to ruin the ecosystems irreparably. By our consumerist greed and waste, if not by our military madness, we are preparing scenarios of increased acid rain, a destroyed ozone layer, a greenhouse effect that melts the polar icecaps and floods huge coastal areas. Each day the newspapers seem to report some new chemical spill or discovery of a toxic dump-site. Each day nuclear power plants chug along, forcing us to contemplate the radioactive corner into which our consumerist lifestyle is painting us. Christians who do not see these issues as directly germane to their lives of faith stand well below the standards of maturity that both history and God are now asking of them. The old adolescent self-centeredness will not do. For the sake of posterity and God's creation, Christians have to grow up, learn self-restraint, think of many other things as more important than their own ease or pleasure.

It is difficult to realize our responsibilities to the future, of course, unless faith pries the present out of our greed and fixation. When the future portends nothing more godly than the past, has no overtones of a parousia and divine fulfillment, it hardly seems worth sacrificing for. To build the earth confidently and vigorously, as Teilhard saw, requires at least tacit faith that evolution will not miscarry. Christians certainly can read their faith in the resurrection of Christ as a strong pledge that evolution has been secured in God's "heaven" (the state of fulfillment to which Christ has preceded us), but one wonders how many do. More perhaps consign the future to God's hands and put their shoulders to the wheel, but just about everyone's work and social service would be enhanced by a shot of what Teilhard called "Christogenesis." This is the notion that evolutionary progress, especially in the realm of thought and culture, is building up the Body of Christ, helping creation to enter more fully into the mysterious pleroma of the risen Lord. More prosaically, it is the hope that increased interdependence will build the nations into a more peaceful and cooperative community.

We leave to others the connections to world government, genetic engineering, space exploration, and similar futuristic topics that Christogenesis ought to conjure up. As a final perspective on the mission of the contemporary Christian community, let us consider the mercuric topic of abortion. Certainly it comes to mind when one raises the matter of reverence for life. Certainly it has been linked to peacemaking through such reflections as Cardinal Bernardin's on the seamless garment that a Christian ethics rooted in reverence for God's gift of life ought to weave. And perhaps it will bridge the way to the next chapter, in which feminist perspectives on church governance will be quite prominent.

Abortion, as most essayists confess from the outset, offers the beholder few victories or reasons for cheer. In the main, the players in the stories of abortion are victims, while the tone is nearly unrelievedly tragic. This judgment, to be sure, depends upon a point of view in which the human fetus is precious. Those who can dismiss a human fetus as having none of the rights or dignities of a person will find it easier to dismiss abortion as a matter of little moment, but in fact few people are so callous or superficial. The majority even of those who consider abortion licit in certain circumstances grieve that the child must be destroyed. They see abortion as the lesser of two evils, having judged that in some cases to have the child would lead to greater woes. They have little doubt, however, that what human beings conceive is at least postentially a person, for they take the commonsensical view that a normal conception only needs nine healthy months to generate a human person. (We ourselves would place personhood soon after conception, precisely to protect fetal life.)

It is hard to think of the church's mission to build the earth as supporting anything like easy abortion. Easy abortion virtually guarantees a devaluation of human life, with dire consequences for a people's views of war, murder, and human beings' general expendability. What one might call "hard" abortion—abortion under very restricted circumstances—entails more ethical problems. Certainly rape, incest, or carrying a child known to be genetically defective is a more complicated case. Similarly, the abortions that in effect are contraceptions differ from the abortions that come as the last resort of otherwise responsible sexual partners. The broadsides of right-to-life groups that admit none of these distinctions, or that fail to appreciate the conscientious struggles that many women who choose abortion have gone through, do little to help create the optimal climate for discussing the public policies our pluralistic countries should develop. "The right to life," too, runs the danger of becoming absolute in an idolatrous way.

Merely to raise these few of the many dimensions of the debate about abortion is to come close to confessing that one has no easy sureties or wisdoms about how to lessen the tragedies. Probably it would be very helpful virtually to prohibit abortion as a morally acceptable choice, but probably it would not be helpful to make this into a legal or criminal prohibition. This disjunction itself is debatable, of course, and we can only propose it tentatively. We do propose it because our general impression of God's way of dealing with human beings is that the Spirit most significantly works through individual people's concrete consciences. Admittedly, this does not mean that murder, theft, and the other breaches of ethical conduct that we proscribe (saying that the Spirit hardly could inspire them) should not be forbidden by legal codes that have criminal sanctions. When a society agrees that a given action is hurtful and threatens its health, that society rightfully passes laws and sanctions against it. However, when a society is divided about the hurtfulness or criminality of a given action, usually it is the part of prudence and wisdom to refrain from passing laws and sanctions until the division of opinion has dissolved.

It is not easy to decide the state of public opinion in large societies, of course, let alone to decide when a deep division has been resolved. Public opinion polls have a limited utility, for they seldom present a problem in its proper complexity. The general impression one receives nowadays about abortion is that the American populace is genuinely divided. The majority certainly consider abortion morally objectionable, but it is not at all clear what legal and criminal consequences they think should be drawn. So many of the women, or couples, brought to the point of abortion are reluctant, wishing there were another viable option, that introducing criminal sanctions, or even legal prohibitions, seems only to compound the problem. Whether abortions should qualify for payment out of public funds is a significant collateral issue. Perhaps such funds should be limited according to an estimate of the fraction of the taxpaying population that approves of public payment. But this notion, too, has its difficulties, running into the general question of how to admit exceptions to overall public policies (for instance, conscientious objection to military draft or to paying taxes to support a buildup of nuclear arms).

The best "solutions" therefore clearly run to a level deeper or prior to the level of law and politics. The church probably will best accomplish its ends by a kindly, patient, reasoned analysis of the dangers latent in permissive abortion, combined with a series of practical helps—with sex education, contraception, perhaps in some situations sterilization, and adoption—that both decrease the incidence of unwanted pregnancies and increase the options that women contemplating abortion have. The demographic and ecological facts of current life make it clear that the human race either will control its increases in population or face massive social problems. The advances of women toward sexual equality with men, when combined with their more central involvement in birth and childrearing, make it clear that women should have the stronger say in how this population control ought to be accomplished. Churches that do not listen to the people most directly involved in population control, but rather try to dictate ethical theory from on high, are not likely to be maximally helpful. Churches that trust their common people to take the full responsibility for sexuality and generativity that the Spirit clearly wants will greatly serve the building of the earth. To make such trust practical, their best resorts likely will be extensions of the evangelical preaching and care for the poor that their overall missionary self-understanding has made primary. In other words, even with such a difficult problem as abortion their first instinct will be to speak of the love of Christ that never fails and of the solidarity with the poor that spiced all of Christ's prophecy.

Summary

We have been considering the missionary dimension of the Christian community, using three main headings. First, we studied the church's imperative to herald the good news by which it stands, the glad tidings of the resurrection of Jesus Christ. A church whose worship does not send it out in joyous proclamation had best reconsider its worship. We noted some of the scriptural foundations for the church's evangelical proclamation, and then we reflected on the missionary presence that groups such as the Little Brothers and Sisters of Jesus have stressed. This in turn helped us appreciate the quite ordinary, every-day aspects of Christian mission, where the basic task is to help others find their burdens bearable, their lives ultimately summoning gratitude. The grace of God always precedes missionaries, and even an apparent lack of meaning or joy can be a form of the divine presence.

Our second main topic was helping the poor, especially those suffering from material want. We noted the church's interest in the injustices and disparities in wealth that bring so much secular division. We also noted the holism of Christ's attacks on injustice and sin. The American Catholic bishops' pastoral letter on the United States economy furnished us both some hopeful signs and considerable stimuli to reflection. The "option for the poor" praised by both the bishops and Pope John Paul II recalls the deep commitment of the Latin American bishops at Medellín, while the understanding of a successful economy that the letter presents implies quite a critical stand toward capitalism. We noted some of the traditional Christian dicta that subordinate material means to humane and religious ends, and then we considered the affiliations and disagreements between Christian ideals and the historical socialisms and communisms. Last, we opined that the bishops would do well to criticize more pointedly the luxury and mammon dominating so many Americans' idea of success.

Our last missionary topic was "building the earth." We reflected on the problem of nuclear war, making it the main impediment to current evolutionary progress. Once again, the American bishops' recent pastoral teaching served us as a hopeful and stimulating guide. We then turned to ecological matters, calling for a less anthropocentric Christian faith. Teilhard de Chardin served us well at several points, especially in the links he forged between physical evolution and Christogenesis. Our final consideration was the knotted problem of abortion, which certainly any program to reverence life and build up creation has to treat. We found few obvious solutions, tending to prefer moral and religious means to laws or criminal sanctions. Probably Christian missionaries best alleviate problems such as abortion by helping people gain the moral maturity, the sensitivity to the Holy Spirit, that makes most of the objectionable options unthinkable or unnecessary.

STUDY QUESTIONS

1. What were the key features of the missionary activity of the worker-priest Egide van Broeckhoven?
2. How does a conviction about God's priority tend to orient Christian missionary activity?
3. What are the advantages in Jesus' holistic approach to poverty, injustice, and sin?
4. What are the goals of the economic systems that Christian social thought can support?
5. What do the scenarios of nuclear winter imply for the Christian mission to build up the earth?
6. Compare ecological pollution and abortion as evolutionary crises.

NOTES

1. Rosemary Haughton, THE PASSIONATE GOD. New York: Paulist, 1981, pp. 312–313.

2. See Chaim Potok, MY NAME IS ASHER LEV. New York: Alfred A. Knopf, 1972.

3. United States Catholic Bishops, "Pastoral Letter on Social Teachings and the U.S. Economy," no. 53. THE NATIONAL CATHOLIC REPORTER, November 23, 1984, p. 14.

4. Ibid., no. 77, p. 15.

Chapter 7

Governance

Serving the Community ◆ Teaching the Faith ◆ Ministering Reconciliation ◆ Summary, Study Questions, Notes

Serving the Community

All the models of the church that are influential in current ecclesiology stress both worship and mission. Virtually without dissent, theologians and ordinary laypeople agree that the community of Christ is unfaithful to its Master when it does not gather regularly to pray and go forth to extend Christ's work. Where both the models and further discussions of the nature or work of the church tend to become controversial is in their implications for church governance. Rather distressingly, Christians historically have shown themselves little better than their secular counterparts in squabbling over institutional power. So the issues of order and polity have contributed as much to Christian disunity as all the doctrinal issues put together. The church has been all too human in its inability to handle problems of law and authority.

For a contemporary theologian such as Karl Rahner, whose sacramental view of the church we have used on several occasions, the best way to regard church power is to keep it quite modest. Power or authority in the community of Christ exists only to enable the church to carry out its key tasks or self-expressions of worship and mission. Bishops, presbyters, and others who hold official responsibility therefore should think of themselves as overseers or facilitators. They are doing their work well when the community is praying deeply and showing itself full of missionary zeal. They are doing their work badly when lines of communication grow jammed, hunger for worship lags, or Christians feel little imperative to proclaim the gospel in season and out. This is a rather straightforward, pragmatic test, in line with Jesus' own dictum that "you will know them by their fruits" (Matthew 7:16).

In a sacramental ecclesiology, therefore, ordination to authority and responsibility in the church is quite functional. One may speak of charismata or gifts of the Spirit that help people accomplish such responsibility, but these merely range themselves alongside such other gifts as wisdom, counsel, prophecy, and so forth. The people who hold authority differ little from the rest of the Christian community. The rest may seem more oriented to the outside, insofar as their missionary imperatives are the basic way that the community will be that city on the hill illumining what all human communities can become. But the more inward orientation of church officials should keep the community's generally outward orientation well in mind. When authority starts to forget the church's overall mission, making infra-ecclesiastical business the community's dominant concern, it has begun to default on its largely instrumental vocation.

This is to say, then, that church leaders are much more like the rest of the community than unlike them. It is to make such sacraments as baptism and the eucharist more basic than the sacrament of holy orders (the rite by which the church commissions its leaders). And it is to deny or call aberrant distinctions between clergy and laity such as those described by Popes Gregory XVI ("No one can deny that the Church is an unequal society in which God destined some to be governors and others to be servants. The latter are the laity; the former, the clergy") and Pius X ("Only the college of pastors have the right and authority to lead and govern. The masses have no right or authority except that of being governed, like an obedient flock that follows its Shepherd").[1]

Not only do views such as these run counter to the basic sacramentality, and so ground-level authority (to worship and exercise Christian missions), of the Christian community. They also run counter to the scriptural imagery bequeathed us by the New Testament. There Jesus explicitly rejects worldly notions of authority and class divisions, proposing that the leaders in his community ought mainly to think of themselves as servants. Of the several texts that one might cite, Mark 10:35–45 can serve our argument: "And James and John, the sons of Zebedee, came forward to him, and said to him,

'Teacher, we want you to do for us whatever we ask of you.' And he said to them, 'What do you want me to do for you?' And they said to him, 'Grant us to sit, one at your right hand and one at your left, in your glory.' But Jesus said to them, 'You do not know what you are asking. Are you able to drink the cup that I drink, or to be baptized with the baptism with which I am baptized?' And they said to him, 'We are able.' And Jesus said to them, 'The cup that I drink you will drink; and with the baptism with which I am baptized, you will be baptized; but to sit at my right hand or at my left hand is not mine to grant, but it is for those for whom it has been prepared.' And when the ten heard it, they began to be indignant at James and John. And Jesus called them to him and said to them, 'You know that those who are supposed to rule over the Gentiles lord it over them, and their great men exercise authority over them. But it shall not be so among you; but whoever would be great among you must be your servant, and whoever would be first among you must be slave of all. For the Son of man also came not to be served but to serve, and to give his life as a ransom for many.' "

In its liturgy for Holy Thursday, the church catholic has recalled both this general memory of Jesus' view of authority and Jesus' example of washing the feet of his disciples (see John 13:3–15). Thus the person presiding at the liturgy is to wash the feet of representatives of the community at large. Alan Paton has shown the explosive power of this symbolism in his wonderful novel of apartheid South Africa, AH, BUT YOUR LAND IS BEAUTIFUL. There a distinguished white judge washes the feet of the black woman who has taken care of his children for many years. It is a simple enough gesture, one that over the centuries has helped Christians recall their basic equality before God and the ministerial character of all Christian faith. But in a land where distinctions between races have become supposedly predestined, rooted in God's eternity, it is a startling rebuke to the leaders of the establishment. At a stroke, it levels their pretensions to be sanctioned by the biblical Christ or to be carrying out a divine commission. By their fruits of arrogance, racism, and self-importance, the white establishment is shown to be unChristian. Paton suggests the problems that such dramatically biblical expressions of Christian service give regimes like that of Pretoria: "And on Saturday two of the great papers of the world, THE TIMES of London and the NEW YORK TIMES, told the story. Stories like that place the South African ambassador in Washington in a most unsatisfactory position. In the White House such an event is regarded as a redeeming act in the history of a wayward nation, but in the embassy it is regarded as an act destructive of the tireless propaganda that goes out in praise of separate coexistence and separate education and separate worship and separate lavatorial accommodation."[2]

Of course, the egalitarian or ministerial (servant) character of Christian faith and authority is meant to be destructive of all the tireless propaganda, inside the church and outside, that denies the radical equality of human beings and the cruciform pattern of God's redeeming love. Jesus came into conflict with the religious establishment of his day, in which class distinctions were significant, because he championed the common people and kowtowed not a whit to the scribes and Pharisees. Christians distinguished themselves in the Roman empire for their egalitarian love, and their ranks swelled because they admitted all people, including women and slaves, as equal in dignity before God. True enough, by the second century church fathers such as Ignatius of Antioch were writing paeans to the the office of the bishop and centering the church around episcopal leadership. But one must recall that Ignatius' bishop held primacy mainly in his willingness to suffer martyrdom for the faith. In no way was he a power-bearer on the model of secular power-bearers bent on polishing their own privileges and distinctions.

The symbol of a servant leadership is tricky, of course, and church leaders may be excused some of their historical failures. Common people tend to foist upon their leaders baggage accumulated in struggles with parents and school teachers. They also tend to crave the pomp and ceremony that a sacral view of Christian religion can create. Then the leaders of Christian communities become like the leaders of pagan religions, standing between heaven above and earth below as channels of divine power. The Pharaoh who mediated *maat* (divine power and order) to the people of millennial Egypt is one of the purest examples of this cosmological mythology. Not occasionally Christian popes and bishops have been conceived on the analogy of the Pharaoh or the high priests of the Roman Empire. As "Vicar of Christ on earth," for instance, the Pope sometimes has seemed a highly sacralized, even an infallible connection between heaven and earth. At such times the other description of the Bishop of Rome, that he should be the servant of the servants of God, has kept its light under a bushel.

In our time the ministerial character of church authority especially comes to grief on the issues of women's ordination and celibacy. The Roman Catholic and Eastern Orthodox churches suffer many problems of credibility because of their restrictions that limit priestly ordination to unmarried men. (In the case of orthodoxy, married men may be ordained priests but may not be ordained bishops.) Contemporary sensibilities view these restrictions as prejudicial and unjust. Indeed, they are major reasons that the majority of feminists consider the Christian church a sexist institution. Respectable studies such as Edward Schillebeeckx's MINISTRY: LEADERSHIP IN THE COMMUNITY OF JESUS CHRIST[3] indicate the ritualistic foundations of the traditional exclusions. Christianity took from Judaism a sense of ritualistic purity that made it feel its priests should distance themselves from sexual activity. Such activity, like a number of other bodily functions, was perceived to be polluting—to render the person unfit for contact with the holy God. The Christian leaders, lawyers, and theologians who elaborated this instinct into requirements of celibacy and maleness seem rather completely to have forgotten the Incarnation that ought to have been the distinctive feature of their divinity. Had they taken the enfleshment of God's Word fully to heart, they could never have considered femininity or sexual love an impediment to liturgical leadership, let alone to Christian leadership in general.

In saying this we do not forget that Jesus himself was a male and that there is no evidence that Jesus married. Rather we imply that Jesus' maleness and single status were accidental, compared to his complete humanity. However more ordered Jesus' humanity may have been than our sinful own, it was not a real humanity unless it carried with it things that a pollution-minded sense of religion tends to call impediments to union with God: sweat, blood, excrement, sperm, physical dirt, and more. So it was not Christian instincts that led to the historical reservation of official leadership in the Christian community to unmarried men so much as instincts adopted from the surrounding Jewish or Hellenistic worlds. The irony is that this effort to purify the priesthood so often led to segregating it from the people it was supposed to serve. That in itself would have shown a pragmatic church authority it was on the wrong track, but often the authority of the church has forgotten Jesus' criterion and tried to know itself by standards other than the fruits it was generating.

Today a further irony appears. The profiles of church leaders most praised in our time turn out to be stereotypically feminine. Somewhat the way that the washing of the feet should embarrass a leadership grown unservant, the stereotypically feminine profile of the best church leadership ought to embarrass a sexist church authority structure. For every time that they advance personalist values, make themselves enablers or mediators, minister reconciliation, and in general conceive of their main task as nurturing people's faith, church leaders fill out patterns historically more attributable to women than to men. Every time they move away from highly rationalized, bureaucratic, adversarial, or legalistic procedures, they affirm the ways of Taoists and women, rather than the ways of Christian crusaders and power-politicking men. For these ways to have become the standard call of contemporary church reformers while women continue to be forbidden access to official church power in two-thirds of the Christian churches is either tragic or humorous, depending upon one's given dispositions.

To serve the church in a post-modern time, when personalist values, ecological networks, the dysfunctions of power-politics and brutality, and women's raised consciousness have all considerably clarified, authorities simply have to begin to repent of their historical sexism and indenture to overly institutional models. Again and again one hears both angry and sad laments that the official or institutional leadership of the church greatly lags behind the instincts of today's most admirable human beings, Christians and non-Christians alike. For example, in the stories of child abuse by priests that began to be widely known in 1985, a regular refrain of the distraught parents was the impersonal and ineffective response of chancery officials. The pathology of the priests was bad enough, but the refusal of many bishops to deal with the parents straightforwardly, in the ways that a non-institutional model of the church would dictate, was what brought the parents to seek redress in the civil courts. The bishops and other church leaders seemed to place the welfare of the abused children and their parents second to an effort to avoid scandal or any tainting of the church's institutional image. They dealt in "damage control" rather than Christian charity. And they reaped exactly what they deserved: alienation and lawsuits.

There is no saying, of course, that more democratic standards for admission to the priesthood would have completely avoided this problem. Every dictate of common sense, however, is that whatever would humanize the priesthood would lessen such pathology. Equally, whatever would move church authorities to think of their community as a fellowship of disciples, rather than as another institution shaped by the forces of money and advertising, would greatly help both to prevent such problems from occurring and to alleviate the distress they cause when they do occur. Few Christians or other people of good will are surprised by human weakness. Few have any long-lasting inclination to damn people who fail, even in serious moral matters, rather than to try to help them. A servant authority loves this better instinct of so many people and does its best both to nurture it and to keep faith with it. Keeping faith with it would mean explaining the facts to aggrieved parties such as the parents, keeping them informed of what is being done to prevent occurrences in the future, and working with them to obtain the therapies that hold out the best hope of healing for all involved: children and parents first, but also offending priests and church authorities culpable by virtue of their inaction.

It does not speak against this sort of reform or movement toward a more ministerial church authority to cite traditionalists such as Mother Teresa of Calcutta or Pope John Paul II who manifest considerable humanity through conservative religious forms or conservative understandings of church authorities. Not to put too fine a point on it: the humanism of such people occurs despite their notions of how Christian authority must be exercised, not because of them. Analyzed carefully, the humanism in fact calls for forms of authority that are not impersonal, that do consult with laypeople, and that level all institutional roadblocks to justice and love.

Teaching the Faith

To govern the community of Christ well, one must secure a leadership that not only is ministerial but also is wise. The prospering of the church in worship and mission depends on its close connection with the truth that makes it free. Consequently, from as early as the Pastoral Epistles the church worried about sound doctrine and took steps to protect it. The rise of bishops to special authority in the church was in good part an effort to localize and strengthen a magisterial agency that could effectively oppose heretics. The development of a Christian canon of Scripture and the solemn definitions of official church dogma in ecumenical councils sought the same ends. Jesus was remembered to have been a teacher, as well as a prophet, healer, and suffering servant. The Holy Spirit left to the church by the risen Christ was conceived as the first of the community's resources, the main provenance of the inward anointing in truth that could keep the community faithful to its Master and Lord.

It makes sense, therefore, that the hierarchical leaders of the church have considered the defense of the faith one of their major responsibilities. Even when such defense has turned the church toward a conservative bureaucracy, sympathetic viewers could understand the good intentions behind the perhaps quite faulty practices. And, of course, the rights and responsibilities of church leaders to safeguard strong doctrine and command a docile (which should not mean a mindless or uncritical) hearing completely continue today.

One sees a clear expression of this conviction, and a very creative use of it to further ecumenical unity among the different Christian bodies, in the challenging book of Heinrich Fries and Karl Rahner, UNITY OF THE CHURCHES: AN ACTUAL POSSIBILITY. The authors present eight theses whose acceptance and implementation they feel would allow the churches to achieve substantial reunification. The first thesis expresses the minimal doctrinal agreement necessary for serious Christian ecumenism: "The fundamental truths of Christianity, as they are expressed in Holy Scripture, in the Apostles' Creed, and in that of Nicaea and Constantinople, are binding on all partner churches of the one Church to be."[4] The second thesis expresses the opinion that, beyond this minimal doctrinal agreement, no partner church may reject decisively or confessionally what another partner church proposes to its members as binding dogma. In explanation of this second thesis, Karl Rahner calls upon the "epistemological tolerance" that the knowledge explosion and the speedup of history have forced upon us. Today no one can be a universal scholar, able to master all the bodies of knowledge relevant to any significant judgment in matters of serious human import. All of us have been forced to confess a greater mysteriousness in both creation and the divine plan of salvation. Thus even church officials and theologians have to go more cautiously and patiently with opinions of people outside their own ecclesiastical community that at first blush appear unacceptable. Only after considerable study and discussion can they even come close to deciding whether or not such opinions could be compatible with healthy Christian faith.

All the more must theologians and church leaders go slowly and gently with positions that other Christian communities in good faith have imposed upon their adherents as doctrinally binding. In Rahner's use of epistemological tolerance, the churches emerge better able to put up with confessional differences than they were in the eleventh, or the sixteenth, or even in the nineteenth century: "From the viewpoint of dogma, a unity of the churches is already possible today with this kind of epistemological tolerance. A consequence of this tolerance is that one does not cram radically contradictory but definite and explicit teachings together, and yet one makes room for the not-yet-agreed-upon but nevertheless acknowledged as agreed-upon. This sentence may seem daring, utopian, and perhaps even dogmatically controversial. But if one rejects the notion that a unification of the churches is simply impossible in today's intellectual-political circumstances—a notion surely prohibited by the fundamental convictions of Christianity and the Church—then one will have to admit that in today's intellectual climate no unity in faith is possible other than the one just proposed. Therefore it must be legitimate."[5]

Ecumenical doctrinal unity of course must be a major concern of the magisterium or ecclesiastical teaching office, because doctrinal division so badly blurs the church's mission to proclaim the gospel. Historically, the heretical and schismatic splits within the church have greatly hindered the acceptance of the gospel both in the church's cultural basin of Europe and in the fields of foreign missions. Thus serious and creative proposals such as those of Fries and Rahner deserve both welcome and hopeful study. If respected, indeed revered theologians can cut a path through the jungle of sectarianism that has so badly wounded the modern church, the people who have the overall responsibility of serving the church's progress had best get a move on.

The reality, unfortunately, appears to be that the theologians involved in ecumenical discussions have progressed far beyond what such general church leaders are willing to act upon. In bilateral and multilateral studies, theological representatives of most of the main Christian bodies have hammered out substantial agreements on almost all the topics that historically were the causes or occasions of the great church divisions. Thus the trinitarian question of the *filioque,*

with its division of East and West on the matter of how the procession
of the Spirit within the eternal divine mystery relates to the Father
and the Son, today seems reduced to manageable proportions. By a
principle such as the Fries-Rahner second thesis, Roman Catholics
and Eastern Orthodox could both retain their traditional interpretations yet move forward toward actual ecclesiastical reunion. The same
judgment would seem to hold for such historically divisive matters as
justification by faith and the relative authorities of Scripture and tradition. Protestant and Roman Catholic theologians have virtually buried the disagreements that caused such strife in the sixteenth century.
Even on the probably more rudimentary disagreements about church
authority and the Petrine ministry exercised by the Bishop of Rome
the theologians have come up with creative formulas holding great
promise of letting the churches reunite in good conscience. But the
leaders of the main ecclesiastical bodies hold back from acting upon
these formulas, so reunion remains more a dream than a process making steady progress.

It is hard to condemn the top leaders of the churches for trying
to be patient and prudent, of course. Very large issues indeed are in
question. But it is also hard not to fault such leaders as having too
negative or conservative an understanding of their responsibilities to
teach the faith. "The faith" is not a deposit in a bank account that
automatically earns interest year after year. It is the living self-understanding of Christ's people, which either advances or recedes, depending upon a given generation's circumstances, gifts from the
Spirit, courage, and abilities to discern the signs of the times. Certain
central matters give the church stability, but even they have to be re-
translated for each generation. Otherwise the community will not
make Jesus contemporary or experience what salvation can mean for
the present day.

Thus, we think church leaders would be wise to teach the faith
more mystagogically, focusing on the central mysteries of the trinity,
grace, and the Incarnation, and letting the epistemological tolerance
of which Rahner speaks permit them to bracket definitive judgments
in areas of new research. They might then be able to follow the principle of Gamaliel (Acts 5:34–39) and let the work of a Küng, a Schillebeeckx, or a Boff run the gauntlet of experience, both academic and
pastoral, before condemning it.

Much the same advice comes to mind when one contemplates the mandate of the contemporary church to teach about morals. Parallel to the way that today's epistemological situation cautions teachers to home in on the central mystery in virtue of which all Christian doctrine stands clear or confused, today's moral situation bids teachers loosen the hold of laws that are quite historically conditioned and take aim rather at invigorating the charity and prudence that inform all healthy Christian ethics. The result could be that the church would better take to heart its own wise motto "in necessary things, unity; in doubtful things, liberty; in all things, charity."

One thinks, for example, of the harm done, the credibility wounded, by such recent moral teachings as Pope Paul VI's encyclical against artificial birth control and by the edict of the Sacred Congregation for the Doctrine of the Faith against the ordination of women. Both documents asserted as necessary teachings things the Christian community as a whole found contingent or relative or historically conditioned. Both did not win the agreement of the theological community, let alone the agreement of the people most directly affected (Christian spouses and women). The result was a several-sided injury to the church's moral authority. The Christian community as a whole perceived the teaching office of the Roman Catholic church to be arbitrary, nonconsultative, and out of touch with the most creative movements in its own constituency. The right-wing portion of this constituency, to be sure, praised the documents as reasserting traditional wisdom and discipline. However, a teaching authority that pleases only its right-wing, conservative constituency is in bad shape. Unless it can capture the middle ground, winning the support of all but the most extreme conservatives or innovators, it should look itself in the mirror and go back to the drawing board.

By contrast, the good reception given the two recent documents of the American Catholic bishops that we have already cited shows that these bishops' teaching authority is in quite healthy shape. No doubt part of the good reception came from the tentative nature of the bishops' expositions, which frankly acknowledged the complexity of the issues they were treating. Another part certainly came from the wide consultation the bishops employed. Because of it all parts of the spectrum of Christian opinion could feel they had had at least some input. No one claims that either the document on peacemaking in a nuclear age or the (first draft of the) document on the United States economy is perfect. But both documents deserved the high marks they generally received because they showed the magisterium proceeding as Christian wisdom suggests it should: humbly, respectfully, reasonably, and prophetically. And the effect, we would venture to say, was a considerable increase in the respect and docility that the magisterium in fact should command.

We focus on these four cases from recent Roman Catholic ventures in pastoral teaching because our book is oriented toward our own Roman Catholic community. It would be easy, however, to find documents from other churches deserving warm praise because of their courageous efforts to bring traditional faith abreast of current times. For example, the agencies of the World Council of Churches have done yeoman work on the issues of ecology and technology, far outdistancing anything that Roman Catholic agencies have accomplished.[6] Such documents of individual Protestant churches as that of the American Friends on peace in the Middle East can serve all other Christians as wonderful exemplars of what traditional Christian moral instinct can become, when it stays in close touch with the parts of the world most longing for redemption.[7]

We do not mean, either, to neglect the contributions of individual Christian writers, who often are well in advance of their church communities. Thus Alan Paton, whose most recent novel on South Africa we quoted, has probably done more to express the proper Christian moral judgments on apartheid than all the official Christian agencies put together. Somewhat parallel has been the work of the Jewish novelist Elie Wiesel, without which we no doubt would have a considerably duller appreciation of the depth and implications of the Nazi holocaust of so many millions, both Jews and non-Jews.

Only a rather rigidly institutional view of the church would not admit an Alan Paton or an Alexsandr Solzhenitsyn as an authoritative teacher of Christian morality. As long as an appreciation of charismatic teaching authority remains, such people will be honored as doctors and prophets. Similarly, only a viciously restrictive reading of the traditional notion that outside the church there is no salvation would back away from the wisdom of a Wiesel and not consider it a vehicle of divine truth for our time. What Cardinal Newman called "the sense of the faithful" is always subtler and more inventive than the sense of orthodoxy or wisdom enshrined in the church's official teachers. If only because the faithful so greatly outnumber the members of the official magisterium, the Spirit plays more variations in their midst than Rome or Geneva can know. The wisest teaching authorities, in our opinion, do their best to stir up the gifts of the faithful, to help more and more of the faithful become mature and take charge of their own moral lives. A teaching authority that tries to lay down a universal law, or that seems to disregard the gifts of ordinary Christians to discern what love demands in their own concrete circumstances, loses effectiveness precisely in the measure that people come of age in their faith.

St. Augustine is famous for many dicta, but at this juncture one of them seems irresistibly obvious: "Love and do what you will." Certainly this dictum is easily abused, and probably Augustine had no disregard of the official teaching authority in mind. That said, however, it remains true that his dictum gives a priority to individual conscience and the inspiration of the Holy Spirit that Christian tradition as a whole has found highly salutary. For example, the sacramental dealing with sin that focused in penance was based on the individual penitent's self-accusation. The moral codes and catalogues had their place, as did the advice of the confessor, but in the final analysis only the individual was judged competent to say how clear the issues had been and what degree of freedom had been available. Somewhat the same way, the traditional Christian principle of subsidiarity, which said that matters ought to be carried out on the lowest or most local level possible, rather than being referred to higher authorities, spotlighted the significance of concrete, existential information and intuition. General authorities usually are wise to confine themselves to general principles. For the discernment of spirits in particular, specific cases, one has to be on the spot, know the issues at first hand.

This means, of course, that the only truly effective Christian doctrinal or moral teaching is that which enables individuals to decide well for themselves. As long as truths, doctrinal or moral, remain heteronomous to the majority—something "out there" best left to officialdom—Christian teaching must account itself a failure. In this it is not different from other forms of teaching, of course, for no thoughtful teacher wants mere regurgitation or knowledge gained from reference books. All parents and teachers of any maturity know that their charges should be led into greater and greater personal competence and responsibility. Relatedly, all know that laws and principles can never be sufficiently flexible to cover all cases. Only people who have discerned the general drift of the laws, their overall goals and as-

sumptions, stand a chance of becoming responsible citizens, whatever
the community in question. The glory of the magisterium is the many
times it has nurtured such Christian citizens.

Ministering Reconciliation

The third aspect of church governance that needs attention today
is the ministry of reconciliation. As is true of the first and second aspects we have treated, serving the community and teaching the faith,
it is both a responsibility of all Christians and a special charge laid
upon church leaders. Just as all Christians should think of themselves
as obligated to care for the needs of the church and bring up to date
the teaching in which the church has expressed its convictions about
salvation, so all Christians should think of themselves as peace-mak-
ers, reconcilers, mediators who can help rebuild broken bridges between God and human beings as well as among human beings
themselves. Nonetheless, those ordained for leadership in the Christian community have a special or more formally sacramental responsibility to minister reconciliation. In the sacrament of penance they
help people reknit the moral fabric rent by sin. In the sacrament of
the eucharist they celebrate God's redemptive acts, by which the deepest human alienations were overcome. Indeed, all official proclamation of the gospel and help of the poor involves reconciliation, since all
involves trying to reveal the causes of human disorder and reset people's bones for health.

One of the most comprehensive treatments of Christian ministry, Bernard Cooke's MINISTRY TO WORD AND SACRAMENTS, sees reconciliation as both part of the biblical perception of how to heal social
existence and a key aspect of the priestly ministry of building community despite the power of evil. As Cooke puts it, "When we apply
the notion of healing to the social existence of man, we are in contact
with the biblical category of 'reconciliation.' One can see how basic
this ideal is in New Testament thought about salvation when one recalls that the opposite notion, 'alienation,' is the most basic scriptural
designation for sin. If sin is alienation of man from God, of man from
his fellow man, of man from his true self, then salvation must consist
in healing each of these three cleavages; it must involve a threefold
reconciliation.

"Because of the mysterious power of evil, the priestly ministry of building community must be one of achieving reconciliation. The work of Jesus himself was clearly seen in this light by the New Testament writers, perhaps most especially by Paul. Christ's ministry, particularly the supreme service of his death and resurrection, accomplished the reconciliation of men to his Father; it broke down the barriers of division between Jew and Gentile, between social and economic classes, between men and women (Gal. 3:28)."[8]

How ought we most profitably to regard this sinful alienation and gracious reconciliation that biblical theology makes so central to the ministry of Christ, and so to the ministry of the church? Probably as exchanges, "economic" activities, in a system of love. The sinful alienation that cleaves the relationship between God and human beings boils down to a refusal to love. God is always loving, always creative and offering partnership with human beings. We could not presume or assume that God should be so, but the entire burden of revelation forces us to say that God is so. For Christians, the fullest declaration of God's loving nature was the death and resurrection of Christ, through which God worked the definitive conquest of sinful alienation. Where human beings previously had regularly held back, closing themselves to God's creative and restorative love, God used the full humanity of Christ to gain a complete "yes" to the divine loving purposes and so to reset humanity in a new relationship with the divine. If "Adam" could symbolize previous humanity, somehow twisted away from God in its roots, Christ could symbolize a recreated humanity whose roots were straight and responsive to their Creator's love. True enough, human beings retain the capacity to close themselves off from God's love. We can refuse to see our lives as gifts and treasures, refuse to view creation as a marvelous outpouring of the divine beauty. Mired in suffering, well aware of how mottled and hurtful many human experiences can be, we easily lose heart and curse the day we were born.

The church opposes this discouragement, infiltrating hope and renewal, by drawing us back to the love poured forth in our hearts by the Holy Spirit, the love so dramatically displayed by Christ on the cross. In each fruitful sermon, each salutary sacrament, all penetrating teaching, the church explicates the symbol of Christ the new Adam by pointing to both the traditional bases and the contemporary experiences that encourage us to trust that the divine mystery is a pure love.

This may seem rather recondite theology but in fact it is as simple and obvious as the most humble forgiveness that friends or spouses extend to one another, the most ordinary renewal of any sinner's heart. When we were sinners, people closed in on ourselves and not wanting the vistas of the divine love, God continued to love us. When we were sulking or hurt or nursing our grievances, God's was the voice that urged us to stop rubbing salt in our wounds, accept the fact that our friend or lover was weak and deserved our forgiveness.

That is the leitmotif of the human side of reconciliation. If the divine side shows a God only capable of wanting our good, always acting toward us like the good father in Luke's parable of the prodigal son (Luke 15:11–32), the human side shows people who all have sinned and fallen short of the divine glory, who never are not in need of forgiveness. Taken together, the God who always makes the sun to shine and the rain to fall on just and unjust alike and the human partner always in need of forgiveness offer humanity the crucial solution to its most destructive incapacity or weakness. Again and again we human beings fail. By stupidity or moral weakness, we do not do the good we ought to do or we do do the evil we ought not to do. Had God not intervened to offer us a mechanism for overcoming our failures, for getting our train back on the track, we would be condemned to slide further and further into alienation.

But God has offered us such a mechanism, and little is more basic to the mission of the Christian community than getting human beings to use it. The mechanism is displayed as early and dramatically as the description of the beginnings of Jesus' ministry in the Gospel of Mark: "Now after John was arrested, Jesus came into Galilee, preaching the gospel of God, and saying, 'The time is fulfilled, and the kingdom of God is at hand; repent, and believe in the gospel" (Mark 1:14–15). If people will repent, be converted or turned around, and believe in the good news of God, they can haul themselves out of their deadends, make new beginnings and set out again for the common life they know they ought to be building.

The roots of alienation are the forgetfulness, self-concern, and closure of heart that keep us from making the divine love that is the core of the good news our sovereign treasure. When that love stands front and center, almost all the things that trouble us fade into insignificance. We are humbled by our distance from the divine goodness, so we are not surprised that other people also show themselves to be sinners. Even the hurts we suffer from other people, the quite objective evils and injuries, fade considerably, for we are able to recall what other people did to Jesus, the pioneer of our hopes for heaven and the one who sacrificed himself on our behalf. Jesus did not experience life to be a picnic or unadulterated success. He drew close to the ugliest features of human beings, often breathing in the rank stench of the satanic lovelessness. Few of us have more than the slightest sense of the horrors that Jesus intuited. Few of us, therefore, have any excuse for not trying to forgive others seventy times seven and make the church a community conspicuous for fostering new beginnings.

In the light shed by the sacramental model of the church, reconciliation becomes one of the main services that the Christian community offers the entire world. Christian leaders who focus on ministering reconciliation, and Christian laypeople who take such a ministry to heart, bring to the consciousness of the world at large a quite other-worldly potential. For the world at large at most pays lip-service to the idea of rooting out animosities, hatreds, and bloodlust. It sees the internecine strife of the African tribes, or the Middle Eastern nations, or the groups in Northern Ireland as remnants of the jungle or proclivities of the human heart that any realistic politics has to assume will stay in place. The forgiveness that Christ depicts in the Sermon on the Mount therefore comes as a startling revelation. When the church can draw close enough to its master to minister or mediate such forgiveness, its other-worldly, truly holy origins shine forth in unwonted splendor.

Recall the vigor with which Christ taught his disciples the reconciliation implied by the coming of the Kingdom of God. Whereas Torah in the past had sought an admirable justice, the advent of the Kingdom prompted Jesus to say something more. Like a new Moses, Jesus enounces for his community a constitutional law founded on nothing less than an effort to imitate an inconceivably good God: "You have heard that it was said, 'You shall love your neighbor and hate your enemy.' But I say to you, Love your enemies and pray for those who persecute you, so that you may be sons of your Father who is in heaven; for he makes his sun rise on the evil and on the good, and sends rain on the just and on the unjust. For if you love those who love you, what reward have you? Do not even the tax collectors do the same? And if you salute only your brethren, what more are you doing than others? Do not the Gentiles do the same? You, therefore, must be perfect, as your heavenly Father is perfect" (Matthew 5:43–48).

Different exegetes no doubt take this passage in different directions. What strikes us is the revelation of the deepest nature of the Christian community that Christ's words carry. To be converted to the standards of Christ, to enter upon the life that Jesus announced and mediated, one must try to mount up to nothing less than God's own standards. Without forgetting human finitude and sinfulness, one yet must admit as perhaps even more important the divinization that faith implies. Often theologians discourse on this divinization in ontological terms, speaking of the communication of the divine nature (2 Peter 1:4) or *theosis* that grace would develop. In the Sermon on the Mount we catch a glimpse of divinization in terms of morality. People who belong to God are raised up toward something of the divine way of acting and regarding other beings. This divine way, symbolized in the steady offering of sun and rain to all of creation, is an unwavering benevolence or love. Because of what God is, of God's own nature, the divine attitude and intent is always loving and beneficial. Jesus seems to be saying that the Christian ideal can be nothing less than trying to imitate God in this love and benevolence. The outreach of his disciples' good will cannot stop at the border of their families and friends. It must reach across even to their enemies. In fact, it must dissolve such spontaneously generated or deeply rooted categories as "friends" and "enemies," when these would put limits to the sphere of God's action. Nothing less than the universal outreach of God's love can be the model and measure of the disciple's sense of the life that faith entails.

In this context, reconciliation becomes obvious, almost a matter of course. Just as God harbors no grudges or cannot be moved from an unfailing goodness, so the children of God ideally are rooted in an unfailing goodness. The reality, of course, is very different—so different, in fact, that we start to appreciate the awesome distinction between divinity and sinful humanity. What to Jesus' Father is nearly automatic Jesus' disciples find heroic and very rare. If the vast extent of the universe does not convince us of the infinite qualitative distinction between ourselves and our Creator, surely the vast extent of the Creator's goodness should.

The ultimate symbol of this goodness, of course, is Christ on the cross. For his followers, the way that Jesus died made his words about loving our enemies and doing good to those who persecute us indelible. Thus theologians such as Bernard Lonergan understand the Christian doctrine of redemption as proceeding under a "law of the cross." Taking their cue from Jesus on Calvary, they realize that reconciliation with God and our fellow human beings boils down to reversing the law of the jungle, the *lex talionis* that calls for exact retribution. Jesus did not ask God for justice. He did not seek the redress of his sufferings in a punishment of his enemies or those who had done evil to him that would make them suffer similarly. Rather he prayed that the Father would forgive them their sins. That is perhaps the greatest index of the difference between Jesus and most of us. Few of us, when badly hurt by other people, feel as our first reaction a prayer for such people's forgiveness by God. Most of us want evildoers to know how much the pain hurts, how searing and humiliating it is.

The church therefore does much of its best imitation of Christ by suffering evil in love. Again and again it most deeply reconciles enemies by offering all parties the astounding perspective of the divine forgiveness. To do this it clearly has to read some biblical texts against others, since the biblical God sometimes appears quite wrathful or even intent on revenge. It has to prefer the texts in which Jesus urges forgiveness to the texts in which Jesus or the apocalyptic Christ conjures up a heavenly scenario of a final, exacting rendering of justice and punishment. It will keep its convictions of God's justice, of course, but ultimately it will admit that God is more concerned about loving people back to health than about squaring all of their accounts. Again and again the parables of Jesus make this point, so the church has impeccable credentials for such an emphasis. And all of such parables go in the direction of reconciliation. With the coming of the Kingdom God offers all people a chance to make a new beginning and restore their filial connection to heaven. With the coming of the Kingdom the old classes, divisions, and antagonisms ought to wash away. They are out of place, because of the largess God himself has shown.

The implications for the governance of the church are both radical and widespread. Not only should the church insistently call its whole membership back to its bedrock fellowship and ministry of reconciliation. It must as well try with might and main to effect the reconciliation of its alienated parts and renounce all classism and antagonism in its midst. Ecumenically, a church in which doctrinal disputes or historical hurts weigh larger than the law of the cross and the call to imitate a completely good God is a church violating its own constitution in the divine mercy. Administratively, a church in which the first word is legal justice rather than reconstitutive love is a church with an unconverted leadership. As commentators on such church documents as the American bishops' statement on peacemaking occasionally realize, the tradition of the just war falls far short of the standards of reconciling love sketched by the New Testament Christ.[9] As any serious effort to bring the message of Matthew 5:43–48 to spouses, neighborhoods, races, or nations that are at war reveals, humanity is so deeply mired in contrary, vindictive attitudes that a church taking Jesus' teachings to heart will be thrown back on the mysteriousness of its source. Reconciliation to Jesus' proclaimed degree amounts to nothing less than giving God carte blanche. In the moral and political order it is the equivalent of Père de Caussade's "holy abandonment," according to which people serious about contemplative prayer reach a point where they see that they must completely hand their lives over to God. Were the church to be governed or led according to such abandonment, it would be a much brighter city on a much higher hill.

Summary

We have concluded our survey of the main topics under which contemporary ecclesiology tends to prosecute its analyses of the nature and works of the church by focusing on governance. To reflect on the sort of guidance and leadership appropriate in Christ's community, we discussed the calls to serve the community, teach the faith, and minister reconciliation that God issues to both heads and members.

The call to serve the community makes it plain that church leadership exists only to facilitate good Christian living, and not vice versa. People are ordained to office in the Christian community because the community needs facilitators and overseers. It is clear from the New Testament that leadership among Jesus' followers is a primacy in community service, as the foot-washing ceremony of Holy Thursday dramatically symbolizes. When the church has forgotten this primacy of service and followed the different symbolisms of the cosmological religions, it has run the risk of making its leadership sacral in a distorting sense and so quite unlike Jesus of Nazareth, the suffering servant. It is ironic that church leadership today finds itself called to a feminist profile, and certainly the churches that forbid women access to governmental powers risk being hoist on the petard of the contemporary discovery of Jesus' sense of church authority.

A second principal task of church governors is teaching the faith. We noted both scriptural and historical signs that the community has found a magisterial authority important, and we considered some of the contemporary refinements of magisterial authority suggested by forays into ecumenical theology. For example, the theses of Heinrich Fries and Karl Rahner that stress the epistemological tolerance demanded by the contemporary explosion of knowledge and speedup of history might both ease the way for churches to unite despite doctrinal difference and give the magisterium a more tolerant view of diversity and innovation generally. At the present time it is discouraging, if not indeed scandalous, that the ecumenical theologians have made significant progress in removing doctrinal obstacles to the reunion of the churches but the heads of those churches hold back from action. We noted analogies to this doctrinal situation in the area of the church's obligation to teach on moral matters, reflecting on recent church documents dealing with such issues as birth control, women's ordination, peacemaking, and economic justice. In all cases the stance to praise seemed to be that which was properly tentative and open to creative developments of the past tradition. Whether inside the Roman Catholic orbit, or among Protestant churches, or in the orbit of individual charismatic teachers, the Augustinian dictum of "love and do what you will" seemed to spotlight teaching that helps people mature into taking responsibility for the application of Christian faith to their own lives and neighborhoods.

Our final focus was reconciliation, which we found basic to any ministry seeking to follow in Jesus' wake. Such reconciliation seemed most amenable to an interpretation in terms of offerings and rejections of love. We rooted the church's ministry of reconciliation in the constant goodness of God and the equality of human beings in needing God's forgiveness, and then we meditated on Jesus' terribly demanding and revealing teaching about forgiving one's enemies. Such a teaching, when buttressed and exemplified by Jesus' own sacrificial and forgiving death, shows Christians how far their God transcends spontaneous human morality. Taken to the heart of the church's mission to the world, administration of its community, and sense of its dependence upon God, such an understanding of reconciliation would bring something wonderfully unearthly into many places now terribly distorted by hatred.

STUDY QUESTIONS

1. How might one make structural—formative [or destructive] of bureaucratic patterns—the lessons in the Holy Thursday service of footwashing?
2. What are some of the mutual criticisms that a dialogue between Christian and feminist models of leadership might spark?
3. How valid is the notion that today one can be more tolerant of doctrinal diversity among the churches than was true in past centuries?
4. Give an example of a pastoral situation in which St. Augustine's "love and do what you will" might be both liberating and challenging.
5. What does a ministry geared to reconciliation suggest for pastoral approaches to divorce and domestic violence?
6. How might the contemporary church make redemption according to Jesus' law of the cross more credible?

NOTES

1. See Leonardo Boff, CHURCH: CHARISM & POWER. New York: Crossroad, 1985, p. 142.

2. Alan Paton, AH, BUT YOUR LAND IS BEAUTIFUL. New York: Charles Scribner's Sons, 1981, p. 236.

3. See Edward Schillebeeckx, MINISTRY: LEADERSHIP IN THE COMMUNITY OF JESUS CHRIST. New York: Crossroad, 1981, pp. 38–99.

4. Heinrich Fries and Karl Rahner, UNITY OF THE CHURCHES: AN ACTUAL POSSIBILITY. New York: Paulist, 1985, p. 7.

5. Ibid., p. 38.

6. See Roger L. Shinn and Paul Abrecht, eds., FAITH AND SCIENCE IN AN UNJUST WORLD, 2 vols. Philadelphia: Fortress, 1981.

7. See American Friends Service Committee, A COMPASSIONATE PEACE. New York: Hill and Wang, 1982.

8. Bernard Cooke, MINISTRY TO WORD AND SACRAMENTS. Philadelphia: Fortress, 1976, pp. 346–347.

9. See, for example, Sandra M. Schneiders, "New Testament Reflections on Peace and Nuclear Arms," in CATHOLICS AND NUCLEAR WAR, ed. Philip J. Murnion. New York: Crossroad, 1983, pp. 91–105.

Chapter 8

Conclusion: Contemporary Answers

Love ◆ Egalitarianism ◆ Praxis ◆ The Spirit ◆ Summary, Study
Questions, Notes

Love

The movement of our study has been from a survey of the problems facing the contemporary church, through a look at the ecclesiological data of the New Testament and the data of church history, to contemporary treatments of the nature, worship, mission, and governance of Christ's community. To conclude, we return to the problematic with which we began, essaying a program or sketching a network of pastoral emphases that might respond to the church's most pressing needs.

In all ages the community of Christ is as healthy and vigorous as the degree to which it centers itself in the divine love that its Master would have animate it. This love, slow to anger and quick to forgive, was the main resource of biblical Israel. It impressed Paul as the greatest of Christian charismata, John as the nearest index of the divine nature, and the synoptics as the otherworldly power that supported Jesus on the cross. We may read church history as so many advances and recessions in the community's penetration of this love. We may analyze the nature of the Christian community, its worship, its mission, and its governance by love's standards. For any age, the wisdom, healing, and example that human beings most crave is the love of God, poured forth in abundant measure for the flourishing of all people.

Today the divine love couldn't be more needed. The nations' preparations for war call into question the surety of human posterity.

The nations' disparities in wealth make mockery of the notion that all people constitute one human family. According to the technological and secularist horizons that dominate current history, God is at best in eclipse, waiting to reappear if computers and biological engineering should fail. According to the fundamentalist religious horizons that dominate militant if not terrorist Muslims, Hindus, and Sikhs, God sends the faithful out on bloody *jihads,* applauding each latest venture in holy war. Only on scattered islands of the human map does the divine benevolence get a patient hearing, and even there it is hard to be confident that the first rule is Christ's law of the cross. One might therefore tender a hypothesis: the map of current history is bloodied and convulsed in the measure that the love of God, with whole mind, heart, soul, and strength, is not the dominant treasure. The corollary would be: when people do not love their neighbors as themselves their chances of achieving justice—legal, political, economic, or any other—are less than a snowball's chances in hell.

If this description catches anything of the contemporary global situation, the task of the community of Christ is stark and simple. It is not the healthy who have need of love medicine[1] but the sick souls responsible for most of our troubles. It is not the burghers and bankers that the church should first target but the poor, the marginalized, those discriminated against. Many voices ask the church to cry, and what the church should cry is as old as Isaiah: all flesh is grass. Left to ourselves, we all perish from the heat of human passion, the drought of affection and care. Only the Word of the Lord endures forever. Only the rain that falls from heaven and the sun that shines from the Father of lights can give human beings good measure, pressed down and overflowing.

This may be fine biblical poetry, insight quite familiar and well-borrowed, but what practical changes could it bring to the parishes of Mudville, let alone to the starving hordes of East Africa? That is a telling question of course, and not one that theologians, caught in rhetorical mid-stride, enjoy stopping to face. The parishes of Mudville force one to slow down, observe carefully, not overlook the good work already being done. The starving hordes of East Africa urge one to speed up, get charity into gear, sound the klaxons before the emergency has been accomplished and only the bones remain. Let us try to imagine what both sets of problems could entail.

Christian parishes or local churches of course vary from locale to locale, and what effective love will mean on any given spot depends considerably on the local culture. Because the local culture of most of our readers is likely to be that of people from the middle class of the United States, we shall try to translate into the language of middle class America. So trying, the first thing to be said is that bourgeois assumptions cannot stand on the same level as gospel imperatives. "Bourgeois" does not have to be a completely pejorative term. God does not immediately penalize people for being the average, commonsensical bloc in their nation. God does not immediately favor the elite at the top or the marginal at the sides. But the gospel of Christ does challenge the values that the high and mighty of most societies have espoused, and it does make a preferential option for the sufferings of those shunted to the margins. If the poor, the marginalized, the discriminated against use the freedom from worldly assumptions their condition offers them, they can be the blessed of God. Where does that leave the middle class or bourgeoisie? Rather uncomfortably under the microscope. If they (we) are espousing the inertia of the status quo, are concerning ourselves mainly with tax reform and the PTA, the Kingdom of God is passing us by. If we would repent and believe in the good news of God, tax reform and the PTA could not be our predominant passions.

Take this instinct to Mudville, pen it out into several Sunday sermons, and what would you proclaim? That the predominant passion of the healthy Christian personality is God, the sovereignly beautiful mystery of creation and salvation. That the most human life ever lived stands before us in Jesus Christ, who alone gave his hearers the words of eternal life and who was nailed to a tree as a despicable criminal. That the measure of the humanity in our own lives is the sobering, even frightening criterion of the judgment scene in Matthew 25: "Then he will say to those at his left hand, 'Depart from me, you cursed, into the eternal fire prepared for the devil and his angels; for I was hungry and you gave me no food, I was thirsty and you gave me no drink, I was a stranger and you did not welcome me, naked and you did not clothe me, sick and in prison and you did not visit me.' Then they also will answer, 'Lord, when did we see thee hungry or thirsty or a stranger or naked or sick or in prison, and did not minister to thee?' Then he will answer them, 'Truly, I say to you, as you did it not to one of the least of these, you did it not to me.' And they will go

away into eternal punishment, but the righteous into eternal life"
(Matthew 25:41–46).

Mudville is bound to have its poor, its mentally ill, its naked and
sickly and imprisoned. In any locale, those accounted failures by the
standards of middle class success grow numerous in the measure we
seek them out. The successful may console themselves that they pay
handsomely in taxes and charitable deductions to succor such unfortunates. They may take heart from the good deeds they do to the sufferers in their own families or neighborhoods. But if they hear
genuinely kerygmatic sermons in their parishes or read the words of
the New Testament Christ with any regularity, they won't long keep
their standing among the bourgeoisie. The contentedness or complacency or settledness so central to the mentality of the bourgeoisie (despite all their carping and grasping) collides with the prophecy of
Christ and suffers unsalvageable shipwreck. A church in love with
God, mindful of Jesus, aware of the claims of the poor has here, in
this familiar bit of space and time, no lasting city. A spirit enlivened
by the love of God that is truly holy, mighty, and immortal is bound
to be hungry and thirsty for a justice and peace not on the platforms
of the regnant politicians.

Let us try to express this for Bob Everyman, an amalgam of several of our middle-American neighbors: "You work on your pickup and
your rec room in the basement, Bob, and certainly one can only ap-
plaud the diligence and concern for your family that shows. You go off
to your job on time, soldier no more than the rest, and return home
both sober and cheerful. You don't beat your wife or your kids. You
pay your taxes and never fall too far behind on your Master Charge.
Now and then you read the paper. About half the time you watch the
evening news. You show up at church most Sunday mornings, unless
you have been partying the night before or have an especially early
fishing date. You have contributed to two Reaganite majorities, but in
the last local election you supported a conservative black. It would be
too much to call you a pillar of your community, but you are not one
of its pressing problems. If the majority of the citizenry were like you,
the status quo would purr along in fine shape.

"The trouble is, Bob, there's little distinctively Christian, let
alone prophetic, in the way that you live. There's little interest or concern that extends beyond your own family circle. Your ties of blood

and friendship are strong, so you are very loyal to those you know well, but you care little about those you don't consider family or friends. You've no interest in the side-effects of the economic system that brings you your adequate salary and benefits. As long as we're not at war with a country overseas it couldn't concern you less. You consider most politicians liars, and most preachers leave you cold. Mainly you want to be left alone, to enjoy your color television set and plan your strategy for getting a new camper. It is hard to think of the New Testament Christ paying you a great deal of attention. Because you are neither hot nor cold, he most likely would lump you with Isaiah's herd that have had their eyes blinded so they will not see, their ears stopped so they will not hear. Christ must keep offering you conversion and newness of life, but the statistical laws give him little grounds for optimism."

There are correctives to this sort of speech, of course, and they include prominent mention of God's movement in all people's hearts, no matter how dull they appear, and of God's care for all people's sufferings. Brought low by illness or unemployment, Bob Everyman quickly becomes a prime object for the care of both Christ's Spirit and Christ's church. Unfortunately, until Bob is brought low he probably will be but another part of the inertial problem, but another irreligious Philistine.

There is a time for the church to show its love for the Philistines by going gently with their underdevelopment, and a time for the church to kick them in the butt. The contemporary church seems much more inclined not to disturb its sleepy, thoughtless majority than to try to bring them aflame, so we think the expression of Christian love most needed today in most Mudvilles is a frank, witty, biting attack on the mammon holding so many captive. The television that Bob and Bobbi watch, the camper or Neronian bathroom they covet, the ambitions they have for their children (football and computer programming, cheer-leading and dental hygiene), and the political scenarios dominating their citizenship are enemies of the Christ they profess to follow. Where Christ says they should seek first the Kingdom of God and its justice, they first seek their own comfort and pleasure. Where Christ says their neighbor is anyone in need, they think only of the people on their block. If they are the salt of the earth, creation has gone terribly flat. If their priests and ministers had any gumption, the Word of God would be a two-edged sword, slashing to the marrow of their complacency and conservatism. Each Sunday it would set before them two ways, of death and of life, forcing them to choose. Not to choose would be to choose love of self unto contempt of God.

Without a love of God unto contempt of self, the church has virtually no hope of rousing people to care about East Africans and other sufferers. The middle class almost by definition has a little world carefully sanitized. If possible, it allows no troubled children, no doddering old folks, no people spastic or mentally deficient to intrude. If possible, it leaves the wretched of the earth to the afterglow of television, trusting that the great communicators who dominate the tube will get the right grains to the right gullets. The church agencies that counteract this self-centered carelessness do yeoman work to keep the light shining in the darkness. The freedom-fighters and guerillas who stay at their posts provide much-needed hope for us all.

We say this as people seeing their own words come back at them like boomerangs. Middle-class we were born and middle-class we remain by all the economic indicators. If we are overly educated for middle-class tastes, and liberal to radical in our politics, that hardly qualifies us as champions of the poor, people able to compel credibility because their witness has been bloody and at cost. So if only to shield ourselves from the accusations flying back from our pages we have to add that all things are possible with God, even camels passing through the eye of a needle, even comfortable bourgeoisie nipping in through a narrow gate. God does not ask, we hope, that all of us trek off to East Africa. God does seem to ask that we take the East Africas of our time to heart, make some concrete gestures, consider the economic and political changes that such disasters imply. If we will not, we have grown so deadened to conscience and the gospel that there is little even God can do for us. Only our own stumbling into tragedy will hold out any prospects of turning us around.

Does this mean that Christian love today rings hollow and false unless it is an energy for political, this-worldly liberation? It does indeed. Of course, Christian love also implies prayer and otherworldliness, cultural development and incarnational beauty. But in our time the best and the brightest, both inside the churches and outside, have seen that great quanta of human suffering are man-made. They have therefore concluded that great quanta of human suffering could not be, should not be, and so must be moved against. To move against them is to attack the systems that produce them and, behind the systems, the this-worldly despair and greed. Thus critical Christian communities and churches at the grass-roots regularly read the gospel as a call for new political arrangements, as we have seen on several occasions. Thus people of serious contemplative bent return from their sojourns in the wilderness of God astonished that most of the world's business should be so irrational and ugly. The love of God poured forth in the most exemplary hearts today by the Holy Spirit urges very radical reforms. If the cultural context be middle class America or bourgeois Europe, it urges a thoroughgoing counter-culture.

We need not concern ourselves greatly with the changes urged in totalitarian cultural contexts, except to say for the record that Christian love is the implacable enemy of the godlessness expressed in the gulags and purges of Stalin or the slaughters of Hitler and Mao. The totalitarian regimes usually recognize this very well, so Christian religion becomes their hunted enemy. It is the supposedly more praiseworthy regimes of the free world that offer more fertile ground for prophetic musing about love, and if they wish the citizens of such regimes can consider this judgment a compliment. All is far from lost in contemporary America or the West, although most is definitely in peril. The equation that right wing religion makes between Americanism and Christianity is one of the most perilous of our current notions. Surpassing even it, however, is the fanatical devotion to defending our material prosperity that powers the engines of war and industrial production. Christian charity has little to do with the basic design of the contemporary Western cultures. Its main task, coming clearer every day, is to criticize the soullessness of that culture and show it a much more excellent way.

Egalitarianism

The more excellent way of love, expressed in a radical contemplation and a radical politics, holds out the church's best chances of imitating its provocative Master and getting the lead out of its sedentary majority. Love also pressures the contemporary Christian community to throw off its older cultural and political forms, that it may embrace a radical egalitarianism. It needs to be considerably clearer than it now is in the community of Christ worldwide that there is neither Jew nor Gentile, neither master nor slave, neither male nor female. These Pauline negations are but disjunctive ways of saying that in Christ's community all stand needy before God, all are radically the same in having been called by grace to a life utterly beyond them (the qualitatively different, "supernatural" life of Father-Son-Spirit). In Johannine terms, the branches all depend on the vine for every whit of divine life they enjoy. The hallmark of church life is abiding in Christ the vine. All orders, hierarchies, commissions, charismata, and the rest are secondary and far less important.

This is theologians' talk, of course, and not the talk of sociologists. Sociologists and historians will be quick to say that throughout history it has made an enormous difference whether one has been Jew or Gentile, master or slave, male or female—inside the church every bit as much as outside. Our point is not to deny the truth of such sociologists' and historians' claims but rather to expose the vision of the church, founded in the central tenets of biblical and traditional faith, that we find most compelling today. In that vision sociological distinctions and historical baggage yield pride of place to the theology of grace. Indeed, the main function of past sociological distinctions, past differences in faith stemming from ethnicity or race or sex, is to show how vitiated the ecclesial vision becomes when a primacy of grace does not convince the general church membership that all followers of Christ are sisters and brothers.

Some will quickly press the case for the unmeltable ethnics, the different racial experiences, the complementary practices of women and men, arguing that the church must gather up the richest possible variety of searches for God and findings by God. Fine. As long as one takes care not to canonize the injustices pregnant in many of those distinctions, let variety, diversity, catholicity dance wild and free. Our point again is somewhat different. We are trying to answer the question, "What directions ought the contemporary church to take, if it wants to regalvanize its people, reinvigorate the Body of Christ?" In our view the signs flashing on both highways and byways point to egalitarianism. The way up to the measure of God's gifts is the way down to the reaffirmation of all Christians' dignity, the resolicitation of all Christians' gifts.

Perhaps there are alternate voices, again, that would argue either that this egalitarian renovation is actually occurring, or that in fact it is not what the signs are flashing. Neither argument seems to us very

strong, at least in the admittedly slim or allusive way it is here presented. With notable and encouraging exceptions, the churches of the
Mudvilles we visit are frequented by few live wires. Many good people
they certainly house, but few who so hunger for justice that they can
taste it, so long for union with God that they ache in their bones. The
sermons these good people hear seldom crackle with prophecy or usher
their spirits into silent admiration of the mystery. The social events
the churches sponsor seldom take aim at forming grass roots churches,
new cells of a countercultural faith. The love of God and love of neighbor that Christ used to summarize the Law and the Prophets rarely
etches its way into the community's constitutional tablets, like a smoking acid. The gentle Christ that Luke described seldom is ruthlessly
distinguished from the amiabilities of day-time television. No, in the
churches we visit mammon suffers only few all-out assaults. In the
churches we visit the pastors proclaim and the flocks nod sleepily.

By egalitarianism, then, we mean a direct return to the ecclesiastical model of bands of disciples. For us the term implies small
groups in which people can know one another well and interact with
minimal reference to their sociological roles in society at large. It implies alertness, mobility, criticism, and ongoing discernment of spirits. The bedrock theological assumption is that the Spirit has gifts for
all believers and that the community treasury will only be full as it
should be when all believers are encouraged to pitch in their mites.
Correlative assumptions are that all the members will work together
to strengthen the prayer and social action they agree are central to
what the basic Christian community is about; that genuine authority,
rooted in actual wisdom or learning or political experience or gifts of
prayer, will weigh more heavily than institutional authority; and that
the history of the church will be for all a great storehouse of lessons,
both cautionary and encouraging, so that what the little community is
doing in the present will fold into the prior struggles of Christ's people. (In other words, egalitarianism has a historical dimension: we
stand on an equal footing with the saints and sinners who have preceded us in our tasks.)

Among these many possible topics for further discussion, what
we have called "genuine authority" is the hobby horse we now want
to ride. It calls to mind Bernard Lonergan's discussions of authenticity. For Lonergan we are authentic, in both our humanity and our
faith, when we are following the solicitations (of both grace and na-

ture) to be attentive, intelligent, reasonable, responsible, and loving. These are "transcendental" calls or imperatives, working in all human consciousnesses. In the light of Christ, they reveal the human vocation to be a pursuit of warm light, clear love, that in fact is the gracious presence of God. Generally speaking, love follows upon knowledge, so we progress in authenticity to the degree that we realize the imperatives and then act upon them. For example, we progress when we acquaint ourselves with the data on smoking, or jogging, or cholesterol and adjust our habits for better health. We progress when we understand the further implications of social justice, factor in the systemic dimensions, and adjust our votes, charities, use of our talents, and the like toward a more ecological, networked obedience to Christ's second commandment. Things change, however, when we come to the most holistic dimension, the place where we fall in love, because love at the radical level is the mover rather than the follower. When we fall in love, the world tips over, our horizons shift, and all of our knowledge has to readjust. The deepest falling in love is the unrestricted romance we can have with the divine mystery, for it alone is with full mind, heart, soul, and strength. The deepest falling in love is therefore the deepest guarantor of our authenticity. By what Christians call the love poured forth in our hearts by the Holy Spirit, we can measure all our insights, test all our spirits, listen with acutest ear for whether the tones we are hearing ring false or true.

In Frank Herbert's admittedly often pretentious science fiction novels there is a category of important players called "truthsayers." They have been trained to study the smallest signs of expression and so determine whether what a person is saying is true or false. Something similar occurs with the divine love breathed into us by the Paraclete. 1 John 2:26–27 alludes to it: "I write this to you about those who would deceive you; but the anointing which you received from him abides in you, and you have no need that any one should teach you; as his anointing teaches you about everything, and is true, and is no lie, just as it has taught you, abide in him." The anointing rather poetically recalls both the sacramental signing at baptism and the unction one experiences in spiritual consolation. The "him" probably is Christ, although it could also be the Spirit. The point is plain, if in need of complement by other forms of teaching (as the beleaguered Johannine community finally admitted when it joined the Great Church and accepted a more institutional authority that it had long resisted): there is an inner touchstone, illative sense, fine point of the soul—call it what you will—by which Christians finally fly. It is nice, delicate, dependent on prayer and a lack of turmoil, but it operates as a sixth or spiritual sense that enables one to determine holistically the correctness or health of both people and doctrinal positions.

This anointing by the Spirit comes as the Spirit wishes. It tends to move along with ordinary human experience, maturing as prudence and better judgment mature. And sometimes it certainly comes in special measure to those who have heavy responsibilities because of their office. But one has to grant the Spirit freedom to breathe where it will. One has to be open to the possibility that the least distinguished, titled, official member of the community may have the keenest insight, the freshest solution. Otherwise one has kicked the Spirit out and voted in routine. Otherwise one has become a Pelagian, depending more upon human effort than upon the God who alone can give salvation.

As the church moves toward a more egalitarian model, encouraging people to form small groups where they can discuss the Scriptures and share their insights, it probably will find the anointing of the Spirit expressing itself in quite simple or even vulgar forms. We recall listening to a fellow-student who had spent a year at a prestigious Ivy League seminary. He was part of an experiment in ecumenical cooperation and considerably older than most of the students he met at his new school. When we asked him how he assessed those Ivy League students, he shook his head and gave a wry grin: "They're bright enough kids, that's for sure, but they have no nose for bullshit." One could translate that for middle America by saying that the Spirit had yet to mature the students' ability to distinguish between what might be so and what in fact probably is so.

For students of Lonergan, this is the distinction between intelligence and reasonableness, between insight and judgment. For students of scientific method it is the distinction between a new hypothesis and a well-tested theory. People of common sense and workaday experience use the distinction each time they simply indulge the chattering salesman or brighteyed and bushytailed newcomer who tells them all the wonderful changes that surely will happen next month. People in small Christian groups use the distinction when they agree that the new church documents sound fine but that their proof will be how they are acted upon.

The advantage of egalitarianism is that it supports the anointing of the Spirit and the ability to distinguish the good stuff from the bullshit. Because officialdom has been cut down to size, myth and suspension of judgment play lesser roles. There is a place for myth, of course, since the word can mean the storied, symbolic form of truth that is much better able than simply propositional expressions to elicit our full-bodied support and enthusiasm. There is even a place for the suspension of judgment, so that proposals are allowed to grow the fruits by which they may be assessed. But the history of official authority in the church suggests that balance nowadays lies on the side of demythologizing the tiaras and chasubles. Nowadays, statements of church leaders that rub against the instinct of the majority ought to receive a very critical application of judgment.

The example that leaps to mind, in this context of egalitarianism, is the teaching that renders the vast majority of Christians ineligible for orders or formal ecclesiastical authority. The Roman Catholic position that women and married men may not serve as priests, bishops, cardinals, or popes limits institutional power to perhaps 10 percent of its pool of talent. The majority instinct is that this is a strange point of view, so the egalitarian response is to test quite severely the myths and suspensions of judgments upon which it depends. The historians and theologians who have done such testing have tended to find compelling neither the tradition on which the current practice claims to depend nor the analytical arguments that the current practitioners propose. There are solid signs that women led house churches in the New Testament era, and a contemporary analysis of the core of the Christian message (in light of the patriarchalism of past ages) tends to conclude that Christ, not wanting to demand or forward sexism, would certainly renounce the discriminations against women now practiced in many of his churches.

One could apply this egalitarian outlook retrospectively, in order to secure the confidence of basic communities that they must rely on the anointing of the Spirit if they are to develop an authentic faith and praxis. Such a reliance should not reject official statements, past or present, out of hand, but it should read them critically, testing the spirits very thoroughly. For example, if one considers the debates about slavery that racked the churches of the United States in the mid-nineteenth century, one finds uses of Scripture and tradition that seem tendentious in the extreme. People on both sides of the debate were more in search of proof-texts than in search of genuine Christian instinct and judgment, but the twistings of the slavers certainly were more egregious. Their interpretations of the myth of Ham and of Pauline letters such as Philemon finally were judged unChristian by most of the Christian bodies, but it took a century for this judgment to grow strong enough to rework the civil legislation of our reputedly religious nation and start to move Martin Luther King, Jr. beyond the reach of J. Edgar Hoover and the FBI. The Nobel Prize for Peace that King received shortly before his assassination certainly was a bitter-sweet dosage for both the United States and the American Christian churches. It strongly affirmed the Christian instincts behind King's civil disobedience and non-violent approaches to political change, but it barely veiled a stark condemnation of all the decades of sinful prejudice that both had made it necessary for God to raise up a prophet of King's status and that came to climax in King's martyrdom.

Black people, women, and others who have been kept on the margins of either secular or church power know in their bones, with a surety that we should not separate from the anointing of the Spirit, that many of the things told them by the masters of the times are self-serving bullshit. They do not have to read Marxist critical literature on ideology to be well aware that money and power tilt almost all of the situations in which they work or study or even pray. The people who study marginalized groups often find them much more sophisticated, intuitively, than are the members of the middle class. The members of the middle class, too, are being woefully manipulated, but as long as they have beer in the refrigerator and a patch of grass to mow they tend to go to bed content. So a Robert Coles or a Studs Terkel who interviews ordinary people grows alert to the ways that such people perceive the structures that keep them low, giving higher marks to the more radicalized types who have seen through the smokescreens and folderol. True, they reserve their highest marks for those who have come to this radicalization without having grown so bitter or cynical that the bloom has completely come off their rose. Mental health, faith, and political effectiveness all depend on an ability finally to laugh at the petty perversions, lies, and self-delusions that shape so much of our institutional life. This laughter or irony or satire, however, need not be separated from the sort of anger that burned in the prophetic Christ. The woes he cast upon the scribes and Pharisees whom he found hypocritical embarrass too many of his supposed followers. In the larger churches, they usually have been ousted in the name of gentility, of the emotions and language proper to ladies and gentlemen. In basic Christian communities Christ need not be so sanitized or emasculated. In basic Christian communities Christ can be a prophet rather than a gentleman.

Praxis

One way to mediate between prophets and properly genteel Christians, people who prefer the gentle Christ and mothering images of the Spirit, is to take to heart Christ's own pragmatic criterion of authenticity. The *locus classicus* in Jesus' own teaching is Matthew 7:15–21: " 'Beware of false prophets, who come to you in sheep's clothing but inwardly are ravenous wolves. You will know them by their fruits. Are grapes gathered from thorns, or figs from thistles? So, every sound tree bears good fruit, but the bad tree bears evil fruit. A sound tree cannot bear evil fruit, nor can a bad tree bear good fruit. Every tree that does not bear good fruit is cut down and thrown into the fire. Thus you will know them by their fruits. Not every one who says to me, "Lord, Lord," shall enter the kingdom of heaven, but he who does the will of my Father who is in heaven.' "

The Johannine parallel to this synoptic criterion occurs in the key discussions of Jesus' works. For the author of the Gospel of John "the Jews," Jesus' antagonists, are culpable of bad faith and unbelief because the works that Jesus did in their midst ought to have convinced them of his special status, of his unique mission from God. In the speeches of the Johannine Jesus, these works stand front and center. He does not ask people to accept myths and stories. He does not even stress the newness and power of his teachings. He stresses the works that he does. Indeed, the first half of the Gospel of John is treated by most scholars as "the book of signs." The seven main signs that Jesus performs, for all their sacramental overtones and references to the later life of the Christian community, harken back to how the Word that had taken flesh and dwelt in human beings' midst, full of grace and truth, made his case that he was God's special revealer. He based his case on the things God moved and enabled him to do. His criterion was the same as that of both his synoptic equivalents and our latter-day liberation theologians: praxis, performance, doing.

We find a Pauline equivalent to this New Testament pragmatism in Galatians 5. There Paul is contrasting "flesh" and "spirit," the way that sinful humanity operates in contrast to the operations of humanity led by God's grace: "Now the works of the flesh are plain: fornication, impurity, licentiousness, idolatry, sorcery, enmity, strife, jealousy, anger, selfishness, dissension, party strife, envy, drunkenness, carousing, and the like. I warn you, as I warned you before, that those who do such things shall not inherit the kingdom of God. But the fruit of the Spirit is love, joy, peace, patience, kindness, goodness, faithfulness, gentleness, self-control; against such there is no law" (Galatians 5:19–23).

When we try to appropriate this legacy of discernment today, we find little in it to improve. The psychology of faith that the synoptics, John, and Paul employ is as germane now as it was nearly two thousand years ago. If we have the Spirit of Christ we will show good effects. If our lives do not show good effects, we do not have the Spirit of Christ. Some things do remain constant across the ages.

However, it is also true that some things change across the ages, so while there is little in the traditional psychology of faith that needs improvement there is a sociology of faith that we must add. In the time of the classical New Testament writers, the world seemed stable and predictable. The classical ideal, expressed in the "science" of Aristotle, was certain knowledge of things through their causes. Neither the statistical or evolutionary changes of nature nor the historical variations of human institutions had appeared on the scene, at least in anything like their modern garb. So people living within the Roman Empire, in the aura of the Pax Augustiniana that had brought a time of unusual peace, tended not to question the social arrangements through which they moved. Their economic, political, and institutional forms appeared as parts of a relatively static, predetermined, unchangeable natural order. In addition, Christians were considerably shaped by eschatological expectations. One finds in Paul's ethical passages, for example, a strong sense that present relations between the sexes aren't worth much consideration, since the end of this present age is right around the corner. One finds an acceptance of slavery that would be extraordinary, granted the stark contradiction between slavery and the Christian egalitarianism of such Pauline passages as Galatians 3:28, except for this sense that current history is on the wane.

Since the parousia has not come, and an imperfect, unjust history continues to wax fat, today's theologians have a strong basis, if not indeed a Spirit-given imperative, to approach the discernment of spirits or pragmatism of faith with a keen sociological eye. Tutored by Marxists, feminists, black theoreticians, or any others who offer insights and good analytical tools, they are turning over the relations between money and ideology, power and politics, where one stands in an institution and how one feels about changing it. Their general finding is that people tend to act from considerable measures of self-interest. Those who are unhappy with a situation and feel it to be unjust are much riper ground for change or even revolution than those whom the situation is rewarding handsomely. The number of people who believe and act in ways contrary to their own material advantage is quite small indeed. Analogously, the number of people who act against their own interests in terms of power, espousing theories or policies that are likely to reduce their influence or authority, is quite small indeed. The somewhat saddening fact is that religious institutions offer few exceptions to this general sociological analysis. As a result, many theologians have endorsed Paul Ricoeur's "hermeneutics of suspicion." When they analyze a situation they take into account the self-deception and self-advantage that even high-sounding pronouncements may carry.

An ecclesiology predicated on love, egalitarianism, praxis, and the Spirit therefore runs counter to the theology, as well as the sociology, of many current churches and church officials. It implies changes that those profiting from the status quo will find it hard to call good. If small basic communities were to become the rule, or even to become a significant factor, the current American pattern of large parishes geographically determined would be up for grabs. Up for grabs as well would be the privileges of traditional pastors, which the old code of canon law treated in quite disedifying detail. People would be able to be baptized, married, and buried in communities of their own choosing—in conventicles fashioned more by the Spirit than by the diocesan chancellor or officialis. Pastors and all church personnel would be asked to be ministers, servants, rather than lords of little fiefs.

Egalitarianism plainly has dangers, however, and such dangers suggest the perennial need for officials, supervisors, overseers. The Spirit probably would be sufficient if we all listened carefully, selflessly, wisely, but manifestly we do not. So we authors would understand egalitarianism as an emphasis rather than an ideology or doctrinaire conviction. It is the way we would like the church to move, the governmental stress or style we see as most compatible with adulthood and maturity, rather than a political absolute that we find required by the gospel of the Christ. The pragmatic test enshrined in the gospel of the Christ suggests that we should no more absolutize egalitarianism than past ages absolutized their monarchical or episcopal models of the Christian community. A model is as good as the fruits of faith, hope, love, and service that it grows. The crux is deep prayer and generous work to make a world worthy of God, fit for children of God to live in.

Hung on this crux, doctrinaire views of "the people" seldom hold up. If only because they have for so long been denied the chance to have a say or take responsibility for their faith, the majority of Christians nowadays appear a quite torpid lot. The parallel with the students one meets in most colleges comes readily to mind. We have spent the last decade working with students in large public universities who no doubt are much more representative of the consumer side of American higher education than are the students in smaller private schools. Perhaps one in four of our students has been solidly responsible, reliably committed to learning. Another fourth will perform if exposed to the lash, but half remain disappointing underachievers, people who have no earned right to be taking up space and resources. They are irregular in their attendance, slovenly in their study, at the far end of the spectrum from inner direction or maturity. Their native talent may be passable, but their discipline is prepubescent. They furnish few grounds for being optimistic about democracy or any culture set in the hands of the crowd. We have the American economy, politics, and entertainment we now do largely because they and their older models make money and vote.

To form a church that would be anything like an answer to the sundering questions of contemporary humanity, we obviously would have to convert, reform, and give a new spirit to the American humanity that shows itself en masse. (There is little reason to alter this judgment if the topic is global humanity. The people we have met on the streets of Europe and Asia are as much in need of conversion, reform, and a new spirit as are Americans.) The proper response to this situation, however, is not to opt for more heterogeneity or authoritarian rule. Like the college, with which it shares many of the dynamics of the spiritual life, the church betrays itself when it succumbs to the temptation of trying to form its people by military, monarchical, or bureaucratic methods. Indeed, it betrays itself when it considers its laws to be more than counsels, directives, sketches of the ideal. Just as a college only succeeds when it stresses a mission to provide the best fare that it can, letting students accept (challenge, interact with) this fare as they choose, so the church only succeeds when it offers the most challenging, beautiful, truly religious fare that it can, letting its members, actual or potential, accept (challenge, interact with) this fare as they choose.

Teachers should be personable, kind, interested in their students. They should do their best to be relevant as well as clear, strategic as well as faithful to the encyclopedic outreach of their discipline. But they should not take from students the possibility of failing, the right to meet a demanding test, the clear distinction of good work (understanding, criticizing, creative production) from bad work. Education has to deal in honest coinage. It depends on responsibility flowing back and forth between both sides of the lectern. If teachers are to do their job, they have finally to lay it out there and let students do with it what they will. If students are to have the educational experiences they deserve, they have to suffer the real sanctions that their abuses of freedom call for. Presently too many schools denature education in the name of a false egalitarianism or democracy. Without being elitist in the pejorative sense, we have to make education crackle with the inner fire and sanctions of the spiritual life. In the spiritual life if you don't perform you get burned. If you don't study you remain ignorant. Conversely, if you are given freedom and you use it responsibly you are bound to grow. No one can force you to remain ignorant. Your intellectual fate is in your own hands.

Much of our religious fate is also in our own hands. When we are left free, our maturity or immaturity, wisdom or foolishness, finally lies on our own heads. In deeper perspective, of course, we are always left free in this way. In deeper perspective we choose the masters we serve and accredit, the teachers and priests we follow and depend upon. Not purely or without historical and sociological conditioning, yet nonetheless ultimately, we do choose who we become. So the famous standoff between Christ and the Grand Inquisitor that spices THE BROTHERS KARAMAZOV needs another episode.

The people who surrender their freedom to the Grand Inquisitor still have to come before their own consciences, before the Holy Spirit, and before the King who assembles them at the Last Judgment. At each of those audiences they will be asked what they did with the talent their Creator gave them, with the freedom and responsibility that were their birthrights. And they will be forced to answer, not allowed an incomplete.

All of this is simply an existential way of saying that the egalitarianism we are proposing already occurs in the councils of both God and inner conscience. We do people no favor by shielding them against their own laziness or even underdeveloped faith. Even when our ecclesiastical motivation is concern that they are like sheep without a shepherd, rather than concern for our own power as officials or teachers, we can't wisely deal in any coin but freedom. We have to tell people about the anointing of the Spirit they have been offered, try to fashion cells or small communities in which that anointing can flourish, and pick up the pieces when people abuse such freedom. We have to read church history with an eye wary of enthusiasm, read personalities with an eye sensitive to the patterns of ego-inflation, and read social movements well aware that prophetic personalities can easily become harsh or megalomaniacal, quite concerned that our group not come to think itself a pure army of the righteous. The Puritans of history, as epitomized by Cromwell and his ilk, are nearly the complete opposite of what the contemporary egalitarianism we are proposing should intend.

Still, as the *campesinos* of Solentiname suggest, it is possible to stay in close touch with the evangelical Christ, to offer one another regular correction, to develop political acumen while assuming the humbler, more self- critical posture that we would praise. Where the *campesinos* differ from the average pew-sitter in the mainline North American churches is in the personal responsibility they exhibit. They are much closer to realizing that their church and their nation alike are in their own hands. Those hands may be small or stained or quavering, but the peasants know that Christ calls them to act, expects their faith to lead to praxis. Too many of our pew-sitters think of religion as a pleasant respite, a dip into the balming promises of a good God that just may wash away some of the grime and fatigue they accumulated through the week. Too many of our pew-sitters are under-challenged and under-achieving.

For both those who hold positions of leadership and those who constitute the mass of the Christian rank and file, praxis can be the watchword. The leaders, both formal and de facto or intrinsic, should be judged by the leadership they actually offer: the clarity of their teaching, luster of their example, depth of their counsel, and courageous relevance of their policies. The rank and file should be judged by the prayer and social action that, under the dialectical (back and forth, listening and responding) influence of such leadership, they produce. One can never fashion tests or questionnaires or data bases that accomplish such a judgment adequately. Always the Spirit overspills as well as quickens the letter. But one can make holistic assessments, global discernments of spirits, that are sufficient to fly by. With individuals, one can monitor the peace and joy—solid rather than sporadic or emotional—that are key signs of the Spirit's presence. As well, one can ask for a slowly increasing wisdom, an ever slightly richer blend of stability and creativity, of constancy and innovation. With groups one can monitor commitment to prayer, fraternal and sororal charity, criticism of secular politics, and the like. With groups familiarity with Scripture should be breeding savor rather than contempt, efforts at social action should be fostering sobriety and humility rather than useless rage or self-applause. These are pilgrim ventures, of course, always struggling for their progress. The law of Christ's cross never goes on holiday. But the criterion of praxis, sweetened by divine grace, is God's own index. We finally are the love we want and do. We finally are the church we want and suffer for.

The Spirit

Our last prescription for current ecclesiology is that it greatly needs to promote the presence of the Holy Spirit to all Christians. This is a conviction that charismatic Christians and Pentecostals long have promoted, of course, but now it seems needed across the ecumenical board. If there is anything valid in our foregoing analyses, anything apt in our urging that the future ecclesiological stress be love-egalitarianism-praxis, then the Holy Spirit becomes theologically crucial, since it is the Holy Spirit who best symbolizes the divine, gracious side of such a future ecclesiology.

It would be wonderful to be able to report that current analysts

of concrete church life in the United States have been spotlighting
either an upsurge in appreciation of the Holy Spirit or prescriptions
that bring forward the Holy Spirit as the best comprehensive "answer"
to the church's current needs, but such does not appear to be the
case.[2] Theologians certainly have been rethinking the history of the
theology of the Holy Spirit.[3] Ecumenists such as Kilian McDonnell
have been moved by their encounters with Pentecostals to rethink the
doctrine of the Trinity with a new emphasis on the Holy Spirit.[4] But
few treatments of ministry or lay Christian life have given the Spirit
the rule over basic communities that we find the future soliciting.

Edward Schillebeeckx, however, has suggested that the Spirit
was the dominant force in the religious lives of the earliest generations
of Christians, especially those who were converts from the Greek-
speaking Jewish diaspora. Centered at Antioch, the missionary movement of these churches was thoroughly pneumatological or driven by
the gifts of the Holy Spirit: "The solidarity and equality of all Christians 'in the Spirit' (Acts 2.17–18; II Cor. 5.17), 'living through or in
the Spirit' (Gal. 5.25; 6.1), 'new creation' (Gal. 6.15; II Cor. 5.17)
were the key phrases of this 'Antiochene-Christian,' Jewish-Christian
missionary movement and its theology. This ecclesiology had its
source in the baptism in the Spirit, the foundation of all church
life. . . . 'The power of the Spirit', the key-word of the old pneumatic
Christ movement, was the basic conviction of this generation of Christians. Every member of the community had *de facto* authority in the
community on the basis of his or her own inspiration by the Spirit—
even at that time the leading authority in the Christian churches was
institutionalized, on the basis of the baptism of the Spirit and the
pneumatic phenomena which followed from that and led to the formation of communities. Paul came to know this originally egalitarian
view of the church as a brotherhood and sisterhood from pre-Pauline
traditions. The view of the church warmly shared by Paul is crystal-
lized in Gal. 3.28; a kind of Christian charter of freedom, which according to present-day exegetical studies is not an invention of Paul
but an earlier baptismal tradition from the Hellenistic-Jewish, pre-
Pauline communities."[5]

It is hardly an aberrant innovation, therefore, to call for a Christian egalitarianism rooted in all Christians' possession of the Holy
Spirit. The texts cited by Schillebeeckx are mainly Pauline, but one
certainly could muster Johannine equivalents, for it is John who most

stresses Jesus' gift of another Paraclete. Luke has the church sent out on mission through the influence of the Pentecostal Spirit, and the Lukan Jesus moves through Galilee, on his way to Jerusalem, under the leading of the Spirit. So in the measure that they read their Scripture, New Testament or Old Testament, looking for the presence of the Holy Spirit, Christians of little grass roots communities will find a powerful source of encouragement. When they are dragged before hostile authorities, they can trust that the Spirit will tell them what to say. When they are driven to their knees and cry out their deepest prayer, they can experience the Spirit groaning in their depths, with sighs too deep for words. The love of God which is their treasure has been poured forth in their hearts by the Holy Spirit. The love of neighbor as self is actually a participation in the procession of the Spirit from the Father and the Son, since by God's grace the immanent life of the Trinity has become identical with the "economic" life that brings believers their divinization.

If, as Galatians 5:1 proclaims so boldly, it is for freedom that Christ has set believers free, an ecclesiology that trusts in the Holy Spirit more than in organizational structures or canonical laws ought not to be suspect. True enough, the history of charismatic movements shows many derailments.[6] These, however, may finally be traced as much to abandonment of the Spirit of Christ as to an excessive reliance on purely internal authority. Moreover, if we broaden the "history" that has unfolded under the inspiration of the Holy Spirit, taking the divine desire to communicate salvation and divine life as a universal offer, we note that all creativity and genuine progress has in the final analysis come from people who were emboldened by inner conviction to go beyond the limits officially approved in their time. This notation perhaps deserves more consideration than it has received in average ecclesiology to date.

Average ecclesiology thinks of the church within the parameters of Christian, and so largely recent Western, history. Christianity has had its greatest influence in the West, and the past two thousand years are "recent" indeed if one accepts the notion that human beings have been interacting with the divine mystery for perhaps half a million years (since the rise of reflective consciousness). The Christian church certainly has been an important factor in the rise of the West, with its concomitant shaping of the modern and contemporary cultural horizons. Even today, as we noted earlier, the demographic projections we can make for the twenty-first century show Christians to be a very significant fraction of the world's population, especially of the part of the world's population that presently controls most of the wealth and technology. Nonetheless, ecclesiologists wanting to prepare Christians for the twenty-first century probably are well advised to lay more stress on the Holy Spirit than on Christian sociology. In fact, they probably are well advised to relativize the formalities of Christian groupings, making them less prominent than they have been in the past, when "the church" could be an enclave apart from the rest of God's world.

This would mean, for instance, teaching Christians (and Jews) that they are not chosen or special, at least in the ways they have told themselves they are. The sacramental model of the church, properly developed, makes the divine life that centers the church present in the lives of all people. The job of Christians is to manifest the sort of authenticity that the Spirit is encouraging worldwide. The stories of Jews and Christians of course should be told to keep the biblical promises alive, but they are paradigms for Gentiles, atheists, and people of other religious traditions as well. God is always greater than the interests (let alone the self-interest) of the tiny group of Jews and the larger-yet-still-a-minority group of Christians who like to think of themselves as God's people. The Christ illumines lives that have never heard of Jesus of Nazareth, and both Christians and Jews must mature to the point where they can hear echoes of the Christ in Hindu, Buddhist, Muslim, and Marxist teachings and experiences. It is hard for the institutional church to move to these advanced positions, even when mainstream theologians are saying that these are the next decisive battlegrounds. The institutional church is heavy and slow. The tasks of the Holy Spirit therefore devolve on individual Christians, even more so than they have in the past. In the past the pace of history was slower and the role of the institutional church could seem more crucial, especially when one's cultural horizon was limited to the recent West. Today history is becoming ever more integrated, as what one part of the globe does dictates what another part has to do. The instinct of faith would seem to be to consider whatever is honest, noble, and worthy of respect to be inspired by the Spirit. Whatever brings us the light and love shining most humanly from the face of Jesus deserves our applause and support. We are the church of Christ only to help the day draw nearer when God will be all in all. We have no other business than worship and service, two loves with one root and Spiritual inspiration. Like Jesus, we should come into any situation to minister, not to be ministered unto. Like Jesus, we are children of God because we are moved by the Spirit of God to cry "Abba, Father."

The Spirit of Christ therefore makes ecclesiology a family affair. In its blood, the Body of Christ hears singing the endlessly circling love of the Trinitarian persons. What begins in history as grace continues in heaven as glory. The Johannine Christ, passing over from grace to glory, murmuring farewell speeches so replete with references to the Father and the Spirit, can be our symbolic security. As was true of him, the term of our pilgrimage can be an otherworldliness that makes all of our time sacramental.

We began this exercise in ecclesiology with some reflections on our contemporaries' preoccupation with liberation, and it is fitting that we turn our final reflections on the Spirit toward answering the question implicit in this preoccupation: How can the community of Christ best advance all people's freedom from oppression, all people's fuller sharing in the grace and beauty of creation? When the Spirit is active and felt, the question is two-thirds answered.

A holistic liberation theology asks the church to spread its arms wide enough to embrace all of human life. Matter and spirit, food and prayer, warfare and art all demand care and healing. Still, there is an order among human problems, such that some care and healing is more basic and useful than others. When the human being is open to the mystery of God, able to root itself in a fundamental honesty and love, its intellectual, moral, social, and even physical problems fall into place and become amenable to solution. The first thing, ontologically, is ordering the center of the human spirit, making sure that the community has its heart set on the proper treasure. Working from the inside out, as we might picture it, God takes care of this first thing, this *primum necessarium,* by sending the Holy Spirit into our hearts. If we but open to the Spirit even a little bit, we have the essentials of human health. As a community deeply indebted to the Spirit, ardently trying to discern where the Spirit would lead it, increasingly familiar with the Spirit through deeply contemplative prayer, a little group of Christians can fairly easily experience why the author of Genesis had the Creator gaze on what he had made and pronounce it very good. The love of creation, like the love of community, tells us we are in the right spot. It is self-authenticating, so fully consonant with the hunger and best capacity of our heart that we know its rightness immediately.

But the Spirit also is concerned with the outside of human existence. The order that comes when we have souls open to the divine, loving the truly mysterious God as their prime treasure, would gather humanity suffering hunger or sickness to itself the way that a hen gathers her chicks. So, as we have previously noted, when the Lukan Jesus comes to Nazareth to begin his public ministry, he quotes the classical text of Isaiah to show the concrete and external effects that the Spirit who is upon him intends: "The Spirit of the Lord is upon me, because he has anointed me to preach good news to the poor. He has sent me to proclaim release to the captives and recovering of sight to the blind, to set at liberty those who are oppressed, and to proclaim the acceptable year of the Lord" (Luke 4:18–19). For our day, this sort of concreteness means liberating people from the systematic oppressions and deprivations they suffer. It means searching out the connections among poverty, imprisonment, blindness and oppression of all sorts, to show both the changes of heart and the changes of public policy that the good news of Jesus Christ demands. The name of conversion in our day often is rejecting systems that now discriminate blindly, automatically, by the steady whirring of the bureaucratic gears. The change of heart we most often require is giving up our reliance on weapons, cash, and power-politics—growing bold enough to seek security not in arms or dollars but in the Spirit of God.

Inside and outside, for our souls and for our bodies, the Spirit is in labor with our liberation. And in the zones that mediate between our bodies and our souls, in our psyches and our minds, the liberating inspirations of the Spirit gently move us forward toward what Lonergan calls intellectual and moral conversion. When we are rooted in the creative mystery of God, and have adequate food and shelter, we find it relatively easy to contemplate a life in which we pursue goodness rather than self-interest, a reality in which critical realism predominates over animal extroversion or sensuality. Conversion is the Spirit's liminal zone, the "area" we pass through as we progress from oppression to liberation.

This theology of the Spirit has strong pastoral implications for the church, without doubt, but they will not differ greatly from the implications that other well-intentioned groups will see. All who are led by the Spirit of God, whatever their extrinsic denomination or institutional allegiance, will today realize that they are bound to try to help liberate the poor on all levels of their poverty, from bread and shoes to books and shrines for prayer. Where a liberational pneumatology grows distinctively ecclesiological is in calling the community of Christ to apply liberation high and low in its own household. Until the church is unmarked by the oppressions that afflict secular societies, free of the economic, racial, sexual, and other distinctions and discriminations that scarify life outside its borders, it will be neither the sacramental city on the hill nor a credible grouping of disciples. So judgment has to begin with the household of God, if liberation is to receive from the household of God the impetus we must assume the Spirit now seeks.

At the outpouring of the Spirit commemorated in the account of Pentecost in Acts, one of the earliest Christian interpretations of the impetus of the Spirit reached back to the prophet Joel: "And in the last days it shall be, God declares, that I will pour out my Spirit upon all flesh, and your sons and your daughters shall prophesy, and your young men shall see visions, and your old men shall dream dreams; yea, and on my menservants and my maidservants in those days I will pour out my Spirit; and they shall prophesy" (Acts 2:17–18; Joel 2:28–29).

For the author of Acts the last days began with the death and resurrection of Jesus Christ. The present and last age is the time when the church carries the message of salvation to the ends of the earth. The Pentecostal Spirit assures the church it has the resources to accomplish this mission. The mission depends on the divine inspiration throughout and, if Peter and Joel be the guides, it uses all ranks in the church: sons and daughters, young and old, menservants and maidservants. They all can prophesy how salvation and liberation should occur. They all are competent in the religious life inspired by the Spirit. By inference, they all must be competent in the communal life inspired by the Spirit. Thus, to ignore the potential contribution of any member, or to make any member subservient to laws and customs (to consider any living temple of the Spirit less revealing than a collection of legal letters), is to run counter to the basic charter or birth-pattern of the church: its original pneumatic experience. The crux of the credibility of the Christian Church in the twenty-first century probably will be its ability to read these traditional signs for its new times and let them make it the world's foremost sacrament of liberation.

Summary

By way of conclusion, we have been attempting some answers to the contemporary questions with which we opened our study in the first chapter. To sketch the sort of Christian community we find present times demanding, we reflected on love, egalitarianism, praxis, and the Spirit.

In discussing the divine love that is the life at the center of the church, we found ourselves first noting the contrary horizons of secularists and fundamentalist fanatics, and then recalling the special constituency of the divine love: the poor, the marginalized, and the victims of discrimination. We turned from this recall to imagine the parishes of Mudville, trying to translate the divine love into middle class America. One of our strongest conclusions was that the complacency so common to the bourgeoisie is incompatible with vigorous Christian faith in the divine love. We imagined how to sermonize this conclusion for Bob Everyman, noted the gentling correctives that God's patience suggests, but then were forced to repeat the demands of the divine love that we grow beyond self-concern, because only such growth seemed capable of rousing Christians to practical care about the starving of East Africa, to vigorous political efforts to change the systems now oppressing so many people around the world.

The love of God, in infra-church perspective, seemed also to require our growing beyond paternalistic images of the Christian community and starting to reach out after egalitarianism. The roots of a Christian egalitarianism, we saw, are the leveling effects of both sin and grace. These are not opposed to a pluralism that honors historical or ethnic differences, but they are prior in significance. Again looking at the actual church life across the USA today, we opined that few churches are sponsoring or demanding egalitarianism: there is more sleepiness than prophetic challenge to stir up the grace of God given to each and all, more conservatism than passion for peace and justice. A model of discipleship would probably promote egalitarianism and greater sense of responsibility, while fuller reliance on the love poured forth in our hearts by the Spirit would supply the key to the necessary inner resources. Egalitarianism would of course challenge the churches that exclude portions of their membership from official authority. It would draw strength from textual and historical analyses that showed how regularly people have had to pay more heed to private conscience than to laggard official teaching. Finally, one would hope that a more egalitarian ecclesiology would raise the quotient of criticism and help all exploited people, quite including those of the middle class, to see the bunkum being foisted upon them and get off their butts to revolt.

Our third contemporary answer was praxis. To meet today's needs, theoreticians of the Christian community are well-advised to make very prominent Jesus' own pragmatic test: by their fruits you will know them. We saw some of the synoptic, Johannine, and Pauline variants of this test, and then we considered the "sociological" additions to the perennially wise psychology of praxis that today's cultural sensitivities seem to demand. We wove back to egalitarianism and considered what pragmatism suggests about the elevation of "the people" that liberation theology often proposes, shying away from any doctrinaire position that the mass will always be responsible or wise. Nonetheless, we decided that people doing business in the spiritual life (e.g., people in colleges and churches) have to respect the freedom intrinsic to spiritual transactions, offering their message or gift and letting the audience make of it what it will. The rather stolid mass of pew-sitters in the main-line North American churches offer rather discouraging or at best ambiguous data in this regard, but small communities such as that of the *campesinos* of Solentiname offer data very encouraging.

Our last consideration was the Holy Spirit, the specifically divine and gracious side matching up with the love, egalitarianism, and praxis we had been asking of the church's human side. The Spirit is not as prominent in current ecclesiology as we would like, but there are patches of theology alive with pneumatological interest. Moreover, theologians of church ministry such as Edward Schillebeeckx are harvesting rich implications from the pneumatic stress of some of the most primitive New Testament ecclesiologies, such as that of the Antiochene school. We recalled Johannine and Lukan emphases on the Spirit, and then broadened our vista to reflect on the Spirit's movement through the creativity and conscientiousness that have sparked perhaps half a million years of human existence. We suspected that the integrations being worked in today's global history ask individuals to follow the Spirit in advance of the rather cumbersome church officialdom, and we noted the relevance of the gift of the Spirit to the question of liberation that was the most pressing of our introductory probes. To conclude we turned the light of the liberating Spirit on the church itself, realizing that only when the church lives up to its Pentecostal beginnings, as expressed by the vision of the Lukan Peter and Joel, will it have a chance of being the sacramental community of liberation that the Spirit of Christ surely now wants it to be.

STUDY QUESTIONS

1. Assess the divine love at work in your own local Christian community.
2. How might stressing a love deeply contemplative and deeply political shape an ecclesiology adequate to today's needs?
3. Is the anointing of the Holy Spirit too fragile a reed on which to stake an egalitarian ecclesiology?
4. What do the racism and sexism in Christian history imply for the priority of individual conscience and the discernment of spirits?
5. What are the fruits by which a pragmatic Christianity evaluates church life?

NOTES

1. See Louise Erdrich, LOVE MEDICINE. New York: Holt, Rinehart and Winston, 1984.

2. See, for example, Andrew Greeley et al., PARISH, PRIEST & PEOPLE. Chicago: Thomas More, 1981, and Joan D. Chittister and Martin Marty, FAITH & FERMENT. Minneapolis: Augsburg, 1983. Both are excellent studies of parish life, but in neither does the Holy Spirit stand out.

3. See Yves Congar, I BELIEVE IN THE HOLY SPIRIT, 3 vols. New York: Seabury, 1983.

4. See Kilian McDonnell, O.S.B., "A Trinitarian Theology of the Holy Spirit," THEOLOGICAL STUDIES, 46/2 (June 1985), pp. 191–227.

5. Edward Schillebeeckx, THE CHURCH WITH A HUMAN FACE. New York: Crossroad, 1985, pp. 35, 37.

6. See, for example, Igor Shafarevich, THE SOCIALIST PHENOMENON. New York: Harper & Row, 1980, especially pp. 18–79.

Index

Abortion, 168–70
Ah, But Your Land Is Beautiful, 175
Ahlstrom, Sydney, 92–93
Alive into the Wilderness, 116
All That Is Solid Melts into Air, 97
Anabaptists, 92
Anglicanism, 90
Apostolic Canons, 84
Aquinas, Thomas, 78–79
Augustine, 70, 185

Baptists, 92–93
Berman, Marshall, 97
Bernardin, Cardinal, 168
Berryman, Phillip, 123
Biblical Christian community (*See* Scriptural sources)
Boff, Leonardo, 114–15, 139
Book of Common Prayer, The, 90
Broeckhoven, Egide van, 153
Brown, Raymond E., 44, 51, 54–55
Brown, Robert McAfee, 11, 88
Buddhism, 144–45

Calvin, John, 89
Canterbury Tales, 80–81
Cardenal, Ernesto, 122

Catholicism (*See* Church; Counter-Reformation)
Chalcedon council, 71–72
"Challenge of Peace, The," 3
Chaucer, 80–81
Christianity (*See* Church)
Christianity in European History, 74
Christians (*See also* Church): demographics of, 16-17; in Old Testament, 32–33, 38
Church (*See also* Church history; Ecclesiology; Governance; Mission; Scriptural sources; Theological models; Worship): and community, 22–28; and divine life, 14–16; and ecumenism, 23–24; and egalitarianism, 206–9; and faith, 3–5, 9; and liberation, 3–5, 9; and love, 200–202; in Modernity, 98–100; and post-Christianity, 22; and praxis, 312–15; and reconciliation, 191–92; and sinfulness, 9, 13–14; and Spirit, 219–22

Church: Charism and Power, 115
Church: Communion, Sacrament, Communication, The, 110
Church history: and Eastern Christianity, 81–87; in Middle Ages, 74–81; and Modernity, 94–100; in patristic era, 68–74; and Reformation, 87–94
Church of England, 90
Clebsch, William A., 74, 76
Coles, Robert, 5–6
Community: and church, 22; and discipleship, 119–25; ecumenism in, 23–24; ideal, 25–26; individualism in, 24–25; and Jesus, 27–28; and love, 197–99; occurrence of, 26–27; in Old Testament, 33, 38; in post-Modernity, 22–23; and reconciliation, 190–91
Comte, Auguste, 95
Contras, 12–13
Cooke, Bernard, 186–87
Counter-Reformation, Catholic, 93
Covenant, 34–35, 37–38

Dante, 80
Discipleship: and community, 119–25; Dulles' view of, 118; and gospel proclamation, 151; importance of, recent, 118–19; and institutionalism, 113; and Jesus, 119
Divine Comedy, 80
Divine life: and church, 14-16;

and Johannine churches, 57–58; and sinfulness, 14–16
Docetists, 69
Donatists, 73
Duling, Dennis, 47
Dulles, Avery, 111-13, 118
Duryea, John S., 115–17
Dvornik, Francis, 82

Eastern Christianity (*See also* Church): canons of, 84–85; and divisions with Western Christianity, 81; doctrine of, 81–82; Eastern view of, 83–84; ecclesiology in, 81; and icons, 87; and sacramentality, 84, 86–87; and salvation, 85–86; theology of, 82–83; Western view of, 83
Ecclesiology (*See also* Church): in Eastern Christianity, 81; and egalitarianism, 204; ideal, 211; in Middle Ages, 77, 77–78; in New Testament, 39, 42, 45, 51; in Old Testament, 34; in patristic era, 73–74; and Spirit, 217–19
Ecology, 166–67
Ecumenism, 23–24
Egalitarianism: and church, 206–9; dangers of, 211–12; and ecclesiology, 204; and eucharistia, 134–35; in Johannine churches, 54; Lonergan's view of, 204–5; and love, 202–3; and

mystagogy, 142–43; and
Spirit, 205–6; visions of,
203–4
Election, 11, 35–36
"El Norte," 6–7, 9, 123
Epanagoge, 83–84
Eucharistia: and egalitarianism,
134–35; and liberational
model, 130–31; and
politics, 133–34; and praise
of God, 131–33; purpose of,
128; and salvation, 128–30;
and sinfulness, 131–33
Eusebius, 72

Faith: and church, 3–5, 9; and
Coles' interviews, 5–6;
defense of, 180; and
doctrinal divisions, 183;
and doctrinal unity, 180–
82; and "El Norte," 6–7;
importance of, 179–80; and
mystagogy, 182–83; and
pastoral teachings, 183–86;
and praxis, 210–11; and
sinfulness, 14; and
subversion, 7–8
Fedotov, George P., 85–86
Foundations of Christian Faith,
107
Frend, W. H. C., 69, 72
Fries, Heinrich, 180
*From Enlightenment to
Revolution*, 97

Gibbon, Edward, 72
Gnostics, 69–70
God Is New Each Moment, 120
Gospel in Solentiname, The, 122

Governance: faith, teaching,
179–86; reconciliation,
ministering, 186–92;
service, 173–79
Greenberg, Moshe, 36–37
Gregory the Great, 76
Gutierrez, Gustavo, 114–15

Harnack, Adolf Von, 83
Haughton, Rosemary, 153
Haustafeln, 43
Heilbroner, Robert, 7
Herbert, Frank, 205
Heresies (*See* specific names of)
Hesed, 38 (*See also* Covenant)
Hinduism, 144–45
Household codes, 43
Humani Generis, 96
Humanism, 17–18

Imitation of Christ, The, 78
Institutes, 89
Institutionalism: and American
clergy, 115–17; changes in,
118; and discipleship, 113;
Dulles' view of, 111–13;
and feminists, 117; history
of, 113–14; and Rome
authorities, 114–15; and
Vatican II, 117
Irenaeus of Lyons, 69–70
Islam, 145–46
Israel, 32–38

Johannine churches:
characteristics of, 51–52;
contributions of, 56; and
divine life, 57–58;
egalitarianism in, 54;

evolution of, 54–56; and
Jesus, 52–53; and Peter,
53–54; theology of, 52–53
John Paul II, 159, 161
John XXIII, 117
Judaism, 145–46

Kant, Immanuel, 94
Kee, Howard Clark, 62–63
Knowles, David, 79
Kress, Robert, 110
Kung, Hans, 114–15

Lawrence, Fred, 119–20
Leo XIII, 96
Lewis, C. S., 12
Liberation: and church, 3–5, 9;
and Coles' interviews, 5–6;
and "El Norte," 6–7; and
subversion, 7–8
Lonergan, Bernard, 105, 191,
204–5
Love: and church, 200–202; and
community, 197–99;
divine, 196–97; and
egalitarianism, 202–3; and
individual, 199–200; and
Word of God, 138–39
Lumen Gentium, 110
Luther, Martin, 87–89
Lutherans, 92

Marcionites, 70
McDonnell, Kilian, 216
McGucken, Joseph T., 115–17
McKenzie, John L., 37–38
McNeill, John T., 89
Meeks, Wayne, 42
Meier, John, 48–49, 51

Methodism, 91
Metz, J. B., 11
Meyendorff, John, 84
Middle Ages: doctrine in, 79–
80; ecclesiology in, 77–78;
Germanic kingdoms in, 74–
76; literature of, 80–81;
mystics in, 78; prelacy in,
76–77; theodicy in, 76–77;
theologians in, 77–79
Ministry: Leadership in the
Community of Jesus Christ,
177
Ministry to Word and Sacraments,
186
Mission: earth, building, 164–
70; gospel, proclaiming,
151-57; poor, helping, 157–
64
Missionaries, 98–99, 152–57
Modernity (See also Post-
Christianity): church in,
98–100; definitions of, 94;
historical analyses of, 95;
political affairs of, 94–95;
and post-modern culture,
96–97; and psychology, 96;
and Reformation, 93;
studies of, 97–98; theology
in, 95–96
Mystagogy: definition of, 141;
and divine mystery, 143–
44, 147; and
egalitarianism, 142–43; and
ethical matters, 147–48;
and faith, 182; making of,
141–42; and non-Christian
religions, 144–47; and
salvation, 144

New Testament: Acts, 45;
ecclesiology in, 39, 42, 45,
51; Hebrews, 58–59;
Johannine writings, 51–58;
Luke, 45–46; Mark, 46–47;
Matthew, 47–51; Pauline
letters, 38–45; Peter, 58;
Revelation, 59–61; and
sacramentality, 105–6; and
Spirit, 217; and Word of
God, 135–36
Nicaea councils, 71-72
Nicaragua, 12–13
Nobili, Roberto de, 99
Nuclear weapons, 166

"Oath Against Modernism," 100
Old Testament: Christians in,
32–33, 38; and community,
33, 38; and covenant, 34–
35, 37–38; ecclesiology in,
34; and election, 35–36;
and Israel, 32–38; and
Spirit, 217; and Word of
God, 135
Oosterhuis, Huub, 120
Origen, 70
Outler, Albert C., 91

Paton, Alan, 175–76, 184
Patristic era: doctrinal problems
in, 69–71; Eastern empire
in, 72–73; ecclesiology in,
73–74; ecumenical councils
in, 71–72; and expansion of
church, 68–69; and marks
of church in, 71; and
Roman Empire, 68–69, 72;
Western empire in, 72

Pauline churches: changes in,
39; Colossian, 40–41, 43;
Corinthian, 40; diversity
of, 38–39; Ephesian, 41–
43; in Pastoral Epistles, 45;
Thessalonian, 39–40
Perrin, Norman, 47
Pius X, 100
Pius XII, 96
Plato, 147
Pollution, 166–67
Population control (See
Abortion)
Post-Christianity (See also
Modernity): and
alternatives to Christianity,
20–21; and bastardization
of Christianity, 19–20; and
church, 22; and
demographics, 16–17; and
humanism, 17–18; issue of,
16; and Marxism, 20–22;
and modernity, 21–22; and
Thomas' writings, 18–19
Potok, Chaim, 157
Poverty: and Beatitudes, 163–
64; characteristics of, 158;
and economic system, 160–
62; and pastoral letter of
1984, 158–61; and
preaching, 157–58
Praxis: and authenticity, 209;
and church, 212–15; and
egalitarianism, 211–12; and
faith, 210–11; and Jesus,
209–10
Preaching: and disciples, 151;
and divine mystery, 154–
55; essence of, 157; in

everyday life, 153–54; and
hopelessness, 154;
missionaries, modern, 152;
to poor, 157–58
Prelacy, 44–45, 76–77 (*See also*
Church)
Prescriptions: egalitarianism,
202–9; love, 196–202;
praxis, 209–15; Spirit,
215–22
Protestantism (*See* Church;
Reformation; specific sects
of)
Puritan tradition, 89–90

Rahner, Karl: and church
power, 173; and
eucharistia, 128; and faith,
180; and feminism, 117;
and sacramentality, 106–9;
and Vatican II, 99
Ratzinger, Joseph Cardinal, 118
Reconciliation: and alienation,
sinful, 187–89; and
church, 191–92; and
clergy, 186; and
community, 190–91;
Cooke's view of, 186–87;
and sacramentality, 189–
90
Reformation, Protestant: and
Anabaptists, 92; and
Anglicanism, 90; and
Baptists, 92–93; and
Calvin, 89; and Counter-
Reformation, 93; and
Luther, 87–89; and
Methodism, 91–92; and
modernity, 93; and Puritan

tradition, 89–90; result of,
93–94
*Religious Roots of Rebellion:
Christians in Central
American Revolutions, The,*
123
Ricci, Matteo, 99
Romero, Oscar, 134–35

Sacramentality: advantages of,
109–10; disadvantages of,
110; and Eastern
Christianity, 84, 86–87;
and history, 110–11; and
Kress, 110; and New
Testament, 105–6; and
Rahner, 106–9; and
reconciliation, 189; and
sinfulness, 108
Salvation: and Eastern
Christianity, 85–86; and
eucharistia, 128–30; and
Luther, 87–88; and
mystagogy, 144
Sandmel, Samuel, 35
Scharbert, Josef, 34
Schell, Jonathan, 165
Schillebeeckx, Edward: and
church, 59; and clashes
with Rome, 114–15; and
discipleship, 120–21; and
service, 177; and Spirit,
216-17
Schmemann, Alexander, 83–84
Schüssler-Fiorenza, Elisabeth,
117
Screwtape Letters, The, 12
Scriptural sources: Acts, 45;
Hebrews, 58–59;

Johannine writings, 51–58;
Luke, 45–46; Mark, 46–47;
Matthew, 47–51; Old
Testament, 32–38; Pauline
letters, 38–45; Peter, 58;
Revelation, 59–61
Service: and church authority,
173–74; exclusions from,
177–79; and Jesus' view of
authority, 174–76; and
symbols of leadership, 176
Shepherd, Massey, 131–32
Sin (See Sinfulness)
Sinfulness: and church, 9, 13–
14; and divine life, 14–16;
and election, 11; and
eucharistia, 131–33; and
faith, 14; and Godlessness,
10–11; and holocaust, 9–
10; and modern issues, 12–
13; and post-Christianity,
17; and sacramentality, 108
Social issues: abortion, 168–70;
in biblical times, 164–65;
ecology, 166–67; and faith,
167; Nicaragua, 12–13;
nuclear weapons, 166; and
pastoral letter for peace,
165–66; and Teilhard, 165;
and war, 165-66
"Social Teachings and the U.S.
Economy," 158–59
Spirit: biblical emphases on,
216–17; and church, 219–
22; and ecclesiology, 217–
19; and egalitarianism,
205–6; importance of, 215–
16; Schillebeeckx's view of,
216–17

Synoptic churches: Lucan, 45–
46; Marcan, 46–47;
Matthean, 47–51

Taoism, 145–46
Teilhard de Chardin, Pierre,
165, 167
Theological models:
discipleship, 118–25;
institutionalism, 111–18;
sacramentality, 105–111;
use of, 105
Thomas, Lewis, 18–19
Transubstantiation, 80
"Treatise on Christian Liberty,"
88

Unity of the Churches: An Actual
Possibility, 180

Vatican Councils
First, 100
Second, 99, 108, 110, 117
Voegelin, Eric, 81, 97–98

War, 165–66
Weil, Louis, 130
Weinfeld, Moshe, 37
Wesley, Charles, 91
Wesley, John, 91
Wiesel, Elie, 9–10, 13
Williams, Roger, 92
Word of God: and clergy, 139–
40; connotations of, 136–
37; distinguishing, 137–38;
and Johannine writings,
135–36; and laity, 140; and
love, divine, 138–39; and
Old Testament, 135; in

Pastoral Epistles, 136; and Pauline letters, 136; and Protestant churches, 135; in synoptic gospels, 136; and worship, 140–41
Worship: eucharistia, 128–35; mystagogy, 141–48; Word of God, 135–41

Xavier, Francis, 99, 147

Youngest Science, The, 18

Zwinglians, 92